P9-BTY-888

AMONG FRIENDS

Rotary Polio Plus Fundraiser

An International Collection of 500 Delicious Recipes

DEDICATION
Among Friends is lovingly dedicated
to all the children of the world

BY

Rotary International District 536

FRONT COVER
Beef and Burgundy Casserole, page 104
Gourmet Wild Rice, page 89
Caesar Salad, page 70

AMONG FRIENDS
By Rotary International District 536

First Printing — April, 1987 (10,000 copies)
Second Printing — May, 1987 (10,000 copies)
Third Printing — September, 1987 (15,000 copies)
Fourth Printing — November, 1987 (30,000 copies)

Copyright © 1987 by
Verneil Martin, Publisher
Among Friends
Attention: G. Watkins C.A.
P.O. Box 6127, Station "A"
Calgary, Alberta
Canada T2H 2L4

All rights reserved

Canadian Cataloguing in Publication Data
Main entry under title:

Among Friends

Coordinator: Verneil Martin
Includes index.
ISBN 0-919845-50-9

1. Cookery International. I. Rotary International.
District 536 (Calgary, Alta.) II. Martin, Verneil.
TX725.A1A56 1987 641.59 C87-098042-4

We wish to thank and acknowledge the contributors who so generously donated items for our photography sessions:

Boyds Lobster Shop, Calgary - Mr. Blaise Boyd
D'Annes Flowers, Roxboro House, Calgary - Mr. Robert Todesco
Foodvale Stores Ltd., Calgary - Larry and Jack Kwong
Kensington Kitchen Co., Calgary - Mrs. Shirley McCallum
Shamrock Irish Linen Shop, Calgary - Sandra Gowda
Mr. Robert Simpson, Calgary
The Wine Shop, 17th Ave. S.W., Calgary - Mr. John Klemp

Photography by
Ross C. (Hutch) Hutchinson
Bolli & Hutchinson Photographic Design Ltd.
Calgary, Alberta

Designed, Printed and Produced in Canada by
Centax
Publishing Consultant and Food Stylist: Margo Embury
Design by: Blair Fraser
1048 Fleury Street
Regina, Saskatchewan, Canada S4N 4W8
(306) 359-3737 Toll Free 1-800-667-5844

PolioPlus
A Rotary International Campaign
TO IMMUNIZE THE CHILDREN OF THE WORLD

Thank you for buying this copy of "Among Friends". The proceeds from your purchase will go to Polio Plus to provide polio vaccine to help immunize the estimated 275,000 children in the developing countries of the world stricken each year by this dread disease.

Poliomyelitis is an almost forgotten word in North America, even to those of us who were around before the mid-1950's and saw the crippling effects and deaths resulting from this now preventable disease.

Rotary International has pledged to raise $120,000,000 to be spent on polio immunization projects worldwide and, working with governments and international health agencies such as the World Health Organization (WHO) and United Nations Children's Fund (UNICEF), shares the goal of conquering not just polio but five other targeted childhood diseases.

Each year 4,000,000 children die from the six dreaded diseases that could be prevented by immunizations: polio, measles, diptheria, tuberculosis, tetanus, and pertussis (whooping cough). Rotary, through its worldwide network of more than 23,129 clubs in 161 nations, is in a unique position to help organize and carry through this massive project.

Your participation by buying this book will help us to help them - it's nice to be "Among Friends".

MY PRAYER FOR A FRIEND

I said a prayer for you today and know God must have heard.
I felt the answer in my heart, although he spoke no word.
I didn't ask for wealth or fame, I knew you wouldn't mind.
I asked him to send treasures of a far more lasting kind.

I asked that he be near you at the start of each new day
To grant you health and blessings and friends to share your way.
I asked for happiness for you in all things great and small
But it was for His loving care for you my friend
I prayed the most of all.

ACKNOWLEDGEMENTS

My sincere thanks and gratitude goes out to all the wives of Rotarians and to the Rotarians of District 536 who truly believed in Verneil's concept for this worthwhile project for Polio Plus.

Through their unselfish, individual or group efforts in response to her request for recipes, etctera, this book "Among Friends" has become a reality.

My sincere thanks and gratitude to my wife, my Rotary Ann and best friend, Verneil, for truly believing that friends in Rotary would support an important project of this magnitude.

> District Governor Doug Martin
> Rotary International District 536
> 1986/87

We wish to give special thanks to our friends to Rotary, Mrs. Frieda Hamm and Mrs. Lucille Steinhauer for the volunteer efforts they so willingly, unselfishly and efficiently offered at all times, without question.

Our sincere gratitude goes to two very pleasant and amiable ladies, who unselfishly lent their time and expertise helping with the preparation of the many dishes for photography, also for the multitude of hours spent in proofreading:

> Rotary Ann, Marian Magee, B.Sc. (H. Ec.) R.D.
> Volunteer Marian Burrus, B.Sc. (H. Ec.) R.D.

To Margo Embury, Publishing Consultant, food designer and artist and to "Hutch" Hutchinson, Bolli & Hutchinson Photographic Design Ltd., our many thanks and gratitude for your combined expertise and for your patience.

Special acknowledgement to Rotary Ann, Roma Nowakowski, an accomplished artist and a loyal friend to Rotary. We offer a special bouquet of thanks and gratitude for her generous volunteer art designs, designating the various categories throughout the "Among Friends" cookbook.

TABLE OF CONTENTS

MEASUREMENT ADAPTATIONS

Food measurements in this cookbook are given in both U.S. standard and metric. Recipes have been tested in standard and the rounded metric equivalents are given as a convenience for those who are more familiar with metric. Most North American cooks tend to measure food, other than meats, cheeses, etc. by volume. Cooks in other parts of the world tend to measure dry ingredients, fats, etc. by weight. The following adaptations should be helpful in converting measurements.

Equipment

				exact		rounded
1 tsp.			=	(5 mL)		5 mL
3 tsp.	=	1 tbsp.	=	(15 mL)		15 mL
4 tbsp.	=	¼ cup	=	(59.12 mL)		50-60 mL
5⅓ tbsp.	=	⅓ cup	=	(75.6 mL)		75 mL
8 tbsp.	=	½ cup	=	(118.25 mL)		125 mL
16 tbsp.	=	1 cup	=	(236 mL)		250 mL
1 fl. oz.	=	2 tbsp.	=	(29.56 mL)		30 mL
4 fl. oz.	=	½ cup (1 gill)	=	(118.25 mL)		125 mL
8 fl. oz.	=	1 cup	=	(236 mL)		250 mL
16 fl. oz.	=	2 cups (1 pint)	=	(473 mL)		500 mL
32 fl. oz.	=	4 cups (1 quart)	=	(946 mL)		1000 mL (1 L)

Weight Measure

				exact		rounded
1 oz.			=	(28.3 g)		30 g
4 oz.	=	¼ lb.	=	(113.4 g)		125 g
8 oz.	=	½ lb.	=	(226.8 g)		250 g
16 oz.	=	1 lb.	=	(453 g)		500 g
32 oz.	=	2 lbs.	=	(917.2 g)		1000 g (1 kg)

Food Equivalents

biscuit/cookie crumbs	1 cup	=	236 mL	=	4 oz.	=	114 g
bread/cracker crumbs, dry pkg.	1 cup	=	236 mL	=	5 oz.	=	144 g
bread crumbs, fresh	1 cup	=	236 mL	=	2 oz.	=	60 g
butter/margarine/lard	1 cup (2 sticks)	=	236 mL	=	½ lb.	=	227 g
cheese, grated Cheddar	1 cup	=	236 mL	=	1/4 lb.	=	114 g
eggs	1 cup	=	236 mL	=	4-5 whole large or extra large or 8 egg whites or 12 egg yolks		
flour, all-purpose	1 cup	=	236 mL	=	4 oz. (¼ lb.) =		114 g
	4 cups	=	946 mL	=	1 lb.	=	453 g
flour, whole-wheat	3¾-4 cups	=	890-946 mL	=	1 lb.	=	453 g
fruit, dried mixed or raisins	1 cup	=	236 mL	=	6 oz.	=	170 g
gelatin, 1 envelope (unflavored)	1 tbsp.	=	15 mL	=	¼ oz.	=	7 g
honey, golden syrup, treacle	1 cup	=	236 mL	=	12 oz.	=	340 g
lemon, 1 medium (juice)	3 tbsp.	=	45 mL	=	1½ fl. oz.		
nuts, chopped	1 cup	=	236 mL	=	4 oz.	=	114 g
rice, uncooked	1 cup	=	236 mL	=	8 oz. (½ lb.) =		227 g
sugar, brown, firmly packed	2¼ cups	=	532 mL	=	1 lb.	=	920 g
sugar, granulated (castor)	1 cup	=	236 mL	=	8 oz.	=	227 g
sugar, icing (confectioner's)	3½-4 cups	=	828-946 mL	=	1 lb.	=	920 g

HIGH-ALTITUDE BAKING

Too much sugar and low humidity are the two major problems in high-altitude baking, over 3,000 feet (900 metres).

Butter Cakes or Quick Breads — use ½ the amount of sugar as flour (in chocolate cakes cocoa counts as flour), e.g. 1 cup (250 mL) sugar to 2 cups (500 mL) of flour.

Sponge/Angel Cakes — use 1½ cups (375 mL) sugar to 1½ cups (375 mL) of egg whites.

Other Tips — underbeat eggs, as compared to sea level, or keep them refrigerated until use.
— over 5000 feet (1500 m), decrease baking powder or baking soda by ⅛-¼ tsp. (0.5-1 mL) for each teaspoon (5 mL) called for in recipe.
— over 5000 feet (1500 metres), raise baking temperature by 25°F (10°C).

Low Humidity — store flour in moisture-vapor-proof containers. Seasonal variations also increase this problem.
— bread recipes may vary from 6 cups (1.5 L) of flour at sea level to 4½-5 cups (1.125-1.25 L), over 3000 feet (900 metres) in low-humidity areas.
— cakes, quick breads and pastries: try reducing flour 1-3 tbsp. (15-45 mL) from recipe amount.
— alternatively, liquid may be increased 2-4 tbsp. (30-60 mL) for each cup (250 mL) of liquid in the recipe as altitude varies from 3000-10,000 feet (900-3,000 metres).

Brunch, Lunch & Breads

BRUNCH & LUNCH

ALOHA DIP

12	soft coconut macaroons, crushed into small pieces	12
¼ cup	firmly packed light brown sugar	50 mL
2 cups	dairy sour cream	500 mL
1	large pineapple assorted berries and fruits	1

Mix together macaroons, sugar and sour cream. Chill several hours to soften macaroon pieces, or crumbs. Do not stir again or macaroon crumbs will break into smaller pieces. • Slice a cap-shaped piece off the top of the pineapple, about 1″ (2.5 cm) below bottom of the leaves. Hollow out pineapple center with a sharp knife. Leave a firm shell to hold the macaroon dip. • Cut hollowed-out pineapple and other fruits into small pieces. Fill pineapple shell with the dip. Replace top if you like. • Place in center of a large platter. Arrange pineapple chunks, and assorted other berries and fruits in groups around pineapple. If you desire, sprinkle fruit with kirsch or brandy. • To keep apples, peaches, pears, etc. from browning dip in lemon juice.

Here's a great sandwich suggestion: place cucumber and tomato slices over Philadelphia creamed cheese on brown bread. Season lightly with pepper and salt. Nutritious and yummy!

1 cup	whipping cream	250 mL
¼ oz.	pkg. Whip it	10 g
1 cup	plain yogurt	250 mL
1 tsp.	vanilla	5 mL
3 tbsp.	icing sugar	45 mL
¼ tsp.	cinnamon	1 mL
dash	nutmeg	dash

FRUIT DIP

Whip cream with Whip it. Add remaining ingredients except for nutmeg. Stir and sprinkle nutmeg on top for garnish. • Serve in crystal bowl. • Delicious with an assorted fruit tray or with a watermelon "basket" filled with fresh fruit in season.

1½ cups	cottage cheese	375 mL
1½ cups	cream cheese	375 mL
1 tsp.	curry powder	5 mL
2 tbsp.	chopped chutney	30 mL
½ cup	very thinly sliced water chestnuts	125 mL
2 tbsp.	white sultana raisins	30 mL
3	papayas, cut in half and seeded	3
¼ cup	cinnamon-sugar	50 mL
¼ cup	melted butter	50 mL

BAKED PAPAYA MAUNA KEA

Increase the amount of the above ingredients if papayas are extra large. • Mix and blend the cottage cheese, cream cheese, curry powder and chutney. When these ingredients are well blended and smooth, add the water chestnuts and raisins. • Fill papayas with the cheese mixture. Sprinkle tops with cinnamon-sugar and melted butter. Bake approximately 15 minutes in 450°F (230°C) oven.

½ lb.	shrimp	250 g
1 tsp.	sherry, cognac OR wine vinegar	5 mL
½ tsp.	cornstarch	2 mL
½ tsp.	salt	2 mL
2 tbsp.	vegetable oil	30 mL
6	eggs, beaten lightly salt, to taste	6

SHRIMP OMELET

Marinate shrimp in mixture of sherry, cornstarch and salt for 15 minutes. • Heat oil in skillet. • Sauté shrimp at medium heat for 2 minutes. Remove from pan. • Add salt to beaten eggs and add shrimp to egg mixture. • Add more oil to skillet. Heat to medium-high. • Pour in egg-shrimp mixture. Cook and stir until done. • May add ½ cup (125 mL) grated Swiss or mozzarella cheese. • Yields 3-4 servings.

The best household hint I know is to "train your husband and children" to share the load.

9

OVEN APPLE OMELET

4	eggs, separated	4
3 tbsp.	flour	45 mL
1 tsp.	cinnamon	5 mL
½ tsp.	salt	2 mL
½ cup	milk*	125 mL
1	large apple, washed, cored, chopped	1
2 tbsp.	sugar	30 mL
¼ cup	butter	50 mL
¼ cup	grated sharp Cheddar cheese	50 mL

Preheat oven to 350°F (180°C). • Beat egg yolks until thick; combine flour, cinnamon and salt and add to the yolks. Continue beating and add milk gradually, then add the chopped apple. • Beat the egg whites until soft peaks form, then add the sugar and continue beating until stiff, but not dry, peaks form. Stir a little of the meringue into the yolk mixture, then fold the yolks into the whites carefully. • Melt the butter in deep pan. Gently pour in the omelet and sprinkle grated cheese over the top. Allow to cook about 5 minutes, then transfer to the preheated oven and bake for approximately 15 minutes, or until the top is puffed and nicely browned. • Cut into wedges and serve. • This recipe may be doubled successfully. • *Milk may be substituted with 1 tbsp. (15 mL) powdered milk and ½ cup (125 mL) white wine. • Yields 4 generous servings.

A. J.'s CHRISTMAS BREAKFAST

A great make ahead for a brunch!

¼ cup	butter	50 mL
¼ cup	flour	50 mL
¼ tsp.	EACH thyme, marjoram, basil	1 mL
1 cup	half and half cream	250 mL
1 cup	milk	250 mL
1 lb.	old Cheddar cheese, grated	500 g
18	eggs, hard-boiled, quartered	18
1 lb.	bacon, fried and crumbled	500 g
½ cup	chopped parsley	125 mL

Melt butter, blend in flour and spices; add milk and cream. Stir until smooth and fairly thick. Add cheese and stir until melted. • In a 2½-quart (9″ x 12″ or 3 L) casserole, or round equivalent, place half each of eggs, bacon, sauce and parsley. Repeat. • Bake for 30 minutes at 300°F (150°C). • Serves 8-10.

Wet the shells of eggs with cold water before placing into boiling water. They will not crack! When cracked eggs are to be boiled, add a little salt or vinegar to the water, to prevent the white from boiling out. To peel hard boiled eggs easier, dip them into cold water immediately after taking them out of the boiling water. This also tends to prevent the yolks from turning dark.

2	celery stalks, minced	2
3 tbsp.	minced onion	45 mL
2 tbsp.	minced green pepper	30 mL
2 tbsp.	minced red pepper	30 mL
¼ cup	butter OR margarine	50 mL
2 tbsp.	flour	30 mL
2 cups	canned tomatoes	500 mL
6-8	eggs	6-8
	salt and pepper	
	hot buttered toast	

SPANISH EGGS

To make Spanish sauce sauté mixed chopped vegetables in 2 tbsp. (30 mL) of the butter or margarine. Stir in flour, add canned tomatoes and cook until thick.
• Scramble eggs in remaining butter, spread on hot buttered toast and cover with Spanish sauce. • Delicious for brunch or a family supper. • Serves 4.

4 lbs.	potatoes	2 kg
1	dry bun	1
2	onions	2
3½ oz.	Gouda cheese	100 g
2 tbsp.	butter	30 mL
½ lb.	ham, cubed	250 g
½ cup	cream	125 mL
	salt and pepper	
	nutmeg	
2-3	eggs	2-3

POTATO CAKE

Grate potatoes, bun, onion and cheese into a buttered pan. Add ham. Stir cream and seasonings into beaten eggs and pour over top of ingredients in pan. • Bake 35-40 minutes in 350°F (180°C) oven.

12	slices bacon, cooked and crumbled	12
¼ cup	chopped onion	75 mL
1 cup	grated cheese, Swiss OR Cheddar	250 mL
2 cups	milk	500 mL
1 cup	biscuit mix	250 mL
4	eggs	4
¼ tsp.	salt	1 mL
⅛ tsp.	pepper	0.5 mL
	bacon and tomatoes for garnish	

IMPOSSIBLE BACON QUICHE

Lightly grease a 10″ (1 L) pie plate. • Sprinkle bacon, onion and cheese on plate. • Beat milk, eggs, biscuit mix and seasoning together until smooth, approximately 1 minute. Pour into pie plate. • Bake in 400°F (200°C) oven for 35 minutes, or until golden and knife inserted comes out clean. Let stand 5 minutes. • Garnish if desired. • Serves 4-6.

CHICKEN 'N' BROCCOLI PIE

1½ cups	chopped broccoli, fresh OR frozen	375 mL
3 cups	grated Cheddar cheese	750 mL
1½ cups	cut-up cooked chicken, tuna OR turkey	375 mL
⅔ cup	chopped onion	150 mL
1¼ cups	milk	325 mL
3	eggs	3
¾ cup	biscuit mix	175 mL
¾ tsp.	salt	3 mL
¼ tsp.	pepper	1 mL

Heat oven to 400°F (200°C). • Grease pie plate. • If using fresh broccoli, boil in salted water for 5 minutes, drain well. If frozen rinse and drain thoroughly. Mix broccoli, 2 cups (500 mL) cheese, chicken and onion in plate. Blend milk, eggs, biscuit mix, salt and pepper until smooth. Pour into pie plate. • Bake until knife inserted in center comes out clean, 30-40 minutes. Top with remaining cheese. Bake just until cheese is melted, 1-2 minutes longer. • For a vegetable pie, use 1 cup (250 mL) of partially cooked chopped cauliflower and ½ cup (125 mL) of chopped green pepper instead of chicken. • Serves 6-8.

VEGETABLE QUICHE

10"	unbaked pie crust	25 cm
2	fresh tomatoes	2
1	onion	1
½ cup	butter	125 mL
¼ lb.	mushrooms	125 g
¼ lb.	zucchini	125 g
¼ lb.	green beans	125 g
¼ lb.	broccoli	125 g
1 cup	light cream	250 mL
3	large eggs	3
	salt and pepper, to taste	
1 tsp.	thyme	5 mL
1 tsp.	dry mustard	5 mL
¼ cup	parsley	50 mL
½ cup	grated cheese	125 mL

Prepare crust. • Peel, seed and chop tomatoes, drain through sieve. Peel and chop onion. Fry until brown in ¼ cup (50 mL) butter. Trim mushrooms; slice zucchini. Heat remaining butter, add mushrooms and zucchini, brown lightly. Trim beans, cook together with broccoli 3-4 minutes in steamer. Drain. • Beat together cream, eggs, salt, pepper, thyme, mustard, and parsley. • Spread onion over crust; add other vegetables except tomatoes. Cover with cream mixture. Spread tomatoes on quiche and sprinkle with cheese. • Bake 45 minutes or until set in 400°F (200°C) oven.

What do you do with leftover bits and pieces of cheese? Grate them together to make a cheese ball or serve over spaghetti or lasagne.

QUICHE LORRAINE

The cheese crust is a hit!

¾ cup	flour	175 mL
½ tsp.	salt	2 mL
½ tsp.	dry mustard	2 mL
½ cup	grated Cheddar cheese	125 mL
¼ cup	melted margarine	50 mL

FILLING

½ cup	thinly sliced onion	125 mL
½ cup	cubed ham OR bacon	125 mL
½ cup	grated Cheddar cheese	125 mL
2	eggs	2
1 cup	milk	250 mL
dash	salt	dash
dash	pepper	dash

Mix first 3 ingredients, add cheese and then margarine. Mix thoroughly and pack in 10″ (1L) pie plate. Spread onion, ham and cheese evenly in crust. • Beat eggs and add milk. Pour over cheese. • Sprinkle with salt and pepper, if desired. • Bake at 350°F (180°C) for 1 hour. • Serves 4-6.

SALMON QUICHE

1	unbaked pie shell	1
1½ cups	grated Gouda cheese	375 mL
1 cup	cooked OR canned salmon	250 mL
1 tbsp.	finely chopped chives	15 mL
1 tbsp.	finely chopped celery	15 mL
1 tbsp.	chopped parsley	15 mL
1 tbsp.	whole-wheat flour	15 mL
½ tsp.	salt	2 mL
3	eggs	3
1¼ cups	light cream OR ½ cup (125 mL) milk plus ¾ cup (175 mL) sour cream	300mL

Line pie shell with wax paper, fill with dried beans. Bake at 425°F (220°C) for 5-8 minutes. Remove paper and beans and put shell back in oven for 2 minutes. • Reduce heat to 325°F (160°C). • Toss together cheese, salmon, chives, celery, parsley, flour and salt. Beat eggs slightly and gradually stir in cream. Add cheese mixture to eggs. Pour into pie shell. • Bake 40-45 minutes, or until a knife inserted in center comes out clean. Cool 5 minutes and serve. • This works well in tart shells and is great served hot or cold!

SALMON LOAF

1 tbsp.	gelatin	7 g
½ cup	cold water	125 mL
1	loaf French bread	1
1½ cups	soft bread crumbs	375 mL
2 x 7½ oz.	tins salmon	2 x 220 g
4 oz.	cream cheese	115 g
3 tbsp.	ketchup	45 mL
3 tbsp.	mayonnaise	45 mL
¼ tsp.	pepper	1 mL
¼ tsp.	dry mustard	1 mL
3 tbsp.	pimiento	45 mL
½ cup	sweet pickle	125 mL

Dissolve gelatin in the water. • Cut French bread in half and hollow out the middle for your bread crumbs, leaving 1½″ (3.75 cm) crust. • Combine gelatin, salmon, cheese, ketchup, mayonnaise, pepper, mustard, pimiento, pickle, and bread crumbs and mix well. Fill the French loaf with the salmon mixture. • Chill in refrigerator before slicing. This loaf freezes well!

KING CRAB FLAMBÉ

1 lb.	crab legs, shelled	500 g
1	whole pineapple, cored, peeled	1
	tempura batter (below)	
6 oz.	rum	170 mL
12	barbecue skewers	12
	orange sauce (below)	

Cut pineapple, the long way, in 6 pieces. Slice remaining pineapple into chunks. • Cut crab legs in 4-5″ (10-12 cm) pieces and string on small barbecue skewers. Garnish with pineapple chunk on each end. • Dip in tempura batter and deep fry until golden brown. • Alternate skewers and pineapple slices on serving plate. Ignite rum, serve with sauce. • Serves 6. • See photograph page 16A.

TEMPURA BATTER

1 cup	flour	250 mL
1 cup	ice water	250 mL
1	whole egg	1
	salt and pepper	

Combine all ingredients until smooth. Tempura batter must be ice cold.

ORANGE SAUCE

2 cups	bitter orange marmalade	500 mL
1 tbsp.	horseradish	15 mL
½ tsp.	English mustard	2 mL
1 oz.	sherry	30 mL

Combine all ingredients in blender, then serve.

Swallow your pride occasionally, it's nonfattening.

7 tbsp.	unsalted butter	105 mL
1 tbsp.	finely chopped onion	15 mL
½ cup	raw shrimp, cut into bite-sized pieces	125 mL
½ cup	frozen canned OR fresh crab meat, well picked over and flaked	125 mL
½ cup	bay OR sea scallops, cut into bite-sized pieces	125 mL
2 tbsp.	sherry	30 mL
½ tsp.	salt	2 mL
¼ tsp.	freshly ground black pepper	1 mL
3 tbsp.	flour	45 mL
1 ½ cups	milk	375 mL
1 ½ cups	bread crumbs grated Swiss and Parmesan cheeses	375 mL

COQUILLE ST JACQUES (BELGIAN STYLE)

In large skillet, heat 4 tbsp. (60 mL) butter and add onion. Sauté for a minute, add seafood and cook 4-5 minutes, stirring occasionally. Sprinkle with sherry, salt and pepper. • In saucepan, melt remaining butter, add flour and stir with a wire whisk until well blended. Meanwhile, bring the milk to a boil and add at once to the butter-flour mixture, stirring vigorously with the whisk until the sauce is thickened and smooth. • Combine the sauce with the seafood. Spoon the mixture into individual coquilles of desired size, dot with butter and sprinkle with fine dry bread crumbs mixed with cheese. • Can be made ahead to this point. • If desired, sliced mushrooms can be added. • To serve, bake 12-15 minutes or brown under a broiler. Can be served with lemon. • Recipe can be doubled as needed. • Duchess or whipped potatoes may be piped around edge of shell. • Yields 8.

1	large loaf French bread	1
10 oz.	Swiss cheese	285 g
10 oz.	medium Cheddar cheese	285 g
1	bunch green onions, chopped	1
½ cup	mayonnaise, (or more)	125 mL

CHEESE BREAD

Cut loaf in half lengthwise and place foil around base of each half loaf, leaving the tops open. • Grate cheeses, add onions and enough mayonnaise to hold mixture together. • Spread half cheese mixture on each half loaf. Place both loaves on baking sheet. DO NOT COVER. • Bake at 350°F (180°C) for 30 minutes. • Cut in big slices and serve hot. • May be prepared ahead and frozen before baking.

At mealtime at our house — everyone has 2 choices — take it or leave it.

BREADS PLUS

WELSH CAKES — PICE AR Y MAEN

½ cup	butter OR margarine	125 mL
½ cup	sugar	125 mL
1	egg	1
2 cups	flour	500 mL
pinch	salt	pinch
1 tsp.	baking powder	5 mL
¼ tsp.	mace OR mixed spice	1 mL
½ cup	currants	125 mL

Cream butter and sugar and add egg. ● Sift flour, salt, baking powder and spice and work into creamed mixture. ● Add currants. ● Roll out to ¼" (0.6 cm) thickness and cut small circles with cookie cutter, about 2" (5 cm) across. ● Can be cooked in lightly greased iron frying pan or heavy-duty pan, 3-4 minutes on each side. If they brown too quickly, lower the heat to allow the inside to cook thoroughly so that they have a slightly brittle, sandy texture. ● Welsh cakes are known in South Wales as "South Wales Cakes" and regarded there as a specialty of that part of the country. Essentially, they are griddle cakes (called a bakestone in Wales), but they can be cooked in a heavy pan or skillet.

IRISH BRACK

A tea bread!

1 cup	brown sugar	250 mL
1 lb.	mixed dried fruit	500 g
1 cup	cold tea	250 mL
1	egg, beaten	1
2 cups	self-raising flour	500 mL

Soak the fruit and sugar in the cold tea, overnight. ● Next day, preheat oven to 350°F (180°C). ● Line loaf pan with buttered paper. ● Fold egg and flour into fruit mixture. ● Turn into loaf pan and bake for 1¼-1½ hours. ● Cool and slice thinly; serve with butter.

BRUNCH
Papaya Seed Dressing Salad, page 74
King Crab Flambé, page 14
Mai Tai, page 204

2-2½ cups	all-purpose flour	500-625 mL
1 tsp.	EACH salt, baking powder, baking soda and cream of tartar	5 mL
2 tbsp.	sugar	30 mL
3 tbsp.	butter OR margarine OR lard	45 mL
1	egg	1
	milk	

SCONES

Combine dry ingredients and cut in butter or shortening. • Beat egg in measuring cup and fill to 1 cup (250 mL) with milk. • Add egg mixture to dry ingredients. • Turn out on floured board and knead lightly. Press by hand, or roll out, to about ½" (1.3 cm) thickness. Cut with floured cookie cutter, or cut into squares with knife. • Bake on ungreased cookie sheet for 10-15 minutes, or until lightly browned, in 400°F (200°C) oven. • **Variation:** Cheese Scones — add a pinch of cayenne pepper and ½ cup (125 mL) grated cheese, after adding the butter.

1	egg	1
¼ cup	sugar	50 mL
¾ cup	milk	175 mL
1 cup	flour	250 mL
1 tsp.	baking powder	5 mL
¼ tsp.	salt	1 mL
2 tsp.	butter (optional)	10 mL

PICKELETS

Little pancakes from New Zealand and Australia.

Beat the egg and sugar until thick and add with the milk to the sifted flour, salt and baking powder. Lastly, add melted butter. • Mix until smooth and cook in spoonfuls on a hot greased griddle or frying pan. • Serve with butter, jam or sliced strawberries and/or whipped cream, or as desired.

½ cup	flour	125 mL
¼ tsp.	salt	1 mL
¼ tsp.	baking powder	1 mL
1	egg	1
½ cup	milk	125 mL
½ cup	water	125 mL

YORKSHIRE PUDDING

Sift dry ingredients twice. • Break egg into dry ingredients, combine milk and water and add a little at a time to dry ingredients. Beat smoothly until like thick cream. Let stand 1 hour. • Put a dessertspoon of fat into a 9" (2.5 L) square pan. • Heat fat in pan until it is very hot in a 450°F (230°C) oven. • Pour mixture into hot fat and bake for 20 minutes. • Serve immediately.

Reheating pastry: sugary buns, such as doughnuts, bismarks, cinnamon buns and all kinds of pastry heat from the inside out. Care must be taken not to heat too long. 10-15 seconds on high for one is sufficient.

CHEESE KUCHEN

2 cups	flour	500 mL
2 tsp.	baking powder	10 mL
2 tbsp.	shortening	30 mL
2 tbsp.	sugar	30 mL
	milk, to make a soft dough, like pie crust	

TOPPING

3 cups	dry cottage cheese	750 mL
¾ cup	sugar	175 mL
2	eggs, beaten	2
1½ cups	sweet cream	375 mL
1 tsp.	vanilla	5 mL
pinch	salt	pinch
	sugar	
	cinnamon	

Combine first 5 ingredients to make dough. • Roll out dough and put on a 10" x 16" (25cm x 38 cm) pan. • Combine next 6 ingredients and spread on top. • Sprinkle with sugar and cinnamon. • Bake at 350°F (180°C) for 40 minutes or until done. • Makes 2 dozen squares.

CHAPATI (OR ROTI)

1 tbsp.	lard	15 mL
2 tbsp.	margarine	30 mL
1½ cups	vegetable oil	375 mL
3 lbs.	flour	1.5 kg
3½ tsp.	baking powder	17 mL
pinch	salt	pinch
3 cups	water	750 mL

An East Indian flat bread.

Melt lard and margarine and mix with the oil. • Sift flour, baking powder and salt. Combine flour mixture with the water to make dough. • Use a little oil on hands to knead the dough. Leave for 20 minutes. • Cut into small pieces and form into balls. Roll out each ball flat using a rolling pin. Brush with oil mixture, using a pastry brush. Fold into balls again and leave for 10 minutes. • Roll out very flat and round. • Cook on a hot pan. • After 1½ minutes, brush with oil, turn over and brush with oil. • Cook for another minute. Remove from pan, clap between hands while still hot. Fold in half and fold again. • Place in a dish, cover with foil, or wax paper, and a towel. • Serve with Curries.

Here's a wonderful way to give your home an aromatic scent that friends or company will always compliment you on. Fill a pot ¾ full of water. Add allspice, cinnamon, cloves, nutmeg, orange and lemon rinds (you can add about 1-2 tsp. [5-10 mL] of each of the spices). Boil slowly and check occasionally to see if you require more water. Add more of the same spices to strengthen mixture as needed. This mixture can be kept in the refrigerator and used when a nice fragrance is required. Be sure to add more water and stir before heating.

1 cup	whole-wheat flour	250 mL
1 cup	rolled oats	250 mL
1 tsp.	baking powder	5 mL
1 tsp.	baking soda	5 mL
2 tbsp.	sugar	30 mL
1 tsp.	salt	5 mL
2	eggs	2
3 tbsp.	vegetable oil	45 mL
2 cups	buttermilk	500 mL

OATMEAL PANCAKES

Combine flour, rolled oats, baking powder, baking soda, sugar and salt. • Combine eggs, oil and buttermilk. • Add liquid ingredients to dry ingredients and mix only until blended. • Cook the pancakes on a hot, lightly oiled, griddle. • Serve hot with maple syrup, or honey-butter, or Lemon Sauce below:

½ cup	sugar	125 mL
1 tbsp.	cornstarch	15 mL
⅛ tsp.	salt	0.5 mL
1 cup	boiling water	250 mL
2 tbsp.	butter	30 mL
2 tbsp.	lemon juice	30 mL
1	egg yolk	1

LEMON SAUCE FOR PANCAKES

Mix sugar, cornstarch and salt. • Add boiling water slowly, stirring constantly. • Boil for 5 minutes. • Take from heat and add butter, lemon juice and beaten egg yolk.

1½ lbs.	cottage cheese	750 g
	salt, to taste	
2	egg yolks, beaten	2
1 tbsp.	butter	15 mL
1 tbsp.	sugar	15 mL
1 cup	milk	250 mL
1 tsp	salt	5 mL
4	eggs	4
1 cup	flour (scant)	250 mL
	sour cream	
	strawberries	

BLINTZES

Elegant cottage cheese pancakes.

To make filling, press cheese through colander. • Add salt to taste, 2 egg yolks, butter and sugar. • Make batter by adding milk to salt and eggs, stirring in the flour gradually until smooth. • Heat heavy 6″ (15 cm) skillet and grease with oil. • Pour only enough batter to make a very thin pancake, tipping pan from side to side to cover the bottom. Cook on 1 side only until it blisters. Tip onto board, cooked side up. • Place rounded tablespoon (15 mL) of cheese mixture on pancake and fold over like an envelope. • Fry on both sides until golden brown. • Serve with sour cream and strawberries.

CORNMEAL PANCAKES

1 cup	cornmeal	250 mL
2 cups	milk	500 mL
1¼ cups	flour	300 mL
1 tbsp.	baking powder	15 mL
½ tsp.	salt	2 mL
¼ cup	sugar	50 mL
2	eggs	2
¼ cup	butter OR margarine, melted	50 mL

Mix cornmeal and milk in bowl and let stand 5 minutes. • Blend together flour, baking powder, salt and sugar. • Beat eggs and add to cornmeal mixture. • Add melted butter. • Mix in dry ingredients until smooth. • Cook on hot greased griddle. • Makes 12 medium pancakes.

PECAN WAFFLES

2	eggs	2
1½ cups	milk	375 mL
¼ cup	vegetable oil	50 mL
1½ cups	all-purpose flour	375 mL
2 tsp.	baking powder	10 mL
½ tsp.	salt	2 mL
½ cup	chopped pecans	125 mL

In blender, combine eggs, milk and oil. Process until blended. • Add flour, baking powder and salt; mix just until blended, scraping sides of blender, if necessary. • Add pecans and process in 3, 1-second on/off motions. • Pour batter onto preheated waffle iron in batches and cook until waffles stop steaming. • Serve with maple syrup. • Serves approximately 4.

BELGIAN WAFFLES

1 tbsp.	dry yeast (1 pkg.)	15 mL
2½ cups	lukewarm milk	625 mL
6	eggs, separated	6
1 tsp.	vanilla	5 mL
2 tbsp.	brandy	30 mL
2½-3 cups	flour	625-750 mL
1 tbsp.	powdered sugar	15 mL
1 tsp.	salt	5 mL
½ cup	melted butter	125 mL

Sprinkle yeast over warm milk; stir to dissolve. • Beat egg yolks and add to yeast mixture with vanilla and brandy. • Sift flour with sugar and salt. • Add flour mixture to liquid mixture; beat until well blended. • Stir in melted butter; combine thoroughly. • Beat egg whites until stiff, stir ¼ of the beaten whites into batter. Carefully fold in remainder. • Let mixture stand in warm place to rise for at least 45 minutes or until doubled. • Bake slowly in well-heated waffle iron until done, approximately 4-5 minutes. • Delicious with sliced strawberries and whipped cream.

2	overripe bananas	2
½ cup	dark brown sugar	125 mL
¼ cup	soft shortening	75 mL
1	egg	1
1 tsp.	vanilla	5 mL
1½ cups	sifted all-purpose flour	375 mL
1 tsp.	baking powder	5 mL
1 tsp.	baking soda	5 mL
½ tsp.	salt	2 mL
¼ cup	water	50 mL
½ cup	chopped walnuts	125 mL
¼ cup	granulated sugar	50 mL
1 tsp.	cinnamon	5 mL

CRUNCHY BANANA MUFFINS

Mash bananas a little, then add the brown sugar, soft shortening, egg and vanilla. Beat until well blended. • Add flour, baking powder, baking soda, salt and barely mix in. • Add water and nuts. Stir just enough to blend. Do not overstir. • Spoon into 12, 2½″ (6.5 cm) greased muffin tins, filling nearly to the brim. • Mix the sugar and cinnamon for the topping. Sprinkle all of it evenly over top of unbaked muffins. • Bake at 350°F (180°C) for 25 minutes. • Serve hot. • These muffins freeze well. • Makes 12.

½ cup	canned milk	125 mL
¾ cup	canned pumpkin	175 mL
½ cup	honey	125 mL
¼ cup	melted butter	75 mL
1	egg	1
¾ cup	all-purpose flour	175 mL
1 tbsp.	baking powder	15 mL
½ tsp.	EACH salt, cinnamon, cloves, nutmeg	2 mL
1 cup	rolled oats OR bran	250 mL
½ cup	raisins	125 mL
¼ cup	chopped nuts	50 mL

PUMPKIN MUFFINS

Combine milk, pumpkin, honey, butter and egg. • Sift dry ingredients together and stir rolled oats, raisins and nuts into them. • Add liquid ingredients to dry mixture and stir just until moist. • Fill greased muffin tins ¾ full. • Bake at 400°F (200°C) for 20 minutes. • Makes 12.

THE LATEST IN HERBS
BASIL — *great for rice, cheese, mushrooms, peas, squash, green beans and lamb.*
BAY LEAF — *spaghetti sauce, pot roast, chicken, fricassee and fish chowder.*
DILL — *peps up potatoes, cream soups, fish and vegetables.*
MARJORAM — *lima beans, peas, green beans, omelets and chicken.*
OREGANO — *chili, salads, pork or lamb*
ROSEMARY — *is appealing in spinach, green beans, corn bread and fish.*
THYME — *takes to lamb, carrots, creamed onions and chicken and stew.*

RHUBARB MUFFINS

1	egg	1
1¼ cups	firmly packed brown sugar	300 mL
½ cup	salad oil	125 mL
2 tsp.	vanilla	10 mL
1 cup	buttermilk	250 mL
2½ cups	flour	625 mL
1 tsp.	baking soda	5 mL
1 tsp.	baking powder	5 mL
½ tsp.	salt	2 mL
2½ cups	diced rhubarb	625 mL
½ cup	chopped walnuts	125 mL

TOPPING

1 tbsp.	melted butter OR margarine	15 mL
¼ cup	white sugar	50 mL
1 tsp.	cinnamon	5 mL

Combine egg, sugar, oil, vanilla and buttermilk. • Add flour sifted with baking soda, baking powder and salt. • Add rhubarb and nuts. Do not overstir. • Fill muffins tins ¾ full. • Combine topping ingredients and sprinkle evenly over muffins. • Bake at 375°F (190°C) for about 20 minutes or until muffins are lightly browned. • Makes approximately 20.

CARROT AND APPLESAUCE MUFFINS

3 cups	flour	750 mL
2½ tsp.	baking powder	12 mL
1 tsp.	baking soda	5 mL
½ tsp.	salt	2 mL
2 tsp.	cinnamon	10 mL
1 tsp.	cloves	5 mL
½ tsp.	nutmeg	2 mL
1 cup	brown sugar	250 mL
1 cup	vegetable oil	250 mL
1 cup	applesauce	250 mL
3 cups	grated carrot	750 mL
3	eggs, beaten	3
1 cup	raisins	250 mL

Sift first 8 ingredients and put in large bowl. • Add last 5 ingredients. Stir only until combined. • Bake at 350°F (180°C) for 15-20 minutes. • Makes 24 large muffins.

To ripen peaches, pears or tomatoes quickly, place them in a brown paper bag, with a ripe apple. Poke a hole in the bag and put it in a cool, dark place, the apple will give off ethylene gas and cause the other fruit to ripen.

⅔ cup	white flour	150 mL
1 cup	whole-wheat flour	250 mL
4 tsp.	baking powder	20 mL
½ tsp.	baking soda	2 mL
½ cup	bran	125 mL
¾ cup	oat flakes	175 mL
½ tsp.	salt	2 mL
¼ cup	wheat germ	50 mL
1-2 tsp.	cinnamon	5-10 mL
¼ cup	brown sugar	50 mL
1½ cups	raisins OR dates	375 mL
½ cup	chocolate chips	125 mL
2	eggs, beaten	2
1 cup	milk	250 mL
4 tbsp.	vegetable oil	60 mL
¼ cup	molasses	50 mL

JOGGERS' MUFFINS

Mix together dry ingredients, add fruit and chocolate chips. • Combine beaten egg, milk, oil and molasses. • Stir into dry ingredients until mixture is moistened. • Fill greased muffin pans. • Bake at 350°F (180°C) for 18-20 minutes.

¼ cup	shortening	50 mL
½ cup	firmly packed brown sugar	125 mL
¼ cup	molasses	50 mL
2	eggs, unbeaten	2
1 cup	milk	250 mL
1¼ cups	natural wheat bran	300 mL
¼ cup	natural wheat germ	50 mL
1 cup	flour	250 mL
1½ tsp.	baking powder	7 mL
½ tsp.	baking soda	2 mL
¾ tsp.	salt	3 mL
14 oz.	can blueberries	398 mL

BLUEBERRY BRAN MUFFINS

Cream shortening and sugar together. • Add molasses and egg, beat well. • Add milk, then bran and wheat germ. • Combine flour, baking powder, baking soda and salt. Add to liquid ingredients. • Mix well, fold in drained blueberries. • Place in greased muffin pans. • Bake at 400°F (200°C) for 20 minutes. • Makes 12 large muffins.

Variations:

1. Omit blueberries; add to dry ingredients: ⅛ tsp. (0.5 mL) EACH: nutmeg, cloves and cinnamon. Fold in ½ cup (125 mL) grated carrots and ½ cup (125 mL) chopped walnuts. • 2. Omit blueberries; add ½ cup (125 mL) chocolate chips. • 3. Omit blueberries; add ½ cup (125 mL) crushed pineapple.

CRANBERRY MUFFINS

2 cups	all-purpose flour	500 mL
1 cup	white sugar	250 mL
1½ tsp.	baking powder	7 mL
½ tsp.	baking soda	2 mL
½ tsp.	salt	2 mL
¼ cup	shortening	50 mL
¾ cup	orange juice	175 mL
1 tbsp.	dried orange rind	15 mL
1	egg, well beaten	1
½ cup	chopped walnuts	125 mL
1-2 cups	cranberries	250-500 mL

Sift together first 5 ingredients. • Cut in shortening until mixture resembles coarse cornmeal. • Combine orange juice and rind with well-beaten egg. • Pour in all at once; mix just enough to dampen. • Fold in nuts and berries. • Fill muffin cups ¾ full. • Bake in 400°F (200°C) oven, 20-25 minutes.

CARROT-BRAN MUFFINS

6 cups	flour	1.5 L
1 tbsp.	baking soda	15 mL
3 tbsp.	baking powder	45 mL
3 tbsp.	cinnamon	45 mL
1 tsp.	salt	5 mL
4 cups	bran	1 L
4 cups	brown sugar	1 L
2 cups	vegetable oil	500 mL
8	eggs	8
6 cups	grated carrot OR zucchini	1.5 L
1 lb.	raisins OR currants	500 g

Combine dry ingredients. • In a separate bowl, combine oil and eggs. • Stir into dry mixture and add remaining ingredients. • Bake at 350°F (180°C) for 18 minutes. • Frozen, shredded zucchini, is excellent. • Makes 4 dozen.

LIGHT APPLE BRAN MUFFINS

Gluten-free muffins.

¼ cup	margarine	50 mL
⅜ cup	sugar	85 mL
2 tbsp.	molasses	30 mL
2	eggs	2
1	small apple	1
1¼ cups	brown rice flour	300 mL
¼ cup	rice bran	50 mL
pinch	salt	pinch
2 tsp.	baking powder	10 mL
½ tsp.	baking soda	2 mL
½ cup	buttermilk	125 mL

Cream margarine and sugar, add molasses. • Add eggs and beat well. • Add peeled, chopped apple. • Sift dry ingredients and mix in alternately with buttermilk. • Stir just until blended. • Bake at 425°F (200°C) for approximately 15-18 minutes in greased muffin pans.

1 cup	oatmeal	250 mL
1 cup	milk	250 mL
1 cup	flour	250 mL
1 tsp.	baking powder	5 mL
½ tsp.	baking soda	2 mL
	salt, to taste	
⅔ cup	brown sugar	150 mL
1	egg, beaten	1
4 tbsp.	melted butter OR margarine	60 mL
½ cup	chocolate chips	125 mL
¼ cup	chopped walnuts	50 mL
1	orange, rind of	1

OATMEAL CHOCOLATE CHIP MUFFINS

Let oats stand for 10 minutes in milk. • Combine flour, baking powder, baking soda, salt and brown sugar. • Add egg and butter. • Mix well and add oat mixture. • Add chocolate chips, walnuts and orange rind. • Bake in greased muffin tins at 400°F (200°C) for 20 minutes.

2 cups	boiling water	500 mL
2 cups	natural bran	500 mL
3 cups	white sugar	750 mL
2 cups	margarine	500 mL
4	eggs	4
1 qt.	buttermilk	1 L
5 cups	flour	1.25 L
4 cups	bran flakes	1 L
2 tsp.	baking soda	10 mL
1 tsp.	salt	5 mL
2 cups	raisins OR dates	500 mL

BRAN MUFFINS

Combine water and natural bran, let stand for a few minutes. • Add sugar, margarine and eggs and beat until smooth. • Add buttermilk, flour, bran flakes, baking soda, salt and raisins. Mix until moist. • Bake at 375°F (190°C) for 15 minutes. • This batter may be stored in a closed container and refrigerated and baked as needed. Will keep 3-4 weeks. Age improves flavor.

6	eggs, separated	6
2 cups	packed brown sugar	500 mL
2 cups	flour	500 mL
1½ tsp.	nutmeg	7 mL
2 tsp.	cinnamon	10 mL
2 tsp.	cloves	10 mL
1 tsp.	salt	5 mL

DUTCH BREAKFAST CAKE

Beat egg yolks with sugar. • Add flour, spices and salt. • Fold in stiffly beaten egg whites. • Bake in 3″ x 5″ (2L) loaf pan at 350°F (180°C) for 45 minutes.

BISHOP'S BREAD

1 cup	sugar	250 mL
4 tsp.	baking powder	20 mL
3 cups	flour	750 mL
½ tsp.	salt	2 mL
1	egg, beaten	1
1 cup	milk	250 mL
½ cup	melted butter	125 mL
½ cup	raisins	125 mL

Sift dry ingredients together. • Add beaten egg and milk. • Add melted butter and raisins. • Pour into greased and lightly floured 3" x 5" (2L) loaf pan. • Bake in 375°F (190°C) oven for 40-50 minutes.

APRICOT BREAD

½ cup	dried apricots	125 mL
1 cup	sugar	250 mL
2 tbsp.	melted shortening	30 mL
1	egg, beaten	1
2 cups	flour	500 mL
1 tbsp.	baking powder	15 mL
¼ tsp.	baking soda	1 mL
¾ tsp.	salt	3 mL
½ cup	orange juice	125 mL
¼ cup	water	50 mL
½ cup	chopped Brazil nuts OR walnuts	125 mL

Soak apricots in cold water for ½ hour; drain; put through blender or food chopper. • Add sugar and melted shortening to beaten egg. • Sift together the flour, baking powder, baking soda and salt. • Combine orange juice and water. • Add flour mixture alternately with liquids and apricot pulp. • Add chopped nuts. • Pour batter into prepared loaf pan. • Bake at 350°F (180°C) for 1 to 1½ hours.

CRAB APPLE LOAF

2 cups	chopped crab apples	500 mL
1 cup	sugar (half brown, half white)	250 mL
2-3 tsp.	cinnamon	10-15 mL
1 ½ cups	flour	375 mL
1 tsp.	baking soda	5 mL
pinch	salt	pinch
1	egg	1
½ cup	melted butter OR margarine	125 mL

Mix first 3 ingredients and let stand ½ hour. • Combine remaining ingredients. • Add apple mixture and blend. • Bake 1 hour at 375°F (190°C). • Makes 1 medium loaf.

¾ cup	rice flour	175 mL
½ cup	potato flour	125 mL
1½ tsp.	baking soda	7 mL
2 tsp.	baking powder	10 mL
¼ tsp.	salt	1 mL
1 tbsp.	unflavored gelatin	15 mL
3	large eggs, separated	3
½ cup	margarine	125 mL
½ cup	sugar	125 mL
1 tsp.	vanilla	5 mL
1 tsp.	grated lemon peel	5 mL
¾ cup	mashed banana (2)	175 mL
4 tbsp.	sour cream OR yogurt	60 mL
½ cup	chopped nuts (optional)	125 mL

BANANA BREAD

Gluten-free.

Grease a 9″ x 5″ x 3″ (2 L) loaf pan. • Heat oven to 350°F (180°C). • Sift flour, baking soda, baking powder, salt and gelatin together 3 times and set aside. • Beat egg whites until stiff. • Cream margarine and sugar until light, add egg yolks, vanilla, and lemon peel and beat well. • Add mashed banana and yogurt, mix well. • Sift flour mixture in gradually while stirring gently. • Fold in egg whites. • Add nuts. • Put mixture into pan. • Bake at 350°F (180°C) for 1 hour or until toothpick inserted in centre comes out clean. • Cool for 10 minutes on rack and remove from pan.

3 cups	flour	750 mL
2 tsp.	baking powder	10 mL
½ tsp.	baking soda	2 mL
¾ cup	sugar	175 mL
¾ tsp.	salt	3 mL
1 tbsp.	grated orange rind	15 mL
¼ cup	orange juice	50 mL
¼ cup	melted butter	50 mL
¾ cup	milk	175 mL
1	egg, beaten	1
1 cup	blueberries, fresh OR canned, drained and dried	250 mL
½ cup	chopped walnuts	125 mL

BLUEBERRY-ORANGE LOAF

Place flour, baking powder, baking soda, sugar and salt in bowl. • Combine next 5 ingredients. • Add to flour mixture and beat well. • Grease 9″ x 4″ x 3″ (1.5 L) loaf pan. • Spread ¼ mixture in pan. Sprinkle with ½ of the blueberries and nuts. • Add another ¼ batter, then remaining fruit and nuts and place remaining batter over fruit and nuts. • Bake at 350°F (180°C) for 50 minutes. • Frost when cool, if desired, or serve with orange butter.

Of all the things you wear, your expression is the most important.

CRANBERRY-ORANGE BREAD

This loaf is very colorful, perfect for the Christmas season!

2 cups	sifted flour	500 mL
1½ tsp.	baking powder	7 mL
½ tsp.	baking soda	2 mL
½ tsp.	salt	2 mL
1 cup	sugar	250 mL
2 tbsp.	butter OR margarine	30 mL
1	orange, grated rind, plus juice to make ¾ cup (175 mL)	1
1	egg, beaten	1
1 cup	halved raw cranberries	250 mL

Sift together first 5 ingredients • Mix together butter, rind, juice and egg. • Combine with dry ingredients. • Fold in cranberries. • Pour into greased 5″ x 9″ (2L) loaf pan. • Bake at 350°F (180°C) for 1 hour.

PUMPKIN BREAD ROLLS

1½ cups	sugar	375 mL
2 cups	flour	500 mL
2 tsp.	baking powder	10 mL
2 tsp.	cinnamon	10 mL
	salt, to taste	
½ cup	raisins	125 mL
½ cup	coconut	125 mL
½ cup	walnuts OR pecans	125 mL
3	eggs, beaten	3
2 cups	cooked pumpkin	500 mL
1 cup	vegetable oil	250 mL

Combine dry ingredients. Combine eggs, pumpkin and oil; add to dry ingredients and let stand for 20 minutes. • Grease 6 x 14 oz. (398 mL) vegetable cans well with shortening. • Fill cans about ⅔ full. • Bake at 350°F (180°C) for 1 hour.

LEMON LOAF OR CAKE

6 tbsp.	butter	90 mL
1 cup	white sugar	250 mL
2	eggs, beaten	2
½ cup	milk	125 mL
1½ cups	sifted flour	375 mL
½ tsp.	salt	2 mL
1 tsp.	baking powder	5 mL
1	lemon, grated rind of	1

TOPPING

1	lemon, juice of	1
¼ cup	white sugar	75 mL

Cream butter and sugar and add beaten eggs, milk, flour, salt, baking powder and lemon rind. Beat well. • Bake in wax paper-lined 3″ x 5″ (2 L) loaf pan or a small bundt pan at 350°F (180°C) for 1 hour. • Remove from pan, take paper off immediately and pour the topping mixture over the loaf. • Makes 1 loaf.

1½ cups	all-purpose flour	375 mL
½ tsp.	nutmeg	2 mL
1 tsp.	baking powder	5 mL
1 tsp.	baking soda	5 mL
½ tsp.	salt	2 mL
1 tsp.	cinnamon	5 mL
½ tsp.	ground cloves	2 mL
¾ tsp.	ground ginger	3 mL
2	eggs	2
¾ cup	sugar	175 mL
¼ cup	golden corn syrup	50 mL
½ cup	corn oil	125 mL
1 cup	pumpkin	250 mL
½ cup	chopped walnuts OR pecans (optional)	125 mL
½ cup	raisins	125 mL

SPICY PUMPKIN LOAF

Preheat oven to 325°F (160°C). • Grease and line the bottom of a 9″ x 5″ (2 L) loaf pan with waxed paper. • Sift flour, then stir together the first 8 ingredients. • Beat eggs until light. • Add sugar, corn syrup, corn oil and pumpkin; beat until thoroughly combined. • Make a well in the dry ingredients; add the liquid ingredients all at once and stir until well mixed. • Add the raisins and chopped nuts and combine well. • Pour the batter into the prepared loaf pan and bake for 80 minutes, or until cake tester (toothpick) inserted in the center comes out clean. • Remove from pan after 10 minutes, peel off the waxed paper and cool completely on a cake rack. Wrap tightly to store. • Loaf will slice more easily if stored for at least 8 hours. • Enjoy!

4	eggs	4
2 cups	brown sugar	500 mL
1½ cups	cooking oil	375 mL
3 cups	grated carrots	750 mL
1 cup	mixed fruit	250 mL
1 tsp.	vanilla	5 mL
1 cup	walnuts	250 mL
1 cup	raisins	250 mL
2 tsp.	baking soda	10 mL
2 tsp.	baking powder	10 mL
½ tsp.	EACH: nutmeg, allspice, cloves	2 mL
2 tsp.	cinnamon	10 mL
1 tsp.	ginger	5 mL
½ tsp.	salt	2 mL
3 cups	flour	750 mL

CARROT LOAF

Beat eggs until light. • Add brown sugar and cooking oil. Beat again. • Add grated carrots, mixed fruit dredged in ½ cup (125 mL) of the flour, and remaining ingredients. • Bake in 2 loaf pans for 1-1½ hours at 350°F (180°C), 325°F (160°C) for glass. • Makes 2 loaves.

29

SOUR CREAM COFFEE CAKE

½ cup	butter OR margarine	125 mL
1 cup	white sugar	250 mL
2	eggs	2
1¼ cups	commercial sour cream	300 mL
2 cups	all-purpose flour	500 mL
1 tsp.	baking powder	5 mL
1 tsp.	baking soda	5 mL
pinch	salt	pinch
1 tsp.	vanilla	5 mL
¼ cup	light brown sugar	50 mL
2 tsp.	cinnamon	10 mL
1 cup	chopped walnuts OR pecans	250 mL

Cream together butter and sugar. • Add eggs and beat well. • Add sour cream, combining well. • Sift flour; add baking powder, baking soda and salt and sift again. Add to creamed mixture, beat for 3 or 4 minutes. • Add vanilla and combine well. • In a small bowl, combine brown sugar, cinnamon and chopped walnuts. • In a greased and floured 10″ (25 cm) tube pan, put ½ the batter. • Spread ⅔ of the walnut mixture over the batter. Score and mix in with a knife. • Pour rest of batter on top and remaining ¼ of walnut mixture, scoring and mixing as before. • Bake in a 350°F (180°C) oven, [375°F (190°C) in Calgary], for 45 minutes. • Cool, turn out and cool completely. • Slice and spread with butter. • Serves 14-16.

ZUCCHINI LOAF

2 cups	grated peeled zucchini	500 mL
½ cup	chopped walnuts	125 mL
1½ cups	steamed raisins	375 mL
1½ cups	white sugar	375 mL
2	eggs	2
1 cup	vegetable oil	250 mL
1 tbsp.	vanilla	15 mL
3 cups	flour	750 mL
1 tsp.	salt	5 mL
1 tsp.	baking soda	5 mL
2 tsp.	baking powder	10 mL
1 tsp.	cinnamon	5 mL
½ cup	mixed fruit (optional)	125 mL

Prepare the first 3 ingredients ahead of time. • Beat together the next 4 ingredients. • Add the zucchini. • Sift together the next 5 ingredients. • Combine the creamed mixture and dry ingredients. • Add walnuts, raisins and mixed fruit to sifted ingredients. • Bake at 325°F (160°C) for approximately 1 hour and 10 minutes. • Makes 2 loaves.

Toast the nut meats and while hot add a little butter. Your nut bread will take on a new aristocracy.

¾ cup	margarine	175 mL
2 cups	white sugar	500 mL
2 tsp.	vanilla	10 mL
3	eggs	3
1½ cups	white flour	375 mL
1½ cups	whole-wheat flour	375 mL
½ cup	cocoa	125 mL
2½ tsp.	baking powder	12 mL
1½ tsp.	baking soda	7 mL
1 tsp.	cinnamon	5 mL
2 cups	grated raw zucchini	500 mL
½ cup	milk	125 mL
1 cup	chopped nuts	250 mL

CHOCOLATE ZUCCHINI LOAF

Cream margarine, sugar and vanilla. • Beat in eggs, 1 at a time. • Sift flours, cocoa, baking powder, baking soda and cinnamon. • Add flour mixture to creamed mixture in thirds, alternating with zucchini and milk. • Add nuts. • Divide mixture between 2 greased large loaf pans. • Bake 1 hour at 350°F (180°C). • May frost with chocolate icing. • Freezes well. • Makes 2 loaves.

3 cups	flour	750 mL
2 tsp.	baking soda	10 mL
1 tsp.	cinnamon	5 mL
½ tsp.	EACH: allspice and cloves	2 mL
2 cups	chopped dates	500 mL
1 cup	chopped walnuts	250 mL
1 cup	butter OR margarine	250 mL
2 cups	packed brown sugar	500 mL
2	eggs	2
2 cups	beer	500 mL
	confectioner's (icing) sugar (optional)	
½ cup	softened butter OR margarine, whipped with:	125 mL
2 tbsp.	rum	30 mL

GERMAN BEER COFFEE CAKE WITH RUM BUTTER SPREAD

RUM BUTTER SPREAD (optional)

Mix flour, baking soda, cinnamon, allspice and cloves. Set aside. • Combine dates and nuts. Stir in a small amount of flour mixture to coat. Set aside. • In a large bowl, cream butter and sugar. Add eggs, 1 at a time, beating well after each addition. Add flour mixture alternately with beer, blending well after each addition. Stir in dates and nuts. • Pour into a well-greased and floured 12-cup (3 L) fluted tube pan. • Bake in preheated 350°F (180°C) oven for 1¼ hours, or until toothpick inserted in center of cake comes out clean. • Cool pan on rack 10-12 minutes, then turn out onto a rack to cool completely. • Wrap in foil. Let stand 24 hours before serving. • Sprinkle with confectioner's sugar stirred through a strainer. • Serve with Rum Butter Spread, if desired. • Serves 18.

MOM'S BREAD

1 tsp.	sugar	5 mL
1 cup	warm water	250 mL
2 tbsp.	active dry yeast (2 x 7 g pkgs.)	30 mL
9 cups	white flour	2.25 L
2 cups	whole-wheat flour	500 mL
2 cups	scalded fresh milk OR 1 cup (250 mL) evaporated milk plus 1 cup (250 mL) hot water	500 mL
¼ cup	sugar	75 mL
1 tsp.	salt	5 mL
¼ cup	vegetable oil	75 mL
2 cups	cold water	500 mL

In a small bowl dissolve 1 tsp. (5 mL) sugar in 1 cup (250 mL) warm water. Sprinkle yeast onto water mixture and let work for about 10 minutes. • Measure the white flour and whole-wheat flour into a large kneading bowl. • In a large mixing bowl, add the scalded milk, ¼ cup (75 mL) of sugar, salt and vegetable oil. Stir until dissolved, then add the cold water to make the solution lukewarm. • Add 2 cups (500 mL) of the measured flour to the milk mixture and make a smooth batter with a rotary hand beater. • Add the dissolved yeast mixture to the batter and beat with the rotary beater. • Keep on spooning the measured flour into the batter and mixing until the rotary beater is working too hard. • Scrape the batter into the remaining flour in the kneading bowl and knead until the dough becomes smooth. Small handfuls of extra flour might be needed so that the dough is elastic and no longer sticky. • Grease the kneading bowl lightly and cover the dough with a greased piece of plastic. • Let the dough rise in a warm place until doubled. • Turn the dough onto a greased surface and divide it into 6 large or 8 smaller loaves. • Shape and place in greased bread pans and cover with the piece of plastic. • Let the loaves rise in a warm place until just about double in size, about 1-1½ hours. • Bake in a preheated 400°F (200°C) oven for 10 minutes, lower the heat to 325°F (160°C) and cook for 20 minutes more. The top of the loaf should be golden brown, and the sides should be leaving the pan. • Remove from the pans immediately and let cool on wire racks. • Makes 6 large, or 8 small loaves.

RULES FOR USE OF LEAVENING AGENTS

1. *Use 2 tsp. (10 mL) of baking powder to leaven 1 cup (250 ml) flour. Lessen this amount for every egg used after the first.*
2. *Use ½ tsp. (2 mL) baking soda to 1 cup (250 mL) of sour milk.*
3. *Use ½ tsp. (2 mL) baking soda to 1 cup (250 mL) molasses. If milk or molasses are very acid, use in addition 1 tsp. (5 mL) baking powder to each cup (250 mL) flour.*
4. *Use 1 tsp. (5 mL) cream of tartar with ½ tsp. (2 mL) baking soda to 1 cup (250 mL) flour.*
5. *More leavening is needed if coarse flours are used.*

1 tsp.	salt	5 mL
5 tbsp.	brown sugar	75 mL
½ cup	molasses	125 mL
2 cups	rolled oats	500 mL
3 cups	boiling water	750 mL
3 cups	white flour	750 mL
1	yeast cake OR 1 tbsp. (15 mL) dried yeast	1
1 tbsp.	sugar	15 mL
½ cup	lukewarm water	125 mL
2 tbsp.	melted lard	30 mL
3-3½ cups	whole-wheat flour OR combination of white flour, wheat germ and bran	750-875 mL

TASTY MARITIMES BREAD

Stir salt, brown sugar, molasses and rolled oats into boiling water. Cool mixture to lukewarm. • Stir in white flour. • Dissolve yeast and sugar in lukewarm water and let stand for 10 minutes. Add to flour mixture and beat well. • Beat in melted lard. Add whole-wheat flour to make soft dough. • Knead for 3 to 5 minutes. • Let rise in warm place until doubled in bulk (about 1½ hours). • Punch down, shape, put in greased pans and let rise again. • Bake at 350°F (180°C) for 45 minutes. • Makes 2 large or 3 small loaves.

2 tsp.	sugar	10 mL
½ cup	warm water, 105-115°F (40.5-46°C)	125 mL
2 tbsp.	dry yeast (2 x 7 g pkgs.)	30 mL
¾ cup	warm milk	175 mL
¼ cup	sugar	50 mL
2 tsp.	salt	10 mL
¼ cup	shortening	50 mL
2	eggs	2
4½ cups	whole-wheat flour	1.125 L
1½ cups	raisins	375 mL

WHOLE-WHEAT RAISIN BREAD

Dissolve 2 tsp. (10 mL) sugar in ½ cup (125 mL) warm water. Sprinkle in yeast and let stand 10 minutes, then stir well. • Mix warm milk, salt, sugar, shortening, eggs and 1 cup (250 mL) flour. Beat smooth, add raisins, then add 3 cups (750 mL) flour gradually. If necessary, add more flour to make soft dough. • Knead for 10 minutes adding enough flour to make dough smooth and elastic. • Place in greased bowl and grease top of dough. • Let rise in warm place, 75-80°F (24-26.5°C) until doubled in volume, 1-1½ hours. • Turn out on floured board and divide in half. • Shape into round flat loaves and place on cookie sheet. • Cover and let rise 1 hour. • Bake on middle rack of oven at 350°F (180°C) for 25 minutes. • You can use regular loaf pans, if you prefer. • Makes 2 loaves.

BROWN BREAD

2 tsp.	white sugar	10 mL
1 cup	lukewarm water	250 mL
1 tbsp.	yeast (7 g pkg.)	15 mL
3 cups	scalded milk	750 mL
¼ cup	molasses	75 mL
4 tsp.	salt	20 mL
¼ cup	margarine	50 mL
2 tbsp.	brown sugar	30 mL
4-9 cups	whole-wheat flour	1-2.25 L
5 cups	all-purpose flour (optional)	1.25 L

Dissolve white sugar in lukewarm water and add yeast. Let stand 15 minutes.
• Mix milk, molasses, salt, margarine, and brown sugar until smooth. • Add 4 cups (1 L) whole-wheat flour and mix well with a beater. • Add 4-5 cups (1-1.25 L) white or whole-wheat flour. • Knead well. • Let rise until double in bulk. • Knead down and shape into loaves, place in pans and let rise until double in bulk again. • Bake at 425°F (220°C) oven for 35-40 minutes. • I use both brown and white flour; if you use all whole-wheat, the bread is heavier.

ONE-BOWL FRENCH BREAD

3-3½ cups	unsifted all-purpose flour, divided	750-875 mL
4 tsp.	sugar	20 mL
1½ tsp.	salt	7 mL
1 tbsp.	active dry yeast, (7 g pkg.)	15 mL
2 tbsp.	soft margarine	30 mL
1¼ cups	very hot tap water cornmeal	300 mL
1	egg white, slightly beaten	1
1 tbsp.	cold water	15 mL

Combine 1 cup (250 mL) flour, sugar, salt and undissolved dry yeast in a large bowl. Mix thoroughly. Add soft margarine. Add very hot tap water gradually to dry ingredients. • Beat 2 minutes at medium speed on electric mixer, scraping bowl occasionally; add 1 cup (250 mL) flour, or enough to make thick batter.
• Beat at high speed for 2 minutes, scraping occasionally. • Stir in enough additional flour to make a soft dough. • Cover bowl tightly with plastic wrap. Let rest 45 minutes. • Stir dough down, turn out on floured board. • Mold into oblong 15" (37.5 cm) long loaves; taper ends. • Place on greased sheet. Sprinkle with cornmeal. Cover. • Let rise until doubled, approximately 40 minutes. • Make 5 diagonal cuts on top of loaf with knife. Bake at 400°F (200°C) for 25 minutes. • Brush with combined beaten egg white and water. Return to oven. Bake 15 minutes longer, or until done. • Remove and cool. • See photograph on back cover.

1 cup	milk	250 mL
1 cup	hot water	250 mL
¼ cup	honey	50 mL
3 tbsp.	butter	50 mL
1¼ tsp.	salt	6 mL
2 tbsp.	dry yeast (2 x 7 g pkgs.)	30 mL
¼ cup	lukewarm water	50 mL
½ cup	instant, dry skim milk	125 mL
1	egg, lightly beaten	1
4 cups	whole-wheat flour	1 L
2 cups	unbleached white flour OR more	500 mL
1 cup	sultana raisins	250 mL
2 tbsp.	rum	30 mL
	melted butter	

RUM RAISIN BREAD

In a saucepan scald milk, add hot water, honey, the 3 tbsp. (50 mL) of butter cut in bits, and the salt. Stir the mixture until the butter has melted. Transfer to a large bowl and cool. • Proof the dry yeast in the lukewarm water for 10 minutes.
• Add to the bowl the instant dry skim milk, the egg and the yeast mixture.
• Stir in 2 cups (500 mL) whole-wheat flour (preferably hard wheat or bread flour) and 1 cup (250 mL) unbleached white flour. • Beat the dough at least 100 strokes. • Stir in remaining 2 cups (500 mL) whole-wheat flour and 1 cup (250 mL) unbleached white flour and beat the dough until it leaves the sides of the bowl. • Turn the dough onto a lightly floured surface and knead it, adding more flour if necessary, for 10-15 minutes. • Put the dough in a large buttered bowl, brush it with melted butter, cover and let rise in a warm place for 1 hour, or until doubled in bulk. • While the dough is rising, macerate the sultanas in the rum for 1 hour and drain. • Punch down the dough and, on a lightly floured surface, knead in the sultanas, a handful at a time. • Knead in more flour if dough becomes too sticky. • Divide the dough in half, cover and let rest for 10 minutes. • Shape the dough into 2 loaves and put each loaf into a buttered 8" x 4" x 3" (1.5 L) pan. Brush the loaves with melted butter, cover and allow to rise in a warm place for 45 minutes or until doubled in bulk. • Bake in a 350°F (180°C) oven for 50 minutes or until the bottom sounds hollow when tapped. • Remove loaves from pans and allow to cool on a rack.

HOUSE RULES

If you drop it — pick it up,
If you sleep on it — make it up,
If you wear it — hang it up,
If you spill it — wipe it up,
If you turn it on — turn it off,
If you open it — close it,
If it rings — answer it,
If it whines — feed it,
If it cries — love it!!!

CHEESE BREAD

1 tbsp.	yeast (7 g pkg.)	15 mL
¼ cup	warm water	50 mL
¼ cup	sugar	50 mL
¼ cup	shortening	50 mL
1 tsp.	salt	5 mL
¾ cup	milk, warmed	175 mL
2 cups	flour	500 mL

TOPPING

¾ cup	grated cheese, partly old OR nippy	175 mL
1	egg, beaten	1
5 tsp.	milk	25 mL
2 tsp.	grated onion caraway OR poppy seeds	10 mL

Dissolve yeast in warm water. Let stand for 10 minutes. • Mix sugar, shortening, salt and warm milk. Add yeast and stir. • Work in flour, adding more if necessary to make soft dough. • Spread out on a cookie sheet (butter fingers if it's too sticky to spread). • Mix first 4 topping ingredients and spread over dough. • Top with caraway or poppy seeds. • Cover with cloth and let rise in warm place for 1-1½ hours. • Bake at 375°F (190°C) for ½ hour. • Serve hot.

ONION BREAD

1 tsp.	sugar	5 mL
¼ cup	lukewarm water	50 mL
1 tbsp.	yeast (7 g pkg.)	15 mL
1½ oz.	onion soup mix (1 envelope)	40 g
2 cups	water	500 mL
2 tbsp.	sugar	30 mL
1 tsp.	salt	5 mL
2 tbsp.	grated Parmesan	30 mL
2 tbsp.	salad oil	30 mL
6 cups	flour (approximately) cornmeal	1.5 L

Dissolve 1 tsp. (5 mL) sugar in ¼ cup (50 mL) warm water and add yeast. Let rise 10 minutes. • Prepare soup mix by adding contents of package to 2 cups (500 mL) water and let simmer for 10 minutes. • Add rest of ingredients except flour and cornmeal to soup and allow to cool to room temperature, then add yeast mixture. • Add 3 cups (750 mL) flour and mix well, then gradually add remainder of flour. Work flour in until dough becomes stiff and easy to work. (Don't worry if you don't use all 6 cups (1.5 L) or if you need a little more.) • Knead dough for 10 minutes then cover and let rise in warm place until double in bulk. • Punch down and divide into 3 parts. • Divide each piece into 3 more parts, roll each piece to be about 12″ (30 cm) long then braid to form loaf. • Place loaves on cookie sheet which has been sprinkled with cornmeal and bake at 400°F (200°C) for 20-25 minutes. • Cool on racks. • Makes 3 loaves.

1 cup	warm milk	250 mL
1 tsp.	sugar	5 mL
1 tbsp.	yeast (7 g pkg.)	15 mL
1 cup	flour	250 mL
¾ cup	milk, at room temperature	175 mL
1½ tsp.	salt	7 mL
¼ cup	sugar	75 mL
1	egg, beaten	1
½ cup	butter, melted and cooled	125 mL
4 cups	flour	1 L
1 cup	cold butter	250 mL
1	egg, beaten with cold water	1

EASY CROISSANTS

In a medium bowl, stir warm milk and sugar together. Add yeast. Let stand 10 minutes. Stir well. ● Add flour, beat well. ● Add milk, salt, sugar and egg. Beat until smooth. ● Add butter, beat and set aside. ● In a large mixing bowl, place the 4 cups (1 L) of flour and the chilled butter. Cut butter into flour until pieces are the size of beans (not too small). ● Pour the liquid batter into the flour mixture; stir until moistened. ● Cover bowl with plastic wrap. ● Refrigerate for at least 4 hours or overnight. ● Remove from refrigerator. ● Press into a compact ball on a floured board and divide into 4 parts. ● Roll each into a circle 12″ OR 16″ (30 cm OR 40 cm). Cut each circle into 6 OR 8 pie-shaped wedges. ● For each croissant, roll a wedge towards the point. Shape into a crescent and place on ungreased baking sheet. ● Let rise at room temperature until doubled in bulk. (Rising time may be up to 2 hours or more). Brush each with egg beaten with cold water prior to baking. ● Preheat oven to 400°F (200°C). Place croissants in oven. Lower temperature to 350°F (180°C) and bake for 15-20 minutes until golden brown. ● Makes 24-32, depending upon size.

1 tbsp.	sugar	15 mL
½ cup	lukewarm water	125 mL
1 tbsp.	yeast (7 g pkg.)	15 mL
1 cup	mashed potatoes	250 mL
2	eggs	2
½ cup	sugar	125 mL
½ cup	butter OR margarine	125 mL
4 cups	flour	1 L

POTATO BUNS

Dissolve 1 tbsp. (15 mL) sugar in ½ cup (125 mL) lukewarm water, add yeast. Let stand for 10 minutes. ● Mix remaining ingredients, except flour, in blender or mixer. ● Add yeast mixture, stir and add flour. ● Roll into crescent rolls, see Croissants method, above, and place on greased cookie sheets. ● Let sit minimum of 4 hours (the longer they sit, the larger and lighter they become). ● Bake at 350°F (180°C) for 15-20 minutes. ● Makes 3 dozen.

REFRIGERATOR ROLLS

2 tbsp.	fast-rising dry yeast (2 x 7 g pkgs.)	30 mL
1 tsp.	sugar	5 mL
½ cup	lukewarm water	125 mL
2	eggs	2
½ cup	white sugar	125 mL
1 tbsp.	salt	15 mL
2 cups	warm water	500 mL
7-8 cups	all-purpose flour, OR half all-purpose flour and half whole-wheat flour	1.75-2 L
¼ cup	vegetable oil	50 mL

Dissolve yeast and 1 tsp. (5 mL) sugar in the ½ cup (125 mL) lukewarm water, according to directions on package. • In a large bowl beat eggs, add sugar, salt, the 2 cups (500 mL) warm water, and lastly the yeast mixture. • Gradually beat in 3-4 cups (750 mL-1 L) flour, then add the oil and mix well. • Gradually add the rest of the flour and knead dough on floured counter, or board, until dough is smooth and elastic. • Place dough in large greased bowl, turning dough to grease the top. • Cover with foil, or plastic wrap, and refrigerate until needed. • Cut off amount of dough required, shape into rolls, place on greased cookie sheet or pan and let rise in warm place until light. • Bake at 375°F (190°C) for 12-14 minutes, depending on size of rolls. • This dough may be kept for 7-10 days in refrigerator, kneading occasionally to prevent overrising.

QUICK BUNS

½ cup	sugar	125 mL
½ cup	vegetable oil	125 mL
2 tsp.	salt	10 mL
1 cup	boiling water	250 mL
1 cup	cold water	250 mL
2 tsp.	sugar	10 mL
2 cups	lukewarm water	500 mL
2 tbsp.	yeast (2 x 7 g pkgs.)	30 mL
2 cups	flour	500 mL
2	eggs, beaten	2
10-11 cups	flour	2.5-2.75 L

Combine the first 3 ingredients in a large bowl. Pour 1 cup (250 mL) boiling water, then 1 cup (250 mL) cold water over. • In a small bowl, dissolve the 2 tsp. (10 mL) sugar in the lukewarm water, add the yeast and let rise for 10 minutes. • To the first mixture add 2 cups (500 mL) flour and the beaten eggs. Beat well. Then add yeast mixture and the additional 10-11 (2.5-2.75 L) cups flour. • Set to rise. Punch down in 15 minutes. • Let rise another 15 minutes. • Shape rolls, put in pans. Let rise about 1 hour. • Bake at 375°F (190°C) for 12-15 minutes.

You never get a second chance to make a first impression.

1 tbsp.	dry yeast (7 g pkg.)	15 mL	
½ cup	lukewarm water	125 mL	**AIR BUNS**
1 tsp.	sugar	5 mL	
3½ cups	lukewarm water	875 mL	
½ cup	sugar	125 mL	
½ cup	lard OR shortening (not margarine)	125 mL	
2 tsp.	salt	10 mL	
1 tbsp.	vinegar	15 mL	
9-10 cups	white flour	2.25-2.5 L	
1 tsp.	sugar	5 mL	
2 tsp.	milk	10 mL	

Soften the yeast in the ½ cup (125 mL) lukewarm water with the 1 tsp. (5 mL) sugar for 10 minutes. • In a large bowl, combine the 3½ cups (875 mL) lukewarm water, the ½ cup (125 mL) sugar, the lard and the salt. Beat well with a wooden spoon or mixer. • Add the yeast mixture and vinegar. • Add the flour, 1 cup (250 mL) at a time, to make a good dough. • Knead well. • Let rise 1 hour. • Shape into buns. • Let rise 3 hours. • Bake in hot oven, 425°F (220°C) for 25 minutes. • Glaze with 1 tsp. (5 mL) sugar and 2 tsp. (10 mL) milk. • May also be made into bread loaves. • Makes 5 dozen buns.

1 tbsp.	fast rising yeast (7 g pkg.)	15 mL	
½ cup	lukewarm milk	125 mL	**KUFFELS**
1 tsp.	sugar	5 mL	
3 cups	flour	750 mL	
3 tbsp.	sugar	50 mL	
½ tsp.	salt	2 mL	
1 cup	margarine	250 mL	
2	eggs	2	
	melted butter		
½ cup	sugar	125 mL	
4 tsp.	cinnamon	20 mL	

Dissolve yeast in warm milk combined with 1 tsp. (5 mL) sugar. • Sift dry ingredients, except cinnamon, ½ cup (125 mL) sugar and melted butter into bowl. Cut in margarine. • Beat eggs into yeast and milk. Add liquid to dry ingredients. • Place dough in covered bowl and refrigerate overnight. • Divide dough into 8 parts. Roll out, part at a time, in a rectangle or circle. • Spread with melted butter; sprinkle generously with sugar and cinnamon. • Cut into wedges. • Dip into cinnamon and sugar. • Place on well-greased cookie sheet. • Let rise 1 hour. • Bake at 350°F (180°C) for 12-15 minutes. • Enjoy!

When making dressings for your chicken or turkey, try using whole-grain or 7-grain bread, and try adding drained mandarin orange sections, raisins and/or shelled unsalted sunflower seeds. Wonderful!

MONKEY BREAD

1 tsp.	sugar	5 mL
½ cup	lukewarm water	125 mL
1 tbsp.	yeast (7 g pkg.)	15 mL
1 cup	milk	250 mL
½ cup	butter OR margarine	125 mL
¼ cup	sugar	50 mL
1½ tsp.	salt	7 mL
3	eggs, beaten	3
5½ cups	flour	1.3 L
½ cup	melted butter	125 mL

Mix together the first 3 ingredients and let stand for 10 minutes. • Heat milk and ½ cup (125 mL) butter to warm, then add ¼ cup (50 mL) sugar, salt and beaten eggs. • Stir in risen yeast mixture. • Mix in flour until a soft dough is formed. • Allow dough to rise until double in bulk. • Roll out dough to ½" (1.3 cm) thickness. Divide into equal pieces. • Melt ½ cup (125 mL) butter and dip each piece of dough in it. (These pieces can be either squares or rounds). • Pile into a bundt pan or angel pan unevenly, to form an odd shape. • Let rise 1 hour, or to double in bulk. • Bake for 1 hour at 350°F (180°C).

CHOCOLATE-FROSTED COFFEE BUNS

½ cup	milk	125 mL
½ cup	granulated sugar	125 mL
¾ tsp.	salt	3 mL
2 tbsp.	instant coffee	30 mL
½ cup	lukewarm water	125 mL
2 tsp.	granulated sugar	10 mL
2 tbsp.	active dry yeast	30 mL
4¾ cups	sifted all-purpose flour	1.2 L
½ cup	butter OR margarine	125 mL
3	eggs, beaten	3

ICING

1½ cups	sifted icing sugar	375 mL
2 tbsp.	cocoa	30 mL
2 tbsp.	boiling water	30 mL
½ tsp.	vanilla	2 mL

Scald milk, stir in ½ cup (125 mL) granulated sugar, salt and instant coffee. Cool to lukewarm. • Measure lukewarm water into small bowl, stir in 2 tsp. (10 mL) sugar; sprinkle with yeast; let stand 10 minutes. Stir well. • Sift 2½ cups (625 mL) of flour into bowl. • Cut in the butter until mixture resembles cornmeal. • Stir in milk, yeast and well-beaten eggs. • Beat until smooth and elastic; work in enough flour to make soft dough, about 2 ¼ cups (550 mL). • Turn out on floured board, knead until smooth and elastic. • Place in greased bowl, grease top; cover. Let rise in warm place until doubled in bulk, about 1¼ hours. • Punch down. Turn onto floured board and knead until smooth. Divide dough into 3 balls, cover, and let rest for 10 minutes. • Shape into small balls and place on greased cookie sheet 2" (5 cm) apart. Cover. • Let rise in warm place until doubled in bulk, about 45 minutes. • Bake in 375°F (190°C) oven for about 12-15 minutes. • Prepare icing by sifting icing sugar and cocoa together. Add hot water for easy spreading; add vanilla. Ice buns while still warm. • If freezing, ice when thawed.

Appetizers
&
Beverages

APPETIZERS

SNACKING DRUMS

5 lbs.	chicken drumsticks	2.5 kg
½ cup	medium dry white wine	125 mL
¼ cup	ketchup	50 mL
¼ cup	vegetable oil	50 mL
1	large lemon, juice of	1
2 tbsp.	brown vinegar	30 mL
1 tbsp.	brown sugar	15 mL
1 tbsp.	paprika	15 mL
1 tbsp.	onion powder	15 mL
2 tbsp.	EACH: molasses, liquid honey and soy sauce	30 mL
2 tbsp.	instant beef bouillon OR 4 beef cubes, crushed	30 mL
1 tsp.	ground ginger	5 mL
¾ tsp.	marjoram	3 mL
1 tsp.	seasoned pepper	5 mL
½ tsp.	celery salt	2 mL
1	large garlic clove, finely chopped	1

Layer chicken pieces in a large roasting pan. ● Simmer remaining ingredients together over low heat just enough to heat through. Pour over chicken. ● Bake covered for 30 minutes at 400°F (200°C), reduce heat to 350°F (180°C), remove cover and bake another 30 to 45 minutes until golden and tender. Baste often. ● May be frozen. To serve, thaw and reheat. ● Serves 10-12.

Ever run out of brown sugar? Try mixing ½ cup (125 mL) of white sugar with ½ tsp. (2 mL) imitation maple flavoring and ½ tsp. (2 mL) molasses. It's the closest substitute you'll ever find.

3 lbs.	chicken wings	1.5 kg
1 cup	soy sauce	250 mL
3 tbsp.	vegetable oil	45 mL
½ cup	honey	125 mL
1 tsp.	dry mustard	5 mL
1 tsp.	ground ginger	5 mL
¼ tsp.	pepper	1 mL
2	garlic cloves, crushed	2

CHINESE CHICKEN WINGS

Cut chicken wings in 3 parts (use tips for soup). This will leave you with 2 pieces from each wing. • Mix soy sauce with remaining ingredients. Brush all sides of chicken, let stand 3 to 4 hours brushing frequently with sauce. (Try to keep well-coated). • Put chicken on rack in shallow pan and bake at 350°F (180°C) for 50 minutes or until tender. Brush often during baking. • This recipe freezes well and can be re-heated for serving or left cold. • See photograph page 48A.

2 cups	all-purpose flour	500 mL
¾ tsp.	salt	3 mL
½ tsp.	baking powder	2 mL
⅔ cup	lard OR shortening	150 mL
5 tbsp.	ice water	75 mL
3 tbsp.	vegetable oil	50 mL
2	garlic cloves, crushed	2
¼ cup	chopped onions	50 mL
1 cup	diced lean pork	250 mL
½ cup	diced potato	125 mL
	salt and pepper, to taste	
¼ cup	water	50 mL
¼ cup	peas (optional)	50 mL
¼ cup	raisins	75 mL

EMPANADAS

FILLING

Dough: Mix flour, salt and baking powder. Cut in lard with a pastry cutter or a fork until mixture resembles coarse meal. Add ice water and gently toss mixture until it comes together in a ball. Wrap and chill for 30 minutes. • On a floured board, roll out pastry about ⅛″ (3 mm) thick and cut into 4″ (10 cm) circles. Place about 2 tbsp. (30 mL) filling slightly off center on each circle. Moisten edge of each with water, fold over and seal. Place on a greased baking sheet. • Bake in preheated 400°F (200°C) oven for about 20 minutes or until pastry is golden brown. Cool on cake racks. • **Filling:** Heat oil and sauté garlic and onions. Add pork and simmer for a short time. Add diced potatoes, salt, pepper, water and peas, if used, simmer until almost dry. Remove from heat, cool. Add raisins last before sealing. • Makes 12 turnovers. See photograph page 48A.

To peel tiny white onions for boiling or cooking, pour boiling water over them and let stand for 3 minutes. Drain and cover with cold water, cut off stem and root ends. Skins will peel off almost in one piece.

43

WELSH PASTIES

4	potatoes, cooked, mashed	4
12 oz.	can Fray Bentos corned beef	340 g
1	large onion, chopped	1
	salt and pepper, to taste	

Put all ingredients through a grinder to mix well. • Cut pastry rounds, place a spoonful of meat mixture on each round, fold over and seal. • Brush with milk. Bake at 350°F (180°C) until golden brown.

PASTRY

1 lb.	lard, OR use half butter	500 g
2 tsp.	salt	10 mL
5 cups	flour	1.25 L
1	egg	1
2 tbsp.	vinegar	30 mL
	cold water	

Blend together lard, salt and flour. Beat together egg and vinegar. Add enough cold water to make 1 cup (250 mL). Add to flour mixture to make soft dough.

GREEK SPINACH PIE

	butter	
1	onion, chopped	1
1 tbsp.	butter	15 mL
8 oz.	feta cheese	250 g
4 oz.	cream cheese	125 g
4 oz.	Monterey Jack cheese	125 g
2	eggs	2
1 tsp.	grated nutmeg	5 mL
2 tbsp.	minced parsley	30 mL
12 oz.	frozen spinach, chopped	340 g
1 pkg.	phyllo pastry (read directions on package)	1 pkg.
¾ cup	melted butter	175 mL

Butter 1 oblong baking dish or large pie plate. • Sauté onion in 1 tbsp. (15 mL) butter until onion is transparent. • Combine feta, cream and Monterey Jack cheeses, onion, eggs, nutmeg, and parsley until evenly blended. Stir in spinach by hand. • Place 12 layers of phyllo in baking dish, 1 at a time, brushing each with melted butter. Spread cheese spinach mixture over phyllo layers and top with 10-15 more sheets, buttering each as you layer. Trim excess phyllo sheets to fit baking dish. • To make cutting easier, place the dish in the freezer for about 20 minutes. Cut into squares, triangles, or diamonds and bake at 350°F (180°C) for 45 minutes, or until brown and crisp. • This dish may be made ahead and reheated. It may also be frozen unbaked, then thawed and baked. • To serve easily, cut through layers again. • A superb appetizer or hors d'oeuvres, also good with lamb, pork, or chicken. • Makes 8 servings.

---

1 recipe	Plain Pastry, see below	1 recipe
6	bacon slices	6
2	eggs	2
1 cup	heavy cream	250 mL
½ tsp.	salt	2 mL
pinch	nutmeg	pinch
dash	cayenne pepper	dash
dash	pepper	dash
	soft butter	
¾ cup	grated Swiss cheese	175 mL

QUICHE TARTLETS

Line 24 - 2″ (5 cm) tart pans with pastry rounds, don't prick bottoms, and don't bake. ● Fry bacon until crisp, then drain, cool and crumble. ● About 40 minutes before serving time, heat oven to 400°F (200°C). Beat next 6 ingredients well. Spread bottoms of unbaked shells lightly with butter. Sprinkle each with bacon bits, then cheese, then fill with egg mixture to just below top. ● Bake 15 minutes, reduce heat to 300°F (150°C) and bake until puffy and brown, about 15 minutes. Serve hot. ● These can be baked ahead, frozen, then reheated at 450°F (230°C) for about 5 minutes. ● Makes 24. ● See photograph page 48A.

---

2 cups	all-purpose flour	500 mL
1 tsp.	salt	5 mL
⅔ cup	lard OR ⅔ cup (150 mL) plus 2 tbsp. (30 mL) shortening	150 mL
¼ cup	ice water	50 mL

PLAIN PASTRY

Sift flour into a bowl. Add salt and mix with a fork. Add lard or shortening and cut in coarsely with a pastry blender. Sprinkle in water, a tablespoon (15 mL) at a time, and mix lightly with a fork, just until all flour is dampened. Try not to add any extra water. Gather into a ball and press firmly together. ● Roll out thinly, cut into 3″ (7.5 cm) rounds. ● Makes 2½-3 dozen 3″ (7.5 cm) rounds.

12	large mushrooms	12
1 tbsp.	margarine	15 mL
1	garlic clove, minced	1
3 oz.	prosciutto ham, minced	85 g
¼ cup	bread crumbs	50 mL
2 tbsp.	chopped parsley	25 mL
¼ cup	grated Swiss OR Jarlsberg cheese	50 mL

PROSCIUTTO STUFFED MUSHROOMS

Wash and dry mushrooms. Remove stems and chop finely. ● Melt margarine until bubbly, add minced garlic and sauté for 1 minute, add chopped mushroom stems and sauté for an additional minute. Stir in ham and bread crumbs and sauté for 2 minutes, remove from heat and stir in parsley. ● Divide mixture among caps and top with cheese. Bake at 350°F (180°C) for 15-20 minutes, or microwave 3 to 4 minutes on high until bubbly. ● Makes 12. ● See photograph page 48A.

CRAB-STUFFED MUSHROOMS

40	bite-sized mushrooms	40
1 tbsp.	butter	15 mL
2 tsp.	all-purpose flour	10 mL
¼ cup	rich milk	50 mL
1 tbsp.	lemon juice	15 mL
1 tbsp.	mayonnaise	15 mL
¼ cup	shredded Cheddar cheese	50 mL
4¾ oz.	crab, membrane removed	125 g
1 tsp.	crushed onion flakes	5 mL

Remove mushroom stems, reserve for another purpose. • Melt butter in saucepan. Stir in flour. Add milk, lemon juice and mayonnaise, stirring until it boils and thickens. • Add cheese. Stir to melt. Stir in crab and onion. • Fill mushroom caps. • Bake in 400°F (200°C) oven for 15 to 20 minutes, until heated through. • Serve as a finger food or as a table appetizer. • Makes about 40. • See photograph page 48A.

RISSOLES

Delicious warm or cold.

1	medium onion, chopped	1
6 tbsp.	butter	90 mL
	parsley, to taste	
¼ tsp.	garlic salt	1 mL
½ tsp.	nutmeg	2 mL
	salt, to taste	
2-3 tbsp.	olive oil	25-50 mL
1½ lbs.	small shrimp, cooked (reserve cooking water)	750 g
½-¾ cup	milk	125-175 mL
3¾ cups	flour	925 mL
6	eggs	6
1	egg white, beaten	1
	bread crumbs	

Filling: In a pan, mix chopped onion with 3 tbsp. (50 mL) of butter, parsley, garlic salt, nutmeg, and salt. When onion begins to brown, add olive oil, and the already boiled shrimp. Add milk, and then to thicken, add a bit of flour, approximately ¾ cup (175 mL). • **Dough:** Take 3 cups (750 mL) of the water in which you boiled the shrimp and add 3 tbsp. (50 mL) of butter and a bit of salt. Heat to a boil. Add 3 cups (750 mL) flour, letting it boil. Keep stirring. When the dough is thick enough to roll into a ball, it is ready. Remove from heat and beat in the eggs, 1 at a time, until dough is thick and shiny. Spread the dough on a flat surface and let cool for about 10 to 15 minutes.. Knead for a few minutes and then spread with a rolling pin. • Put a bit of filling on a small section of dough, close, and cut it to a semicircle using a glass. • Dip each in egg white and then coat with bread crumbs. • Deep fry in vegetable or olive oil until brown. • Makes approximately 50.

2 x 6 oz.	jars marinated artichoke hearts	2 x 170 g
1	onion, minced	1
1	garlic clove, minced	1
4	eggs	4
⅛ tsp.	pepper	0.5 mL
⅛ tsp.	oregano	0.5 mL
¼ tsp.	salt	1 mL
dash	Tabasco	dash
¼ cup	fine bread crumbs	50 mL
2 cups	shredded sharp Cheddar cheese	500 mL
2 tbsp.	parsley	30 mL

ARTICHOKE SQUARES

Drain artichokes, reserve juice from 1 jar. Sauté onion and garlic in juice. Drain. Chop artichoke finely. • Beat eggs, add seasonings, crumbs, cheese and parsley. Add onion, garlic and artichoke. (Watch amount of oil.) • Place in a greased 8″ (20 cm) pan and bake at 325°F (160°C) for 35 minutes. • Cool and cut into squares.

3	large zucchini	3
½ cup	grated Gruyère cheese	125 mL
¼ cup	mashed feta cheese	50 mL
2	eggs	2
1 tbsp.	flour	15 mL
1 tbsp.	parsley	15 mL
1 tbsp.	chopped dill	15 mL
	salt and pepper	
	butter	
	paprika	

ZUCCHINI BITES

Trim ends, then boil whole zucchinis for 8 minutes. Drain and slice zucchinis in half lengthwise. Scoop out center and pat zucchini dry with paper towel. • Combine next 8 ingredients and fill drained zucchini with cheese mixture. Dot with butter and sprinkle with paprika. • This can be done early in day. Cover and place in the refrigerator. • When needed, broil until cheese is bubbly and brown. Slice about 2″ (5 cm) long and eat either as an appetizer or as a vegetable.

½ cup	large shrimp per serving in shells, fresh OR frozen	125 mL
½ cup	white wine	125 mL
2 tbsp.	butter	25 mL
few drops	Tabasco sauce	few drops
1	garlic clove, crushed	1

RIVER BOAT SHRIMP

This is simple, quick and good!

Sauté shrimp, thawed if frozen, in the shell in butter until they begin to turn pink. Add other ingredients and simmer until fully cooked and bright pink. • Serve hot in clam shells as first course, or as a main course with rice and salad. Include lots of napkins and time to enjoy conversation over the shelling.

PRAWN COCKTAIL

An Australian specialty.

1½ lbs.	prawns in shells, cooked	750 g
	lemon slices OR wedges	
½ head	lettuce	½ head
4	shallots	4
2 tbsp.	chopped parsley	30 mL
	Brandy Cocktail Sauce, below	

Shell prawns, remove back veins, wash and pat dry. • Put finely shredded lettuce, chopped shallots and parsley into bowl. Toss lightly. Put lettuce mixture at base of 4 individual scallop shells or dishes. Top with prawns. • Cover and leave in refrigerator until ready to serve. • At serving time, spoon sauce over and garnish with lemon wedges. • Serves 4.

BRANDY COCKTAIL SAUCE

¼ cup	tomato sauce	75 mL
1 tbsp.	tomato paste	15 mL
2 tsp.	lemon juice	10 mL
1 tsp.	white vinegar	5 mL
few drops	Tabasco sauce	few drops
1 tbsp.	brandy	15 mL
	salt and pepper, to taste	
½ cup	whipping cream	125 mL

Put tomato sauce and paste into a bowl and mix well. Stir in other ingredients, except for cream. • Beat cream until soft peaks form and gently fold into tomato mixture. • Serves 4-6.

OTTAWA FISH MOUSSE

5 oz.	can lobster	142 g
4.5 oz.	can crab meat	127 g
7.5 oz.	can red salmon	225 g
4 oz.	can small shrimp	113 g
2	envelopes gelatin, soaked in:	2
¼ cup	hot water	50 mL
½ cup	chili sauce	125 mL
½ cup	mayonnaise	125 mL
½ cup	finely chopped green pepper	125 mL
½ cup	finely chopped celery	125 mL
	green hot dog relish, to taste	
	instant onion, to taste	

Combine all ingredients and set in a mold. • Serve with crackers.

APPETIZERS
Chinese Chicken Wings, page 43
Quiche Tartlets, page 45
Empanadas, page 43
Crab-Stuffed Mushrooms, page 45
Proscuitto-Stuffed Mushrooms, page 46
Lou's Hors D'Oeuvres, page 206
German Wine Punch, page 57

MARINATED SALMON

3 lbs.	center-cut salmon, filleted, sliced into thinnest possible diagonal slices	1.5 kg
¼ cup	salt	50 mL
3 tbsp.	sugar	45 mL
1 tsp.	pepper	5 mL
3 cups	thinly sliced onion	750 mL
3 cups	sliced lemons	750 mL
7-8	carrots, thinly sliced	7-8
12	brandied cherries	12
4	lemons, juice of	4
½ cup	dry white wine	125 mL
½ cup	vinegar	125 mL

Sprinkle salmon slices on both sides with mixed salt, sugar and pepper. ● Make a bed of carrot, onion and lemon slices in an 8" x 12" (3 L) Pyrex dish. Cover with a layer of salmon. Do not let slices overlap. Cover with another layer of carrot, onion and lemon slices. Scatter a few cherries over, then add another layer of salmon. Continue in this way until all ingredients are used. Pat it down as evenly as possible on top. ● Mix together lemon juice, white wine and vinegar. Pour into dish slowly and carefully. All fish should be swimming in liquid. If necessary, add more lemon juice to cover. ● Cover with plastic wrap and marinate in refrigerator. It will be ready to eat in 2 days. ● Serve drained salmon slices as an hors d'oeuvre or as a first course with bread. Garnish with a few slices of carrot and onion and lemon slices.

SURPRISE SPREAD

8 oz.	cream cheese, softened	250 g
½ cup	sour cream	125 mL
¼ cup	mayonnaise	50 mL
2-3	4 oz. (113 g) cans broken shrimp, drained	2-3
1 cup	seafood cocktail sauce	250 mL
2 cups	shredded mozzarella cheese	500 mL
1	green pepper, chopped	1
3	green onions, chopped	3
1	tomato, diced	1

This easy spread gets rave reviews!

Mix first 3 ingredients together; spread over 12" (30 cm) pizza pan. Scatter shrimp over cheese mixture. Add layers of seafood sauce, mozzarella cheese, green pepper, onions and tomato. ● Cover and chill until ready to serve. Supply assorted crackers for spreading. ● Crab meat may be substituted for shrimp. ● Serves 8-10.

Nothing annoys a woman more than to have company drop in unexpectantly and find the house looking the way it usually does.

SMOKED OYSTER SPREAD

8 oz.	cream cheese	250 g
¼ cup	whipping cream	50 mL
1 tbsp.	chopped onion	15 mL
1 tbsp.	chopped parsley	15 mL
3.67 oz.	can smoked oysters, drained, chopped	104 g
1 tsp.	brandy	5 mL
¼ tsp.	Worcestershire sauce	1 mL
2 drops	Tabasco sauce, OR to taste	2 drops
	salt and pepper	

Mix softened cream cheese with whipped cream until smooth. • Add remaining ingredients and blend. • Serve with assorted crackers.

SALMON PARTY BALL

8 oz.	cream cheese	250 g
2 cups	canned salmon, flaked, skin and bones removed	500 mL
1 tbsp.	lemon juice	15 mL
2 tsp.	grated onion	10 mL
1 tsp.	prepared horseradish	5 mL
¼ tsp.	salt	1 mL
¼ tsp.	liquid smoke	1 mL
3 tbsp.	snipped parsley	45 mL
½ cup	chopped nuts	125 mL

Soften cream cheese; add next 6 ingredients and mix well. • Form into a ball, or 2 small balls, and roll in a mixture of parsley and chopped nuts.. • Chill for several hours. • May chill before forming into ball, for easier handling.

JELLIED PÂTÉ

10 oz.	can consommé	284 mL
	salt and pepper, to taste	
1 tsp.	Worcestershire sauce	5 mL
½	envelope gelatin powder	½
¼ cup	cold water	50 mL
1	pkg. Schneider's braunschweiger	1
4 oz. .	pkg. cream cheese	115 g

Heat consommé, salt, pepper, and Worcestershire sauce. Add gelatin to ¼ cup (50 mL) water. When softened, dissolve in hot consommé. • Put ¾″ (2 cm) of mixture in greased mold and let set in refrigerator. • Combine braunschweiger with remaining consommé with electric beater. Beat cream cheese into ¼ cup (50 mL) of this mixture. Put cheese mixture on top of set consommé and let set a few minutes. Put liver mixture on last. • Keep in refrigerator and unmold to serve.

½ lb.	bacon	250 g
1 lb.	ground beef	500 g
1 lb.	ground pork	500 g
2	garlic cloves, crushed	2
½ cup	finely chopped parsley	125 mL
½ tsp.	tarragon	2 mL
½ tsp.	thyme	2 mL
½ tsp.	paprika	2 mL
1½ tsp.	salt	7 mL
¼ tsp.	pepper	1 mL
2	eggs, slightly beaten	2
½ cup	cognac	125 mL
1 lb.	ground ham	500 g
1½ tsp.	dry mustard	7 mL
½ tsp.	nutmeg	2 mL
¼ cup	dry sherry	50 mL
1 cup	finely chopped green onions	250 mL
1 cup	finely chopped parsley	250 mL
½ cup	dry sherry	125 mL

PÂTÉ MAISON

Heat oven to 325°F (160°C). Line the bottom of 2 loaf pans 8½" x 4½" x 2½" (1.5 L), with 3 strips of bacon each. • Combine beef, pork, garlic, ½ cup (125 mL) parsley, tarragon, thyme, paprika, salt, pepper, eggs and cognac, blending very well. Divide into 4 parts. (1 part for bottom and 1 part for top of each.) • Combine ham, mustard, nutmeg and ¼ cup (50 mL) sherry, blending very well. Divide into 2 parts. (Middle layer for each pan.) • Put 1 part of the beef mixture in each of the pans, packing it firmly. Sprinkle each with ¼ cup (50 mL) of green onions and ¼ cup (50 mL) of parsley. Top each with 1 part of ham mixture than another ¼ cup (50 mL) onions and ¼ cup (50 mL) parsley. Add a layer of beef, packing very firmly. Lay the remaining bacon strips on top. Pour ¼ cup (50 mL) sherry over each pan. • Cover pans tightly with aluminum foil and bake 3 hours. Take pans from oven, set on rack, remove foil and pour off excess liquid. Place fresh piece of foil on top of meat and weight down, try heavy cans. Cool completely. Remove weights, refrigerate after unmolding. Serve with crackers or French bread.

2	medium cucumbers	2
1 cup	yogurt	250 mL
dash	vinegar	dash
dash	lemon juice	dash
1-1½	fresh garlic cloves, mashed	1-1½

ANDY'S TZAZIKI SAUCE

Seed cucumbers. Put through food processor until finely chopped, then strain for about 2 hours or until juice is out. • Combine all ingredients. Mix well. • Serve with pita bread as a zesty dip.

Shop with a grocery list and never when tired, hungry or hurried.

PÂTÉ DE FOIE

1 lb.	chicken livers, trimmed, washed and chopped	500 g
½ lb.	uncooked ham, chopped	250 g
1	large onion, finely chopped	1
1	garlic clove, finely chopped	1
¼ lb.	butter	125 g
1 tsp.	unflavored gelatin, soaked in:	5 mL
¼ cup	water	50 mL
1 oz.	dry sherry	30 mL
1 oz.	brandy	30 mL
2	eggs	2
¾ tsp.	salt	3 mL
2 tbsp.	lemon juice	30 mL
1	bay leaf, crushed	1
¼ tsp.	thyme	1 mL
3	juniper berries (important)	3

Sauté liver, ham, onion, and garlic in butter; do not overcook. Stir constantly as liver must be pink inside when you remove it from the heat or your pâté will be sandy. • Partially cool, place in blender and blend until the mixture becomes smooth. Add soaked gelatin gradually while blending. Keep adding all the remaining ingredients, blending well after each addition. • Grease 2 loaf pans, 3" x 7" (1.5 L), or any desired ovenproof mold. Pour pâté into pans, cover with foil, place in slow oven, 325°F (160°C), and cook approximately 45 minutes. Keep checking as you do not want to overcook. Place a low pan of water in your oven while cooking, to prevent burning the bottoms. • Let cool, and remove from pans. Wrap the loaves well in waxed and foil papers. This will keep well for a month. You can freeze it, the texture changes slightly, but the flavor is the same. • Makes 2 loaves.

CURRIED CHEESE SPREAD

A tangy, quick and easy appetizer!

	butter	
6	English muffins	6
1 cup	chopped ripe olives	250 mL
½ cup	thinly sliced green onions	125 mL
1½ cups	shredded sharp Cheddar cheese	375 mL
½ cup	mayonnaise	125 mL
½ tsp.	salt	2 mL
½ tsp.	curry powder	2 mL

Split, toast and butter English muffins. • Combine remaining ingredients, spread on muffins. • Broil to melt cheese. • Quarter and serve. • Serves 12.

16 oz.	cream cheese	500 g
½ cup	snipped chives	125 mL
dash	Worcestershire sauce	dash
dash	salt and white pepper	dash
¾ lb.	snow peas	365 g

SNOW PEAS AND CREAM CHEESE

In a food processor, or blender, a small batch at a time, blend the cream cheese, chives and seasonings. ● Transfer the smooth mixture to a pastry bag with decorative tip. ● Break off ends and remove the strings from the snow peas. ● Blanch in boiling water for 1 minute. Drain in a colander, and freshen under running cold water. Pat dry with paper towels. ● With the tip of a sharp knife, make an incision in the de-stringed side of each pea; cut open to ¼″ (6 mm) from each end. ● Pipe in the filling. ● This is a light and healthful use of a fresh vegetable in season. A nice companion is cherry tomatoes, for color contrast.

1	round loaf pumpernickel OR rye bread	1
10 oz.	pkg. frozen chopped spinach, thawed and drained	283 g
1½ oz.	pkg. Knorr-Swiss Vegetable Soup mix OR Fine Herb Soup mix	45 g
1 cup	shredded Cheddar cheese	250 mL
1 cup	mayonnaise	250 mL
1 cup	sour cream	250 mL
1	small onion, chopped	1
5 oz.	can water chestnuts, chopped (optional)	150 g
4 oz.	fresh mushrooms, sliced	115 g

LAVA LOAF

Cut lid from top of bread. Tear out bite-sized pieces, leaving shell. ● Combine remaining ingredients and fill shell. ● Serve bread pieces to be eaten with filling.

What is Charity?

It is silence — when your words would hurt
It is patience — when your neighbour's curt
It is deafness — when scandal flows
It is thoughtfulness — for other's woes
It is promptness — when duty calls
It is courage — when misfortune falls.

MEXICAN ANTIPASTO

7 oz.	cream cheese	200 g
¼ tsp.	garlic salt	1 mL
½ cup	sour cream	125 mL
1	large avocado, pitted, peeled and mashed	1
¼ tsp.	lemon juice	1 mL
1	tomato, chopped	1
1	green pepper, chopped	1
5	slices crisp bacon, diced	5
3-4	green onions, chopped	3-4
½ cup	coarsely chopped olives (half green, half black)	125 mL
8 oz.	taco sauce, hot OR mild	250 g
1 cup	grated Cheddar	250 mL

Combine the first 3 ingredients and pat into a 9″ (1 L) pie plate. • Mix the next 4 ingredients together and put on top of first layer. • Sprinkle bacon, onions and olives over the second layer. • Pour taco sauce over the third layer and sprinkle Cheddar cheese over all. • Serve with taco or nacho chips.

MEXICAN TACO DIP

Delicious and colorful!

1	tin refried beans	1
1 cup	sour cream	250 mL
⅔ cup	mayonnaise	150 mL
1.25 oz.	pkg. taco seasoning	35 g
8 oz.	can chopped green chilies, (mild or hot)	250 g
4	ripe avocados	4
2 tsp.	lime OR lemon juice	10 mL
¼ tsp.	garlic powder	1 mL
8 oz.	grated sharp Cheddar	250 g
2 cups	chopped green onion	500 mL
2 cups	chopped fresh tomatoes	500 mL
14 oz.	tin pitted black olives	398 mL

A deep glass pie plate works well or any 10″ (25 cm) flat dish with an edge on it. • Spread refried beans; mix sour cream, mayonnaise and taco mix; spread this on beans. • Drain can of chillies and spread on. Mash the avocados, lime juice and garlic; spread that over dish. • Sprinkle the cheese, green onions, tomatoes and olives over the top and refrigerate. • Can be made the day before, but make at least 6 hours before serving. • Serve with any kind of crackers or tortilla rounds or corn nacho chips. • Serves 20 as an appetizer.

One morning as my husband opened the freezer, he asked "What should I take out for dinner? Me, I replied.

1 lb.	ground beef	500 g
1	large onion, chopped	1
dash	salt	dash
dash	Tabasco sauce	dash
1 pkg.	Lawry's Taco Seasoning	1 pkg.
16 oz.	can refried beans	500 g
4 oz.	can green chilies, chopped	115 g
1 cup	grated Cheddar cheese	250 mL
¾ cup	taco sauce	175 mL

SUPER NACHOS

¼ cup	chopped green onions	50 mL
1 cup	sliced black olives	250 mL
	avocado dip (optional)	
	shredded cheese	
1 cup	sour cream	250 mL
1 cup	guacamole dip	250 mL
	chopped tomatoes	

GARNISHES

Fry meat, add onion. Drain. Add salt, Tabasco and taco seasoning. ● Spread beans on an ovenproof pan (a round glass pizza pan is ideal). Top evenly with meat, then green chilies, then cheese, then drizzle taco sauce over. ● Cover and chill if made ahead. ● Bake uncovered at 400°F (200°C) for 20-25 minutes. Remove from oven and add garnishes. ● Serve with tortilla chips as a dip, an appetizer or a full meal.

1 cup	butter	250 mL
8 oz.	Imperial Cheddar cheese (1 tub)	250 g
dash	Worcestershire sauce	dash
1½ cups	flour	375 mL
dash	salt	dash
dash	cayenne pepper	dash
4 cups	rice krispies	1 L

CHEESE KRISPIES

Mix first 3 ingredients well. ● Add flour, salt and cayenne pepper. Mix well, add rice krispies and blend. ● Drop by teaspoonfuls (5 mL) on ungreased cookie sheets. ● Bake at 350°F (180°C) for 10-15 minutes. ● Makes 6-8 dozen.

We may live without poetry, music and art;
We may live without conscience, and live without heart;
We may live without friends; we may live without books;
But civilized man cannot live without cooks.

BEER CHEESE BALLS

2 x 8 oz.	pkgs. cream cheese	2 x 250 g
2 tbsp.	finely snipped parsley	30 mL
1 tsp.	paprika	5 mL
3 cups	shredded sharp Cheddar cheese (12 oz. [370 g])	750 mL
¼ cup	warmed beer	50 mL
	sliced almonds, toasted	
	snipped parsley	
	fresh fruit OR assorted crackers	

Let cheese stand at room temperature about 1 hour. • In large bowl, beat together the cream cheese, parsley and paprika until well blended. Stir in the Cheddar cheese. Gradually add warmed beer, beating until nearly smooth. • Cover and chill mixture for 1 hour. • Divide mixture in half. With hands, mold into ball or log shape, place on baking sheet. Press sliced almonds into molded cheese, arrange as desired. Sprinkle with snipped parsley. • Cover and refrigerate 2 to 24 hours. • Serve with fresh fruit or assorted crackers. Yields 2 balls or logs.

CURRIED NUTS

½ cup	olive oil	125 mL
2 tbsp.	curry powder	30 mL
2 tbsp.	Worcestershire sauce	30 mL
4 cups	almonds, filberts, pecans OR walnuts	1 L

Heat oil, curry, and Worcestershire sauce in heavy skillet. Stir in nuts. Place in roasting pan lined with brown paper. • Bake for 10-15 minutes at 350°F (180°C).

GARLIC PEPPERED PECANS

1 tbsp.	unsalted butter	15 mL
2 tsp.	Tabasco sauce	10 mL
3	garlic cloves, minced	3
2 tbsp.	soy sauce	30 mL
1 lb.	pecans	500 g
¼ tsp.	crushed red peppers	1 mL
1 tbsp.	seasoned pepper	15 mL
	salt, to taste	

Heat oven to 350°F (180°C). • Grease cookie sheet with butter and sprinkle with Tabasco sauce, garlic and soy sauce. Spread pecans over sheet and stir with fork until well coated with seasonings. Sprinkle with crushed red peppers, seasoned pepper and salt. • Bake 10 minutes. Sprinkle with a little more salt if desired, stir with fork and bake 15 minutes longer. • Cool before serving. • Store in jar with tight lid.

To be enduring, a marriage must be endurable.

BEVERAGES

6 oz.	can frozen grapefruit juice	178 mL
6 oz.	can frozen orange juice	178 mL
26 oz.	bottle apricot brandy	750 mL
2 x 26 oz.	bottles champagne	2 x 750 mL
26 oz.	club soda	750 mL

CHAMPAGNE PUNCH

Have ingredients chilled. Mix slightly thawed juices (no water) in punch bowl. Add apricot brandy and mix. Add champagne and soda last. Stir just slightly, don't destroy bubbles. Mix at the last minute. Enjoy!

4 cups	inexpensive German white wine	1 L
4 cups	sweetened apple juice	1 L
2 cups	ginger ale	500 mL
1	small cucumber	1
1	small apple	1

GERMAN WINE PUNCH

Combine liquids in large punch bowl; add ice cubes. • Garnish with very thin cucumber and apple slices. • See photograph page 48A.

48 oz.	can pineapple juice OR orange juice	1.36 L
48 oz.	can orange OR grape juice	1.36 L
26 oz.	bottle of 7-Up OR ginger ale	750 mL
26 oz.	ros OR white wine	750 mL
26 oz.	white rum OR vodka	750 mL

TAHITIAN PUNCH

Combine all ingredients. • Garnish with cherry ice ring. • Serves 45 or more.

When you get to the end of your rope, tie a knot and hang on.

SANGRIA

26 oz.	bottle cheap red wine	750 mL
26 oz.	bottle soda water	750 mL
2 oz.	dark rum	50 mL
1	small orange, thinly sliced	1
2	small limes, thinly sliced	2
	brown sugar, to taste	

Combine all ingredients in large pitcher, stir well and let sit in refrigerator for at least 1 hour.

MERRY BERRY PUNCH

2 cups	fresh OR frozen strawberries	500 mL
3 oz.	pkg. strawberry gelatin	85 g
1 cup	boiling water	250 mL
6 oz.	can frozen lemonade concentrate	178 g
3 cups	soda water	750 mL
1 qt.	cranberry juice	1 L
26 oz.	ginger ale	750 mL

Pure strawberries. • Dissolve gelatin in boiling water. Stir in lemonade. Add soda water, cranberry juice and strawberry pure. Pour over ice in large punch bowl. Slowly pour in ginger ale. • Serves about 30.

CRANBERRY JUICE DRINK

2 qts.	wild cranberries	2 L
4 qts.	boiling water	4 L
2-3	whole cloves	2-3
1-2	cinnamon sticks	1-2
2 cups	sugar OR equivalent sweetener	500 mL
2 tbsp.	lemon juice OR to taste	30 mL

Boil berries and spices 20-25 minutes. Mash with masher. Strain through sieve and then strain through cheesecloth or cotton bag. • Add sugar or sweetener. Add desired amount of lemon juice for a tart taste. Put on stove and simmer 5 minutes. • Put in sterile jars and seal.

You can use the V-shaped juice can opener to remove stems from strawberries.

Save those foam plastic egg cartons. They make excellent ice cube trays when you need an extra supply for a party.

5	pkgs lemon drink crystals	5
5	pkgs. orange drink crystals	5
½ cup	instant tea	125 mL
2 tsp.	cinnamon	10 mL
1 cup	sugar (if desired)	250 mL

FRIENDSHIP TEA

Mix all ingredients in cannister, ready to serve hot or cold. • Use 2 tbsp. (30 mL) of mix per large glass of water.

1 tbsp.	instant coffee	15 mL
2 tbsp.	boiling water	30 mL
1 cup	Irish whiskey	250 mL
10 oz.	can Eagle Brand sweetened condensed milk	300 mL
13 oz.	can evaporated milk	369 mL
1 tsp.	glycerin	5 mL
1 tsp.	vanilla	5 mL

IRISH CREAM LIQUEUR

Dissolve instant coffee in boiling water. Add all remaining ingredients and beat for 2 or 3 minutes. Pour into a jar. • Leave for 7 days and shake once a day.

4 cups	water	1 L
4 cups	sugar	1 L
¼ cup	instant coffee	75 mL
¼ cup	vanilla	50 mL
26 oz.	vodka	750 mL

KAHLÚA

Bring water and sugar to a boil. Slowly add instant coffee, dissolved in a little water. Boil for 5 minutes. Let cool. Add vanilla and vodka. • Yields approximately 2⅔ x 26 oz. (750 mL) bottles.

1	lemon	1
	salt	
1-1 ½ oz.	white tequila	30-45 mL
½ oz.	Cointreau OR Triple Sec liqueur	15 mL
1 oz.	fresh lemon OR lime juice	30 mL

MARGUARITA COCKTAIL

Rub the rim of a chilled glass with a piece of lemon, then turn in a dish of loose salt to encrust the rim. • Combine tequila, Cointreau and lemon juice with crushed ice in a cocktail shaker. Shake until frothy and strain into a prepared glass. • Serve immediately. • These directions are for 1 drink and can be increased according to demand.

ON WINE AND FOOD by John Klemp

From vineyard to barrel to bottle and glass, wine in all its facets is a fascinating subject. The people involved with growing, making and selling wine around the world constitute a most interesting variety of individuals and nature itself assures that each vintage will be different. The basic quality of any wine begins with the grape, but it is the human element along the way that determines the ultimate outcome. It has always been my opinion that the simple, but sound, wine for everyday use is as important as the great wine saved for special occasions. How could one thoroughly appreciate the latter without experience with the former.

Wine is a very sociable beverage, which promotes conviviality among those who share it. Wine is a common bond, creating a proliferation of wine and food societies and tasting groups. There is no "mystique" that surrounds wine, just a little basic knowledge and an appreciation for the finer things of life.

As this is a book of recipes, my brief comment would not be complete without a few words on the subject of wine with food. I should first stress that all strict rules regarding what wine goes with what food are out of place in today's society. People should feel free to choose according to personal preference, there is nothing wrong with drinking white wine (or red for that matter) with everything. There are those who feel that any serious dinner requires fine and complex wines. So be it. Generally speaking, however, there are certain time-honored pairings which have evolved as to how specific wines bring out the best in particular dishes, or vice versa. There are also certain foods where wine should be avoided, particularly where spices may overwhelm even the sturdiest of wines, such condiments as pickles, chilies, citrus fruits, strong mustards, Worcestershire or Tabasco sauces, vinegar, etc. Salad dressing can often kill a wine. Try using dry white wine, or brandy, in the salad dressings instead of vinegar. If cooking with wine, try to serve the wines used for cooking with the meals; this is generally complementary.

If the readers are looking for guidance, may I simply say that white wines are well served with fish, seafood and light white meats; whereas with other meat dishes, cheeses, etc., most people prefer red. As whites and reds are available in many disguises, experiment a little and do remember to drink what you prefer and not what the rules say or other people suggest. White wines are best served chilled but not ice cold, whereas most red wines are at their peak at room temperature.

Wine glasses come in many shapes and forms. An all-purpose 8-10 oz. (250-284 mL) glass will suit most situations. The glasses should be simple and filled only half full so that there is room to swirl the wine about and appreciate the bouquet. With champagne, use the champagne flute, to preserve the bubbles.

Oxygen opens up wines and releases flavors and aromas; therefore, it is a good idea to let wine breathe a little before drinking. Simply pulling the cork and letting the bottle stand for an hour has little effect. Pour the wine into the glasses and allow it a few minutes to breathe in the glasses. Certain wines may need decanting; this is nothing more than pouring the wine from the bottle into another container, a carafe, a pitcher, a decanter, etc. Generally, only red wines should be decanted as there may be sediment which has accumulated in the bottle and it does allow the wine to open up more quickly. Finally, store your wines at a steady temperature, preferably at 55-60°F (13-15°C). Normal household temperatures of 68-70°F (20-22°C) will not harm wines as long as these temperatures are constant year round. Sudden changes in temperature are harmful.

A husband is one who stands by you in troubles you would not have had if you had not have married him.

60

Soups Plus

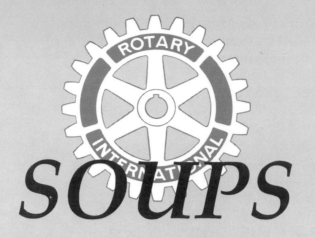

SOUPS

GREEN PEA SOUP WITH PINCHED NOODLES

This Hungarian specialty is unusual and delicious!

8 cups	salted water	2 L
1 cup	diced carrots	250 mL
1 cup	diced potatoes	250 mL
1 cup	diced onion	250 mL
½ cup	diced celery OR parsley	125 mL
1 tsp.	chopped red pepper	5 mL
1 sprig	parsley OR celery leaves	1 sprig
4 tbsp.	flour	60 mL
3 tbsp.	bacon drippings OR fat	45 mL
2 tsp.	paprika	10 mL
2 cups	water	500 mL
4 cups	green peas, fresh OR frozen	1 L
	salt and pepper	
dash	garlic salt, if desired	dash

NOODLES

2 cups	flour	500 mL
1	egg	1
¾ cup	water	175 mL
¼ tsp.	salt	1 mL

In the 8 cups (2 L) salted water, bring to a boil, carrots, potatoes, onions, celery, red pepper and celery leaves. • In frying pan, brown flour in fat, stirring to prevent burning; add paprika and 2 cups (500 mL) of water. Cook, stirring until smooth and thick. Pour mixture in with vegetables. Add peas, season to taste. Turn heat to medium and continue cooking while you prepare noodles. • Combine flour, egg, water and salt. With your hands, mix dough until smooth and velvety. With floured hands, pinch off dough the size of a hazelnut and drop into rapidly boiling water. Noodles will come to the top when done. Drain and rinse with cold water. • Add to soup and simmer until ready to serve. Water may be added if soup is too thick. • Serves 10-12.

3 cups	rich chicken stock	750 mL
3	large carrots, chopped	3
½	large onion, chopped	½
2	medium potatoes, peeled and chopped	2
2 cups	chopped, peeled broccoli stalks, tough ends removed	500 mL
¼ cup	snipped fresh parsley OR 2 tsp. (10 mL) dried parsley	50 mL
1 tsp.	salt	5 mL
1 tsp.	dried dill weed	5 mL
2 cups	boiling water seasoned croutons (optional)	500 mL

BROCCOLI STALK SOUP

In 2-quart (2 L) soup pot, bring 3 cups (750 mL) chicken stock to boil. Add peeled and chopped vegetables plus seasonings. • Simmer and cover for 10 minutes, then purée in food processor or blender. • Add 2 cups (500 mL) boiling water. • Reheat and adjust seasoning to taste. • Delicious served topped with seasoned croutons. • For a party variation, stir in 2 cups (500 mL) crab meat when reheating. • Serves 6. • See photograph page 64A.

1 lb.	fresh mushrooms	500 g
1	medium onion	1
1 tbsp.	butter	15 mL
2 cups	chicken broth	500 mL
2 cups	water	500 mL
1 tbsp.	chicken bouillon powder OR 1 cube	15 mL
1 tsp.	baking soda	5 mL
2 cups	cereal cream OR sour cream	500 mL
	salt and pepper, to taste	

MUSHROOM SOUP

Sauté mushrooms and onions in butter until mushrooms are cooked. Add chicken broth, water and chicken bouillon. Bring to a boil for 10 minutes, then lower temperature to simmer. Add baking soda and then cereal cream or sour cream. Let simmer until heated through. Add salt and pepper to taste. • Serves 6.

Save cooking water from vegetables and potatoes. Store in jars in refrigerator. Use when preparing commercial soups requiring water. The soup will be more flavorful and nutritious.

MUSHROOM AND LEEK SOUP

2	bunches leeks	2
½ cup	butter	125 mL
½ lb.	fresh mushrooms	250 g
¼ cup	flour	50 mL
1 tsp.	salt	5 mL
dash	cayenne pepper	dash
1 cup	chicken broth	250 mL
3 cups	milk	750 mL
1 tbsp.	sherry OR lemon	15 mL
	salt and pepper	

Wash leeks and slice, using only the white parts. Sauté in ¼ cup (50 mL) of butter. DO NOT BROWN. Set aside. • In remaining butter, sauté mushrooms. Blend in flour, salt and cayenne pepper. Gradually stir in broth and milk. Continue stirring as it thickens; add leeks. • Simmer for 10 minutes. • Add sherry or lemon juice before serving. Add salt and pepper to your own taste.

VICHYSSOISE

6	medium potatoes	6
6	leeks, white parts	6
4 tbsp.	butter	60 mL
8 cups	chicken stock	2 L
	cream, as desired	
	nutmeg	
	salt and pepper	
	chopped chives	

Peel potatoes and cut into small pieces. Cook, in boiling water to cover, until tender. Drain and reserve liquid. • Meanwhile, wash leeks, split them and sauté in butter. When leeks are limp, add 2 cups (500 mL) chicken stock and simmer until leeks are tender. • Purée potatoes and leeks and combine. Add the potato water and the remaining chicken stock and heavy cream to the purée. Season with nutmeg, salt and pepper and blend thoroughly. • Chill soup for 24 hours. • Garnish chives. Serve cold. • Serves 8.

MY AUNT TUCKIE'S POTATO SOUP

1 cup	thinly sliced celery	250 mL
2 cups	thinly sliced potatoes	500 mL
1	small onion, chopped	1
¼ cup	elbow macaroni	50 mL
1½ tsp.	salt	7 mL
1 cup	water	250 mL
2 cups	milk	500 mL
	pepper, to taste	
¼ tsp.	dried parsley flakes	1 mL
1 tsp.	flour	5 mL
2 tbsp.	butter	30 mL

Place first 4 ingredients in saucepan. Add salt and water. Cover and boil until potatoes are done. Do not drain. Pour in milk, pepper and parsley. When hot, stir in flour and butter that have been blended together. • Cook for a few minutes and serve. • Great with garlic bread and a salad! • Serves 3-4 big servings.

SOUPS/BREADS
Clam Chowder, page 209
Broccoli Stalk Soup, page 63
Hearty January Hamburger Soup, page 67
85% Whole-Meal Bread, page 228

2 tbsp.	butter	30 mL
1	onion, finely chopped	1
2 cups	fresh oysters	500 mL
4 cups	thin Cream Sauce (see below)	1 L
½ cup	chopped cooked spinach	125 mL
	salt and pepper, to taste	
¼-½ tsp.	Johnny's OR your favorite Seafood Seasoning	1-2 mL
2-3 drops	Tabasco sauce	2-3 drops
½ cup	whipping cream	125 mL

BONGO BONGO SOUP

As served in Trader Vic's!

Melt butter, sauté onion until transparent. Add oysters and cook almost dry. Add 4 cups (1 L) Cream Sauce. Add cooked chopped spinach. • Run ingredients through a blender. Add and check seasonings. • Whip cream until stiff. • Put soup in ovenproof bowls, add a tablespoon (15 mL) of whipped cream. • Put bowls under broiler until cream is lightly browned. • Serves 4-6.

4 tbsp.	butter	60 mL
4 tbsp.	flour	60 mL
4 cups	milk	1 L
	salt and pepper, to taste	

CREAM SAUCE

Make roux with butter and flour. Cook for 2-3 minutes. • Add milk and stir until thickened. • Add seasonings.

1 tbsp.	butter	15 mL
1 tbsp.	vegetable oil	15 mL
1	small onion, chopped	1
2	stalks celery, chopped	2
¼	green pepper, diced	¼
5 cups	chicken broth	1.25 L
8 oz.	stewed tomatoes	250 mL
½ cup	sea-shell pasta	125 mL
	salt and pepper, to taste	
¼ tsp.	sweet basil	1 mL
7½ oz.	can clams	225 g

CLAM AND PASTA SOUP

Heat butter and oil in deep soup kettle. Sauté vegetables for 3 minutes. Add broth and bring to a boil. Add tomatoes and pasta and simmer gently until tender. • Season to taste with salt, pepper and sweet basil. • Add clams and heat through. • Serve with rice crackers. • Serves 6.

To prevent any boiling-over mishaps, just grease the inside of the rim slightly.

CONEY ISLAND CLAM CHOWDER

½ cup	chopped bacon	125 mL
¼ cup	chopped onion	50 mL
	salt and pepper	
¼ tsp.	celery salt	1 mL
½ tsp.	parsley flakes	2 mL
1	bay leaf	1
1 cup	diced potatoes	250 mL
1 cup	diced carrots	250 mL
¾ cup	diced celery	175 mL
1	green pepper, chopped	1
2¼ cups	water	550 mL
2 x 5 oz.	can clams	2 x 142 g
10 oz.	can tomato soup	284 g

Fry bacon, add onion, fry lightly. Add salt, pepper, celery salt, parsley flakes, bay leaf, vegetables and water. • Simmer for 20 minutes. • Add clams, clam juice and tomato soup. • Simmer for another 20 minutes. • Stir before serving.

BASQUE FISH SOUP

1	large onion, chopped	1
½ cup	chopped celery, with leaves	125 mL
1	garlic clove, crushed	1
2 tbsp.	butter	30 mL
2 x 14 oz.	cans stewed tomatoes	2 x 398 mL
½ cup	dry white wine	125 mL
½ cup	minced parsley	125 mL
1 tsp.	salt	5 mL
¼ tsp.	pepper	1 mL
¼ tsp.	thyme	1 mL
1 lb.	frozen fish fillets, cut into chunks	500 g

In a large saucepan, sauté onion, celery, and garlic in butter until tender. • Add remaining ingredients except fish and cover. • Simmer for 30 minutes. • Add fish, cook another 10 minutes and serve.

FRENCH ONION SOUP

3 cups	sliced onions	750 mL
2 tbsp.	butter	25 mL
4 cups	beef broth	1 L
1 tsp.	Worcestershire sauce	5 mL
2	thin slices French bread, toasted	2
	grated Parmesan	

In large saucepan, cook onions in butter over low heat for about 30 minutes, stirring occasionally. Add beef broth and Worcestershire sauce; heat to boiling. Reduce heat; cover and simmer about 30 minutes. • Place ½ slice toasted bread in each of 4 soup bowls; pour soup over bread, sprinkle with Parmesan. • Serves 4.

1 tsp.	butter	5 mL
1 lb.	ground beef	500 g
3	medium onions, sliced	3
14 oz.	can tomatoes	398 mL
	salt, pepper and sweet basil, to taste	
½	bay leaf	½
6 cups	beef stock	1.5 L
3	medium carrots, sliced	3
3	medium potatoes, sliced	3
3	celery stalks, sliced	3
¼ cup	small sea-shell pasta	75 mL
	Worcestershire and Tabasco, to taste	

HEARTY JANUARY HAMBURGER SOUP

Melt butter, add beef and cook slightly. Add onions, tomatoes, salt, pepper, basil, bay leaf and beef stock. Bring to a boil; cover and simmer for 1 hour. • Add remaining vegetables and cook 1 hour longer. • Stir in shells during the last 12-15 minutes of cooking. • Correct seasonings. Remove bay leaf. Test shells to see if tender. • Serve hot. • For a delicious variation: add 6-7 cups (1.5-1.75 L) of cabbage when adding the rest of the vegetables. • Cooking time approximately 2½ hours. • Serves 12. • See photograph page 64A.

3 qts.	water	3 L
1 qt.	canned tomatoes, mashed	1 L
1 cup	diced carrots	250 mL
1	beet, quartered (optional)	1
2 tbsp.	salt	30 mL
2	large potatoes, halved	2
½ cup	Cheez Whiz	125 mL
3 tbsp.	butter	50 mL
1 cup	diced potatoes	250 mL
3 cups	chopped onion	750 mL
1	green pepper, chopped	1
4 cups	shredded cabbage	1 L
2 tsp.	snipped dill	10 mL

LOW-CALORIE BORSCH

Boil water, first 3 vegetables and salt until tender. • Remove potatoes, put in small bowl and mash. Add Cheez Whiz and butter to mashed potatoes; mix well and set aside. • Add diced potatoes to pot and cook for 10 minutes. • Add onions, green pepper and cabbage to pot. Cook until done. • Remove pot from heat. • Add potato mixture to pot and stir well. • Sprinkle with dill and serve. • This recipe can be frozen.

Use instant rice or mashed potatoes to thicken soup.

UKRAINIAN BORSCH

4 cups	beef OR pork stock	1 L
2 cups	shredded beets	500 mL
½ cup	diced carrots	125 mL
1 cup	medium shredded cabbage	250 mL
½ cup	diced potatoes	125 mL
½ cup	peas	125 mL
1 cup	tomato juice	250 mL
1	medium onion, diced	1
	salt to taste	
1	bay leaf	1
1	sprig of dill	1
½ cup	dry beans (optional)	125 mL
	sour cream	

Combine all ingredients except sour cream and simmer gently until well done.
● To serve, remove bay leaf, add a spoonfull of sour cream to each bowl.

SWEDISH FRUIT SOUP

A delicious, cool, summer treat.

11 oz.	dried fruit, apricots OR apples	330 g
1 cup	light seedless raisins	250 mL
3	cinnamon sticks	3
4	whole cloves	4
4 cups	water	1 L
1	large orange, sliced	1
48 oz.	unsweetened pineapple juice	1.36 L
¼ cup	sugar, to taste	50 mL
2 tbsp.	quick-cooking tapioca in water	30 mL

Simmer first 4 ingredients in the water for 20 minutes or until tender. ● Add remaining ingredients and simmer 15 minutes more. ● Put in refrigerator and serve cold. ● Serves 8.

CURRIED PEAR SOUP

3 tbsp.	margarine	45 mL
1	medium onion, finely chopped	1
½ tsp.	curry powder	2 mL
4	ripe pears	4
3 cups	chicken bouillon	750 mL
1 tsp.	lemon juice	5 mL

Melt margarine in a large saucepan, add onion and sprinkle with curry powder. Sauté until onion is soft, about 5 minutes. ● Peel, quarter and core pears. Coarsely chop and add to onion. Add chicken bouillon and lemon and bring to a boil. Cover, reduce heat and simmer 10 minutes or until pears are very tender. ● Blend, half at a time, until very smooth. ● Serve piping hot or very cold.

SALADS

12 oz.	pkg. frozen peas	340 g
1	small head lettuce, iceburg OR romaine, shredded	1
1	large green OR red pepper, finely chopped	1
1	medium Spanish OR red onion, finely chopped	1
3	stalks celery, sliced diagonally	3
1¾ cups	mayonnaise	425 mL
1 tsp.	sugar	5 mL
1 cup	grated Cheddar cheese	250 mL
8	slices bacon, cooked, drained and crumbled	8
	cherry tomatoes	
	black and green olives	
	egg slices	

LAYERED VEGETABLE SALAD

Blanch peas in boiling water for 1-2 minutes. Drain. Cool under cold water. Drain and dry. ● Line the bottom of clear salad bowl with layer of lettuce. Over lettuce, layer separately pepper, onion, celery and peas. Spread mayonnaise over top layer of salad. Sprinkle with sugar and cheese. ● Refrigerate for at least 8 hours, covered. ● Just before serving, sprinkle top with crumbled bacon. ● The top can be garnished with rows of tomatoes, black or green olives and egg slices. ● To serve, spoon down through layers so each serving has some of each layer. ● Serves 8-10.

"To make a perfect salad there should be a spendthrift for oil, a miser for vinegar, a wise man for salt and a madcap to stir the ingredients up and mix them well together."

CAESAR SALAD

1	garlic clove, halved	1
1	large head romaine lettuce (or 2 small)	1
1	lemon	1
¼ cup	olive oil	75 mL
1 tsp.	Worcestershire sauce	5 mL
½ tsp.	salt	2 mL
¼ tsp.	dry mustard	1 mL
1 tsp.	anchovy paste OR anchovies (optional)	5 mL
	ground pepper	
1	coddled egg (very softly boiled)	1
¼	garlic clove	¼
	garlic croutons	
¼ cup	grated Parmesan	75 mL

Just before serving, rub large salad bowl with cut clove of garlic. Tear romaine into bite-sized pieces; squeeze juice from lemon over romaine. ● In blender mix oil, Worcestershire sauce, seasonings, anchovies and coddled egg, as well as ¼ clove of garlic; blend thoroughly; pour over romaine. Toss until leaves are well-coated. Sprinkle with croutons and cheese. ● As a variation, add 6 slices of bacon, cooked crisp and crumbled. ● Serves 6. ● See photograph on front cover.

FRESH SPINACH SALAD

2 tbsp.	cider OR red wine vinegar	30 mL
1 tsp.	sugar	5 mL
1 tsp.	salt	5 mL
1 tsp.	dry mustard	5 mL
½ tsp.	seasoned pepper	2 mL
6 tbsp.	salad oil	90 mL
½	garlic clove (optional)	½
8 cups	crisp spinach, hard stems removed	2 L
3	hard-cooked eggs, grated	3
8	slices bacon, fried and crumbled	8
2-3	green onions, finely chopped	2-3
	fresh mushrooms, sliced "T" shaped	
	fresh cauliflower, sliced "T" shaped	

Beat first 6 ingredients and refrigerate. (At this time, you may add a ½ garlic clove, if so desired). ● Tear spinach into bite-sized pieces and prepare remaining ingredients. ● Add dressing just before serving, having removed the garlic clove. ● Serves 4. ● See photograph page 96A.

1	bunch fresh spinach	1	
1	apple, in 12 slices	1	
4	slices bacon, diced and cooked crisp	4	
½ cup	mayonnaise	125 mL	
¼ cup	orange juice concentrate	75 mL	
	pepper, to taste		

SPINACH APPLE SALAD

Wash spinach in warm water. Remove stems, drain, dry and crisp. Tear into bite-sized pieces. ● Combine spinach, apple slices and bacon pieces. ● Mix mayonnaise and warmed orange juice concentrate, stirring until smooth (emulsion goes very lumpy if orange juice is very cold). ● Pour some dressing over salad. Toss. ● Grate pepper over all.

3	heads of butter lettuce	3	
1	can hearts of palm, drained	1	
14 oz.	can artichoke hearts, drained	398 mL	
14 oz.	can lichee fruit, reserve liquid	398 mL	
1	avocado, peeled and sliced	1	
	purple onion rings		
	black olives, pitted		

SPECIAL SALAD

Tear lettuce into bite-sized pieces. ● Cut hearts of palm and artichoke hearts into bite-sized pieces. ● Combine all salad ingredients and toss with the following dressing. ● This salad is good the next day, minus the lettuce.

1	garlic clove, minced	1	
¼ cup	walnut OR safflower oil	50 mL	
2 tbsp.	lemon juice	30 mL	
2 tbsp.	balsamic vinegar	30 mL	
2 tbsp.	sugar	30 mL	
2 tbsp.	lichee liquid	30 mL	
2 tbsp.	unsweetened apple sauce	30 mL	

BALSAMIC VINAIGRETTE

Blend all ingredients.

Save your old kitchen sponges, cut them into 1-inch (2.5 cm) squares and use them to cover the bottom holes in your flower pots. It keeps the soil in and slows down the drying out process.

MARINATED VEGETABLE SALAD

14 oz.	can small spring peas	398 mL
14 oz.	can white corn	398 mL
14 oz.	can French-style green beans	398 mL
1 cup	chopped onion	250 mL
½ cup	finely chopped celery	125 mL
1	pimiento, chopped	1

MARINADE

½ cup	sugar	125 mL
½ cup	salad oil	125 mL
¾ cup	white vinegar	175 mL
1 tbsp.	water	15 mL
1 tsp.	salt and pepper	5 mL

Mix marinade ingredients and bring to a boil, cool. • Drain canned vegetables thoroughly and mix with onion, celery and pimiento. • Pour marinade over and chill several hours. • Drain before serving on lettuce or as a side dish.

PEA AND BACON SALAD

1 cup	sour cream	250 mL
1 tsp.	seasoned salt	5 mL
¼ tsp.	lemon pepper	1 mL
¼ tsp.	garlic powder	1 mL
20 oz.	frozen peas, thawed	550 g
½ lb.	bacon, cook, crumble	250 g
1	small tomato, cubed	1
¼ cup	minced red onion	50 mL
1 cup	chopped pecans OR almonds	250 mL

Combine sour cream and spices. Add other ingredients except nuts. Chill several hours before serving. • 1 cup (250 mL) of chopped pecans or almonds added just before serving adds a flavorful crunch to this salad. • For a lower-calorie dressing, use half sour cream and half plain yogurt. • Serves 6.

NEW MEXICO POTATO SALAD

4	medium potatoes	4
½ cup	olive oil	125 mL
¼ cup	vinegar	50 mL
1 tbsp.	sugar	15 mL
1½ tsp.	chili powder	7 mL
1 tsp.	salt	5 mL
dash	Tabasco sauce	dash
1	small onion, in rings	1
8 oz.	can kernel corn	250 g
½ cup	shredded carrot	125 mL
½ cup	diced green pepper	125 mL
½ cup	sliced black olives	125 mL

Cook peeled potatoes, cool and dice. • Mix ingredients, except for last 5, and refrigerate for 1 hour, covered. • Remove from refrigerator, add remaining ingredients and serve. • Serves 6-8.

1 lb.	ground beef	500 g
14 oz.	can red kidney beans	398 mL
1	bunch green onions	1
1	medium head lettuce	1
4	medium tomatoes	4
¼ lb.	Cheddar, grated	125 g
8 oz.	Thousand Island dressing OR your choice	250 mL
1	medium bag Tortilla Chips, crushed	1
1	large avocado	1

MEXICAN CHEF'S SALAD

Brown ground beef, drain, add kidney beans. Cook for 5 minutes. Cool. ● Chop lettuce, onions, and tomatoes. Add salad dressing. ● Mix beef and beans into cold salad. Add crushed tortillas. ● Garnish with avocado and tomato wedges. ● Serve immediately. ● If making ahead, add chips when serving.

14 cups	shredded cabbage (about 1½ heads)	3.5 L
½	onion, shredded	½
½	medium green pepper, shredded (optional)	½
3	medium carrots, shredded	3

MAKE-AHEAD COLESLAW

¾ cup	white vinegar	175 mL	
¾ cup	salad oil	175 mL	**DRESSING**
1½ cups	sugar	375 mL	
1 tbsp.	salt	15 mL	
dash	celery seed	dash	

Toss vegetables and set aside. Combine and bring dressing ingredients to a boil. Pour dressing over vegetables and mix. ● Let sit at room temperature for 1½ hours; refrigerate. ● This will keep for weeks. ● This recipe can also be made with sauerkraut instead of cabbage. ● Serves about 50.

4	red apples	4
1	rib celery, diced	1
1 cup	seedless green grapes	250 mL
½ cup	walnut pieces	125 mL
½ cup	mayonnaise	125 mL
¼ cup	dry white wine	50 mL

WALDORF SALAD AU VIN

Core apples but do not peel; chop into cubes. ● In a salad bowl, combine apples, celery, grapes and walnuts. ● Mix mayonnaise with wine and pour over fruit. Toss lightly. ● For a Blue Cheese variation: substitute ¼ cup (50 mL) each, crumbled blue cheese, sour cream and mayonnaise.

73

CHINESE VEGETABLE SALAD

½ cup	sliced almonds, toasted	125 mL
½	small cabbage, shredded	½
3½ oz.	pkg. Ichiban Noodles, broken	100 g
2 tbsp.	sesame seeds, roasted	30 mL
1	pkg. bean sprouts	1
2 cups	chopped green onions	500 mL
2 cups	chopped mushrooms	500 mL
½ cup	sunflower seeds	125 mL
½	pkg. chow mein noodles	½

DRESSING

1	soup seasoning from noodles	1
½ cup	vegetable oil	125 mL
2-4 tbsp.	soy sauce	30-60 mL
3 tbsp.	vinegar	45 mL
1 tbsp.	sugar	15 mL
	salt and pepper	

In large bowl, mix the first 9 ingredients until they are very well blended. • In a jar, mix the next 7 ingredients, shaking very well. • Pour dressing over vegetables in bowl and toss them thoroughly to make sure all the vegetables are coated. Refrigerate until needed. Toss gently before you serve! • Serves 8-10.

PAPAYA SEED DRESSING SALAD

Beautiful colors and unique flavor.

2 qts.	mixed salad greens	2 L
1	papaya, cubed	1
1	avocado, cubed	1
1 cup	Chinese pea pods (just poached)	250 mL
1	small cucumber, diced decoratively	1

DRESSING

1 cup	white wine vinegar	250 mL
½ cup	sugar	125 mL
1 tsp.	dry mustard	5 mL
1 tsp.	seasoned salt	5 mL
2 cups	salad oil	500 mL
1	small onion, minced	1
2 tbsp.	fresh papaya seeds	30 mL

Mix greens with enough dressing to coat. Add rest of ingredients and toss gently. • Dressing: Place vinegar and dry ingredients in blender. Turn on gradually. Add oil and onion and blend until smooth. Add papaya seeds. Blend only until seeds are cut to the size of coarsely ground pepper. • As a variation, when papayas are not available, substitute poppy seeds for papaya seeds and pour over butter lettuce, red onion rings and orange slices. • See photograph page 16A.

¼ cup	vinegar	50 mL
½ tsp.	dry mustard	2 mL
½ tsp.	salt	2 mL
2 tbsp.	grated orange rind	30 mL
1 cup	salad oil	250 mL
½ cup	orange juice	125 mL
2 tbsp.	lemon juice	30 mL
3	large oranges, peeled and sliced	3
2	large avocados, peeled and sliced	2
2	medium onions, sliced, separated into rings (use 1 red for variation)	2
1	head romaine lettuce	1
1	head leaf lettuce	1
1	head iceberg lettuce	1

ORANGE AND AVOCADO TOSS

Combine first 7 ingredients in l-quart (1 L) jar. Cover, shake well. Refrigerate.
• Combine oranges, avocados and onions. Pour vinegar mixture over top.
• Refrigerate for several hours. • Add remaining ingredients. Toss. Serve immediately. • For a flavorful nutty variation: add ½ cup (125 mL) shelled sunflower seeds and ½ cup (125 mL) slivered almonds to this salad. Red wine vinegar is also an interesting flavor alternate for the dressing.

2-3 lbs.	carrots	1-1.5 kg
1	large onion	1
1	red pepper	1
1	green pepper	1
½ cup	salad oil	125 mL
1 cup	sugar	250 mL
10 oz.	can tomato soup	284 mL
¾ cup	vinegar	175 mL
1 tsp.	Worcestershire sauce	5 mL
1 tsp.	dry mustard	5 mL
	salt and pepper, to taste	

CARROT SALAD

Cook carrots 10 minutes. • Chop onion and peppers and set aside. • Combine and bring to a boil, the oil, sugar, soup, vinegar, Worcestershire sauce, dry mustard, salt and pepper. • Remove carrots from stove and drain. Add carrots and rest of vegetables to sauce and cool. • Marinate in refrigerator 24 hours. • Will keep up to 2 weeks refrigerated. • Optional method: Combine all ingredients, place in casserole and bake at 350°F (180°C) until carrots are tender. Cool and store in refrigerator. • This recipe may be served hot if you wish.

Paint the handle of your hoe every 4 inches (10 cm) for a built in ruler for spacing plants.

NOVA SCOTIA SEAFOOD SALAD

6 oz.	crab meat, drained	170 g
4 oz.	medium OR small shrimp, drained	113 g
7 oz.	frozen scallops, cooked as directed	200 g
4	green onions, chopped	4
	salt and pepper, to taste	
½ tsp.	dried oregano	2 mL
½ cup	mayonnaise	125 mL
2	green apples, unpeeled, chopped	2
	lemon OR lime wedges	
	lettuce	

Combine crab, shrimp and scallops (cut in halves or quarters if large), green onions, salt, pepper, oregano and ¼ cup (50 mL) mayonnaise; chill well. • At serving time, add remaining mayonnaise and chopped apples. • Garnish with lemon or lime wedges and serve on lettuce leaves. • Serves 8.

POLYNESIAN SALAD

1½ cups	cooked rice	375 mL
1½ cups	diced celery	375 mL
½ cup	finely chopped green onions	125 mL
½ cup	finely chopped green pepper	125 mL
½ cup	frozen peas, thawed	125 mL
1 cup	small cooked shrimp	250 mL
5 oz.	chow mein noodles	142 g

DRESSING

½ cup	salad oil	125 mL
3 tbsp.	vinegar	45 mL
2 tsp.	sugar	10 mL
½ tsp.	salt	2 mL
½ tsp.	celery salt	2 mL
1-2 tsp.	curry powder	5-10 mL
2 tbsp.	soy sauce	30 mL

Prepare salad ingredients. • Combine dressing ingredients. Add to salad. • Add noodles just before serving, leaving some to put on top.

Try boiling peas in the pods. The pods burst open when done, float to the top, and can be skimmed off, leaving the peas with a fresher flavor.

TOMATO ASPIC RING SALAD

2	envelopes gelatin (2 tbsp. [30 mL])	2
4 cups	tomato juice	1 L
½ tsp.	onion juice	2 mL
	salt and pepper, to taste	
½ cup	mayonnaise	125 mL
8 oz.	cream cheese	250 g
1 cup	finely chopped celery	250 mL
1 tbsp.	chopped pimiento	15 mL
1 tbsp.	chopped green pepper	15 mL
½ cup	chopped pecans	125 mL
1 tbsp.	lemon juice	15 mL
2 tsp.	gelatin	10 mL
¼ cup	cold water	50 mL
	lettuce	

Soften 2 envelopes of gelatin in 1 cup (250 mL) cold tomato juice. Dissolve it over hot water, and add to the remaining cold tomato juice with the onion juice and seasonings. • Pour half of the tomato juice mixture into a 2-quart (2 L) ring mold and chill until firm. • Blend the mayonnaise into the cream cheese. Add the celery, pimiento, green pepper, pecans, lemon juice and the 2 tsp. (10 mL) gelatin softened in the cold water and dissolved over hot water. • Spread this mixture over the firm tomato aspic. • Chill until firm. • Pour the remaining aspic over the cream cheese layer and chill again. • When firm, unmold onto crisp lettuce.

PEAR SALAD

6 oz.	lime gelatin powder	170 g
2 cups	boiling water	500 mL
8 oz.	cream cheese	250 g
14 oz.	canned pears, drained	398 mL
1 cup	whipping cream	250 mL

Delicious with chicken or turkey.

Combine gelatin and water. Put into blender and add cream cheese, process until smooth. Pour into bowl. • Place pears in blender and purée. • Add pears to gelatin and cheese mixture. • Whip cream and fold into previous mixture. • Pour into dish or mold and chill until firm.

PRESERVE: CHOICE CHILDREN

1 large grassy field   *½ dozen children*
2-3 small dogs   *pinch of brooks*
few small pebbles
Mix children and dogs well together and put into field, stirring constantly. Pour brook over the pebbles. Sprinkle the field with flowers. Spread over all a deep blue sky and bake in the hot sun. When thoroughly brown, remove and set away to cool in a bathtub. The result is delightful!

MUSTARD SALAD RING

4	eggs, well-beaten	4
1 cup	weak vinegar (add half water)	250 mL
¾ cup	sugar	175 mL
	salt and pepper	
3 tbsp.	dry mustard	45 mL
1 tsp.	turmeric	5 mL
1	pkg. gelatin in ½ cup (125 mL) water	1
1 cup	whipping cream	250 mL

Beat eggs well. • Mix vinegar, sugar, salt, pepper, mustard and turmeric.
• Add beaten eggs. • Add gelatin and cook in double boiler until thick.
• Cool pan in another pan of cold water. When cool, add whipped cream and
pour into salad ring mold. • Unmold on lettuce. Fill center with coleslaw and
serve with baked ham. • Simply terrific and it keeps beautifully, refrigerated!

FROZEN APPLE SALAD

8 oz.	crushed pineapple	250 mL
2	eggs, beaten	2
½ cup	sugar	125 mL
dash	salt	dash
3 tbsp.	lemon juice	45 mL
2 cups	finely diced, unpared apples	500 mL
½ cup	finely diced celery	125 mL
1 cup	cream, whipped	250 mL

Drain pineapple, reserving syrup. • Add water to pineapple syrup to make ½
cup (125 mL). • Combine eggs, sugar, salt, lemon juice and syrup mixture.
Cook over low heat, stirring constantly until thick. Cool. • Fold in pineapple,
apple, celery and whipped cream. • Spoon evenly into a bundt pan, or shallow
jelly mold. • Freeze. • Remove from pan by dipping pan in warm water and
inverting on suitable dish. Return to freezer until serving time. • We enjoy this
salad with leftover turkey, a tossed green salad and hot buns.

CAMEMBERT DRESSING

2	eggs	2
½ cup	white vinegar	125 mL
½ cup	white wine	125 mL
2 tsp.	lemon juice	10 mL
1 tsp.	Worcestershire sauce	5 mL
1	garlic clove	1
2 ½ oz.	Camembert cheese	75 g
¾ tsp.	salt	3 mL
dash	white pepper	dash
3 ½ cups	olive oil	875 mL

Mix in blender; all ingredients but oil. Process until smooth. Add oil slowly while
blending. • Makes about 4½ cups (1 L).

½ cup	salad oil	125 mL
2 tbsp.	lemon juice	30 mL
¼ cup	soy sauce	50 mL
½ tsp.	sugar	2 mL
½ tsp.	pepper	2 mL
1½ tbsp.	grated onion	22 mL

DEANNA'S SOY SAUCE DRESSING

Put all ingredients in jar with a tight fitting lid. Shake well before each serving.

3	eggs	3
1 cup	vinegar	250 mL
1 cup	milk	250 mL
4 tsp.	mustard	20 mL
4 tsp.	flour	20 mL
1 cup	sugar	250 mL
1 tsp.	salt	5 mL
1½ tbsp.	butter OR margarine	22 mL
½ tsp.	turmeric (for color)	2 mL

GOLDEN SALAD DRESSING

Beat eggs well. Mix vinegar and milk and add to the eggs. • Add dry ingredients to the egg mixture in a double boiler. Cook until thickened, about 30 minutes, or over direct heat at medium for about 10 minutes, stirring constantly. • Remove from heat and add butter. • Cool and refrigerate. • Makes 1 quart (1 L).

2 tbsp.	flour	30 mL
1 tsp.	salt	5 mL
1 tsp.	mustard	5 mL
1 cup	white sugar	250 mL
1 cup	cider vinegar	250 mL
¼ cup	water	75 mL
10	egg yolks	10
1 tbsp.	butter	15 mL

MAYONNAISE

An old-time recipe.

Mix flour, salt, mustard and sugar; add some of combined vinegar and water to moisten; add egg yolks that have been slightly beaten; add remainder of vinegar. • Cook slowly, stirring most of the time. Add butter after mixture thickens. • Store in covered jar in refrigerator.

¾ cup	mayonnaise	175 mL
1 cup	sour cream	250 mL
1	garlic clove, minced	1
½ cup	salad oil	125 mL
1 tsp.	Lawry's salt	5 mL
¼ tsp.	cumin	1 mL
¼ cup	vinegar	50 mL
8 oz.	blue cheese	250 g

ROQUEFORT DRESSING

Mix all ingredients together well.

VEGETABLES

VEGETABLES BAPTISTE

1	green pepper	1
2	medium potatoes	2
1	medium turnip	1
3	medium carrots	3
2	medium sweet potatoes	2
4	medium parsnips	4
3	medium cooking onions	3
1	medium acorn squash	1
	broccoli OR brussel sprouts	
	salt and pepper, to taste	
3 tbsp.	butter	45 mL
¼ cup	brown sugar	50 mL
¼ cup	barbecue sauce (hickory)	50 mL
¼ cup	water	50 mL
1 cup	whole fresh, mushrooms	250 mL
12	cherry tomatoes	12

Slice the green pepper into rings. Peel and cube the potatoes, turnip and carrots into 1″ (2.5 cm) cubes. Peel and cut on the bias the sweet potatoes and parsnips, approximately ½″ (1.25 cm) thick. Quarter the onions; peel and slice the squash into "canoes" (half, quarter, eighth until you have "canoes"). Cut broccoli into large chunks; leave brussel sprouts whole. ● In a 9″x13″ (4 L) or similar pan arrange vegetables, except mushrooms, green pepper and tomatoes, in rows across the dish in alternating colors. Sprinkle with salt and pepper. Place dabs of butter on top, add brown sugar, barbecue sauce and water. Cover with foil and bake at 375°F (190°C) for 50 minutes. Remove from oven and sprinkle with whole mushrooms, pepper slices and cherry tomatoes. Bake another 10 minutes at 375°F (190°C). Remove to table and serve from dish. ● Serves 8.

1 cup	soda cracker crumbs (approx. 30)	250 mL
¾ cup	vacuum-packed regular wheat germ	175 mL
8 tbsp.	butter	120 mL
1	onion, sliced	1
½ lb.	zucchini, sliced (2 medium)	250 g
½ tsp.	salt	2 mL
¼ tsp.	pepper	1 mL
¼ tsp.	crushed tarragon	1 mL
1 cup	grated Monterey Jack cheese	250 mL
½ cup	grated Parmesan	125 mL
2	eggs	2
¼ cup	milk	75 mL
1	medium tomato, thinly sliced	1

VEGETABLE TORTE

Nutritious prize-winning casserole!

Mix crumbs with ¼ cup (50 mL) wheat germ and 6 tbsp. (90 mL) melted butter. Press on bottom and up 1" (2.5 cm) on sides of 8" (20 cm) springform pan, or 9" (1 L) pie plate. • Bake in 400°F (200°C) oven for 8-10 minutes until lightly browned. • Sauté onion and zucchini in remaining 2 tbsp. (30 mL) of butter until tender-crisp. Mix in remaining ½ cup (125 mL) wheat germ and seasonings. Turn half into crumb shell. Sprinkle with half the cheeses. Top with remaining vegetable mixture. • Beat eggs with milk. Pour into center of vegetable mixture. • Arrange tomato slices on top and sprinkle remaining cheeses over all. • Bake at 325°F (160°C) for 40-45 minutes or until set. • Garnish with carrot curls, olives and parsley. • Serve with bread sticks, or buns. No meat is necessary. • If you want to add meat, you can use leftover ham, poultry, pork or beef in this casserole. • Serves 6.

---

2 lbs.	turnips	1 kg
2 cups	chicken stock	500 mL
2 tbsp.	butter	30 mL
1½ tsp.	brown sugar	7 mL
⅛ tsp.	pepper	0.5 mL
⅛ tsp.	mace	0.5 mL
1 tsp.	baking powder	5 mL
2	eggs, separated	2
	salt, to taste	
½ cup	fine dry bread crumbs	125 mL
3 tbsp.	butter	45 mL

TURNIP SOUFFLÉ

Chop peeled turnips into cubes. Place in saucepan with stock. Boil 25 minutes. Drain and mash well. • Add 2 tbsp. (30 mL) butter, brown sugar, pepper, mace, baking powder, yolks of eggs and salt. Stir well. • Sauté crumbs in 3 tbsp. (45 mL) of butter. • Beat egg whites and fold into mixture. • Sprinkle with buttered crumbs. • Bake at 375°F (190°C) for 25 minutes.

CRUSTY PECAN SQUASH

3 cups	cooked squash (may use frozen)	750 mL
¼ cup	melted butter	75 mL
¼ cup	evaporated milk	75 mL
2-3 tbsp.	brown sugar	30-50 mL
1 tsp.	salt	5 mL
½ tsp.	nutmeg	2 mL
½ cup	coarsely broken pecans	125 mL
2 tbsp.	maple OR corn syrup	30 mL

Combine first 6 ingredients. Combine pecans with syrup. Sprinkle over squash. Bake 30 minutes at 400°F (200°C). • Serves 6. • See photograph page 128A.

SHERRIED SWEET POTATO CASSEROLE

8	medium sweet potatoes OR 3 x 19 oz. (3 x 540 mL) cans	8
1 cup	brown sugar	250 mL
2 tbsp.	cornstarch	30 mL
½ tsp.	salt	2 mL
½ tsp.	grated orange peel	2 mL
2 cups	orange juice	500 mL
½ cup	raisins	125 mL
6 tbsp.	butter OR margarine	90 mL
¼ cup	dry sherry	50 mL
¼ cup	chopped walnuts	50 mL

Cook potatoes in boiling salted water until just tender. Peel and cut into thick slices. Arrange in 9″ x 9″ (2.5 L) baking dish. Sprinkle with a little salt. • In a saucepan, combine brown sugar, cornstarch and salt. Blend in grated orange peel and orange juice. Add raisins. Cook and stir over medium heat until thickened and bubbly. Cook 1 minute more. Add butter, sherry and walnuts, stirring until butter has melted. Pour over potatoes. • Bake in 325°F (160°C) oven for 30 minutes or until potatoes are well glazed, basting occasionally. • Serves 8.

ORANGE-GLAZED CARROTS

2 lbs.	baby carrots	1 kg
¼ cup	melted butter	50 mL
¼ cup	brown sugar	50 mL
¼ cup	orange juice concentrate	50 mL
½ tsp.	salt	2 mL
	tiny mandarin orange pieces (optional)	

Prepare ahead to let flavors blend. • Slice carrots thinly and boil until cooked, but still slightly crisp. • Combine remaining ingredients until well blended. • Place carrots in buttered baking dish and cover with sauce. Refrigerate overnight. • Turn carrots to coat with sauce. • Before serving, bake at 350°F (180°C) for 20-25 minutes. • May also be heated in microwave oven.

1	medium onion, sliced	1
1 lb.	fresh mushrooms, sliced	500 g
½ cup	butter	125 mL
¼ cup	flour	50 mL
2 cups	milk	500 mL
1 cup	whipping cream	250 mL
5 oz.	can water chestnuts, drained and sliced	150 g
1½ cups	grated sharp Cheddar cheese	375 mL
⅛ tsp.	Tabasco sauce	0.5 mL
2 tsp.	soy sauce	10 mL
1 tsp.	salt	5 mL
½ tsp.	pepper	2 mL
2 x 12 oz.	pkgs. frozen French beans, cooked and drained	2 x 350 g
½ cup	slivered almonds, toasted	125 mL

FRENCH BEAN CASSEROLE

Sauté onions and mushrooms in butter. Add flour and mix. Add milk and cream and stir until thick. Add rest of ingredients except beans and almonds. Stir until cheese melts. Add cooked beans and sprinkle with almonds. • Bake 35-40 minutes at 350°F (180°C).

5 cups	dried white beans	1.25 L
1 tbsp.	baking soda	15 mL
6 oz.	salt pork, cubed	170 g
1 tsp.	dry mustard	5 mL
2 tbsp.	brown sugar	30 mL
4 tbsp.	molasses	60 mL
5½ oz.	tomato paste	156 mL
¼ tsp.	ground pepper	1 mL
1	medium onion, chopped	1
1 tsp.	salt OR to taste	5 mL

OLD-FASHIONED BOSTON-BAKED BEANS

Wash beans in several washes of cold water. Soak overnight in a large pot, covering well with cold water. Next morning, bring to a slow boil and cook slowly for 20 minutes. Stir in soda and watch carefully that it doesn't foam over. Drain and rinse in cold water. • Place beans in bean pot, layering with the salt pork. Stir enough hot water into the remaining ingredients, except onions, to cover beans in pot. Add extra water to level of lid area. Place onions on top and bake uncovered in a 200-220°F (100-110°C) oven for 6 or 7 hours. • Improves by reheating. • Freezes well.

An overload of suds in the sink settles with a sprinkle of salt.

BAKED PORK AND BEANS — STAMPEDE-STYLE

¼ cup	sugar	75 mL
1 tsp.	instant coffee	5 mL
1 tbsp.	vinegar	15 mL
1 tsp.	dry mustard	5 mL
½ tsp.	salt	2 mL
½ cup	water	125 mL
4	slices bacon	4
1	onion, chopped	1
2 x 19 oz.	cans baked beans	2 x 540 mL
½ cup	crushed pineapple	125 mL
¼ cup	cognac	50 mL

Mix together first 6 ingredients and cook for 5 minutes. • Chop and sauté bacon and onion. • Mix all ingredients together, except the cognac. Put into a casserole dish and bake for 45 minutes at 350°F (180°C). • Add cognac and bake for an additional 30 minutes.

CORN FRITTERS

2 x 12 oz.	whole kernel corn, not drained	2 x 341 mL
⅔ cup	milk	150 mL
2	eggs, beaten	2
2 tbsp.	melted butter	30 mL
1 cup	flour	250 mL
2 tsp.	baking powder	10 mL
1 tsp.	salt	5 mL
½ tsp.	sugar	2 mL
	vegetable oil for frying	

In a large bowl, mix corn, milk, eggs and butter. Sift together dry ingredients and combine with corn mixture. Drop by spoonfuls into hot oil in skillet, or electric frying pan, 375-400°F (190-200°C). Brown on both sides like a pancake. • For a round fritter, deep fry in hot oil. • Serves 5-6.

TOMATO CHEESE BAKE

4	large tomatoes, skinned and sliced	4
	salt and pepper	
½ cup	mayonnaise	125 mL
6	green onions, chopped	6
1 cup	grated Cheddar	250 mL
1 cup	grated mozzarella	250 mL

In a shallow baking dish, arrange sliced tomatoes on bottom. Sprinkle with salt and pepper. Spread mayonnaise over tomatoes and top with chopped green onions. Cover with combined cheeses. • Bake at 350°F (180°C) for 25-30 minutes. • Great with steak, meat loaf, etc. • Serves 6.

Place onion, egg and spices in blender for a delicate, consistent flavor throughout your hamburger or meatloaf.

6	medium tomatoes, firm and ripe	6	***MUSHROOM-***
1 tbsp.	cooking oil	15 mL	***STUFFED***
2 cups	finely chopped mushrooms	500 mL	***TOMATOES***
2-3	finely chopped green onions	2-3	
1 tsp.	salt	5 mL	
¼ tsp.	pepper	1 mL	
½ tsp.	tarragon	1 mL	
2	eggs, slightly beaten	2	
½ cup	yogurt OR sour cream	125 mL	

Preheat oven to 400°F (200°C). • With sharp knife, cut out stem of tomatoes, scoop out pulp and invert. • In a skillet, heat oil and sauté mushrooms and onions for 3-4 minutes. Stir in salt, pepper and tarragon. Combine eggs and yogurt, or sour cream, and add to mushrooms. • Fill tomato shells with the mushroom mixture and place in a shallow baking pan. • Bake for 15 minutes. Do not overcook. • Serve hot for lunch, or as a dinner vegetable. • Serves 6.

4 cups	small cooking onions, in ½" (1.25 cm) slices	1 L	***ONIONS AU***
½ tsp.	salt	2 mL	***GRATIN***
1 cup	boiling water	250 mL	

Cook onions in boiling water with salt for 10 minutes. Drain. Reserve ¼ cup (50 mL) of liquid for sauce. Turn onions into buttered baking dish.

2 tbsp.	butter OR margarine	30 mL	
2 tbsp.	flour	30 mL	***SAUCE***
½ tsp.	salt	2 mL	
dash	pepper	dash	
1 cup	milk	250 mL	
¼ cup	reserved onion liquid	50 mL	
½-¾ cup	grated Cheddar cheese	125-175 mL	
3	slices buttered bread, crumbed	3	

To make sauce, melt butter; add flour; cook 5 minutes stirring constantly. Add milk and onion liquid and cook 5 minutes stirring constantly. Add salt and pepper. Remove from heat and stir in cheese until melted. Pour this sauce over onions. Sprinkle buttered crumbs over sauce in baking dish. • Bake at 375°F (190°C) for 25-30 minutes. • This may be made in the morning, of the day it is to be served, and stored in the refrigerator until baking time. • Serves 6.

To remove coffee, tea and juice stains from counter-tops, rub with a paste made of baking soda and water. Let stand for half-an-hour, then rinse.

BROCCOLI WITH ALMONDS IN WINE SAUCE

1½ lbs.	broccoli	750 g
1	bouillon cube	1
¾ cup	boiling water	175 mL
¼ cup	butter	50 mL
¼ cup	flour	50 mL
1 cup	cream	250 mL
2 tbsp.	sherry	30 mL
2 tbsp.	lemon juice	30 mL
½ tsp.	Accent	2 mL
	pepper, to taste	
¼ cup	Parmesan cheese	50 mL
¼ cup	toasted slivered almonds	50 mL

Cook broccoli lightly. Drain well. Place in shallow baking dish. ● Dissolve bouillon cube in water. ● Melt butter, add flour. Stir until mixture bubbles. Remove from heat and blend in bouillon and cream. Return to medium heat and cook until mixture comes to a boil. Add sherry, lemon juice, Accent and pepper. Pour over broccoli. Sprinkle cheese and almonds on broccoli. ● Bake at 375°F (190°C) for 20 minutes, or until thoroughly heated. ● Serves 6.

LAZY PEROGY CASSEROLE

15	lasagne noodles	15
2 cups	cottage cheese	500 mL
1	egg	1
¼ tsp.	onion salt	1 mL
1 cup	shredded Cheddar cheese	250 mL
2 cups	mashed potatoes	500 mL
¼ tsp.	salt	1 mL
¼ tsp.	onion salt	1 mL
⅛ tsp.	pepper	0.5 mL
1 cup	butter OR margarine	250 mL
1 cup	chopped onions	250 mL
	sour cream	

Cook noodles as directed on package. Drain. Line bottom of 9"x13" (4 L) pan with noodles. ● In medium bowl, mix cottage cheese, egg, and onion salt together. Spread over noodles. Cover with a layer of noodles. ● In same bowl, mix Cheddar cheese with potatoes, salt, onion salt and pepper. Spread over noodles. Cover with another layer of noodles. ● Melt butter in pan. Sauté onions until transparent and soft. Pour over noodles. Cover. ● Bake 30 minutes in 350°F (180°C) oven. ● Let stand for 10 minutes before cutting. ● Serve with sour cream. ● Serves 8 generously.

FREEZING PEPPERS: Remove seeds, wash and dry, cut-up and put in freezer bags. When thawed, they will be limp but are good used in casseroles, stews, chili and spaghetti sauce.

4 tbsp.	melted butter	60 mL
2 cups	mashed potatoes	500 mL
2	egg yolks	2
½ tsp.	salt	2 mL
¼ tsp.	nutmeg	1 mL
1	garlic clove, crushed	1

GARLIC PUFFED SPUDS

Melt butter in saucepan and mix potatoes, egg yolks and butter together. Add all other ingredients, mixing well. • Place spoonfuls of the potato mixture on greased serving dish and place under preheated broiler for 5 minutes, or until golden brown. • Serves 4.

½ cup	cold mashed potatoes	125 mL
2 tbsp.	shortening	30 mL
2	egg yolks	2
1¾ cups	flour	425 mL
1 tsp.	cream of tartar	5 mL
1 tsp.	salt	5 mL
½ cup	lukewarm water	125 mL

PYROHY (PEROGIES)

Mix first 3 ingredients thoroughly. Combine flour, cream of tartar and salt. Mix flour mixture and mashed potato mixture alternately with water. Let stand 10 minutes. • Roll dough fairly thin and cut in rounds with a 3″ (7.5 cm) cookie cutter.

½ cup	cottage cheese	125 mL
½ cup	mashed potatoes	125 mL
2	egg whites	2
	salt and pepper, to taste	
	butter	
	fried onions	
	sour cream for garnish	

FILLING

Combine cottage cheese, potatoes, egg whites, salt and pepper. Place 1 tsp. (5 mL) of potato-cheese mixture on each round, fold and pinch edges together. • Toss prepared pyrohy into boiling water, just enough so they will float on top of water, and cook for approximately 5 minutes or until they puff slightly. Remove from water and smother in butter and fried onions. • Serve piping hot with sour cream. • This recipe comes from Lillian Schreyer, wife of former Governor General, Ed Schreyer.

Save the water in which the potatoes have been cooked. It makes a wonderful gravy or a start for homemade soups.

COTTAGE CHEESE ROLLS (NALYSNYKY)

1 cup	all-purpose flour	250 mL
2	eggs	2
½ cup	milk	125 mL
½ cup	water	125 mL
¼ tsp.	salt	1 mL
2 tbsp.	butter OR margarine, melted	30 mL

FILLING

1 lb.	dry cottage cheese	500 g
2	eggs	2
½ tsp.	salt	2 mL
	sweet OR sour cream	

Place first 6 ingredients in blender container in order given. Blend 30 seconds, stop and scrape down sides. Blend 30-60 seconds until smooth. Let stand for 30 minutes to 2 hours to produce more tender crêpes. • Grease small skillet and pour in small amount of batter, rotate to cover bottom of pan. Brown just 1 side. Remove to a plate. Stack crêpes with waxed paper between them. • Continue frying until all the batter is used. • Combine cottage cheese, eggs and salt. • Spread cottage cheese filling on each crêpe and roll jelly-roll style. Place in greased casserole and pour on sweet or sour cream to cover. • Bake in moderate oven 30-45 minutes. • Serve. • Yields 14 rolls.

BUKOVINIAN NACHYNKA

1	small onion, finely chopped	1
3 tbsp.	butter	45 mL
1 cup	cornmeal	250 mL
1 tsp.	salt	5 mL
1 tsp.	sugar	5 mL
¼ tsp.	pepper	1 mL
¼ tsp.	cinnamon (optional)	1 mL
3½ cups	scalded milk	875 mL
½ cup	light cream	125 mL
2-3	eggs, well beaten	2-3

Cook the onion in butter until it is tender but not brown. Add cornmeal along with salt, sugar, pepper and cinnamon; mix to coat the cornmeal thoroughly with butter. Pour in scalded milk gradually and stir briskly until mixture is smooth and free of lumps. Cook until it thickens. Remove from heat and blend in cream. Beat eggs well and fold into cornmeal mixture. Spoon into a 2-quart (2 L) buttered casserole. • Bake the nachynka, uncovered, at 350°F (180°C) for 1 hour. It should have a crisp golden brown crust. • This is a superior and spicy version of a native Bukovinian Nachynka (dressing) served as an accompaniment to meat, just like Yorkshire Pudding. It is often made in large quantities for weddings and community dinners in Bukovinian settlements in Canada. Excellent with any preparation of meat, or as a meal in itself for lunch or supper. For an aromatic dish, increase the pepper slightly. • Serves 6-8.

3 tbsp.	unsalted butter	45 mL
1	small onion, finely chopped	1
1	rib celery, chopped	1
1 cup	long-grain rice	250 mL
2 cups	hot chicken stock	500 mL
1 tsp.	salt	5 mL
¼ tsp.	black pepper	1 mL
3	green onions, finely chopped	3
¼ cup	chopped fresh parsley	50 mL
¼ cup	finely chopped fresh dill	50 mL
1 cup	frozen peas, defrosted	250 mL
2 tbsp.	unsalted butter	30 mL

FRENCH-STYLE RICE PILAF WITH HERBS

Melt butter in 3-quart (3 L) saucepan. Add onions and cook until tender. Do not brown onions. Add celery and cook 1 minute longer. Add rice and stir to coat with butter. Add chicken stock, salt and pepper and bring to a boil. Cover and cook gently for 20 mintues, or until all liquid is absorbed and rice is tender. Stir in green onions, herbs and peas, replace cover and cook for 3-4 minutes. Remove cover and stir in butter. Toss lightly and taste to adjust seasonings. • Butter a 4-5 cup (1-1.25 L) ring mold, pat rice into it. Cover with serving plate and invert. Fill center with cherry tomatoes. • Serves 4-6. • See photograph page 96A.

1¼ cups	wild rice (natural OR Uncle Ben's)	300 mL
¼ cup	butter OR margarine	75 mL
½ cup	chopped fresh parsley OR flakes	125 mL
½ cup	chopped green onions	125 mL
1 cup	diagonally sliced celery	250 mL
10 oz.	consommé	284 mL
1½ cups	boiling water	375 mL
1 tsp.	salt	5 mL
½ tsp.	dried marjoram	2 mL
½ cup	dry sherry	125 mL

GOURMET WILD RICE

Wash wild rice well. Let stand, covered with water, 1 hour before baking. Drain well. This is not necessary with Uncle Ben's rice. • Melt butter in a medium casserole and lightly sauté the parsley, green onions and celery. • Add rice, consommé, water, salt and marjoram. • Cover and bake about 45 minutes at 300°F (150°C), or until rice is tender and all liquid is absorbed. Stir with a fork 2 or 3 times while baking. • Stir in sherry and continue to bake about 5 minutes longer. • Serves 8. • See photograph on front cover.

Scrub toothpaste into grass stains for removal.

PICKLES PLUS

SWISS CHARD PICKLES

5 qts.	Swiss chard	5 L
	salt	
	white vinegar	
4 cups	white sugar	1 L
2 tbsp.	celery seed	30 mL
3 tbsp.	mustard seed	45 mL
12	onions, finely chopped	12
½ cup	cornstarch	125 mL
1 tbsp.	turmeric	15 mL
1 tbsp.	curry powder	15 mL
2 tbsp.	dry mustard	30 mL

Wash and cut up chard. Sprinkle with salt. Let stand 1 hour. Drain and cover with white vinegar. Add sugar, celery seed, mustard seed, and onions.   •   Cook until tender.   •   Make a dressing of remaining ingredients, moistened with water.   •   Add dressing to chard.   •   Boil 15 minutes.   •   Put in jars and seal.

ALICE'S BEET PICKLES

	beets, to fill 1 qt. (1 L)	
2 cups	white vinegar	500 mL
½ cup	sugar	125 mL
1 tsp.	salt	5 mL
1 cup	water	250 mL

Use even-sized beets for boiling. Put in large pot with tops cut to about 1" (2.5 cm). Leave skins on and boil. When tender, pour off boiling water and pour on cold water until you can handle them. Push off skins; cut off top and tail with sharp knife. Use gloves if desired.   •   Pack into 1-quart (1 L) jars, filling to the top.   •   Boil together remaining ingredients.   •   When brine has boiled, pour over beets in jars and seal.   •   Sugar and salt amounts can be changed to suit individual taste.   •   This recipe can be multiplied.

2 bowls	green tomatoes, finely chopped	2 bowls
	pickling salt	
2 bowls	onions, finely chopped	2 bowls
3 tbsp.	pickling spice	45 mL
	vinegar	
1 bowl	sugar, brown OR white	1 bowl

NOVA SCOTIA'S BEST CHOW

This recipe is over 100 years old!

In a large glass or plastic container, place tomatoes in 1″ (2.5 cm) layers. Sprinkle each layer lightly with pickling salt. Let stand overnight. • In the morning, drain in jelly bag. Measure tomatoes after draining, place in large saucepan. Add onion, pickling spice, tied in a bag, and enough vinegar to cover. Cook tomatoes and onion until just tender, before adding the sugar. Simmer slowly for 2-2½ hours. • Fill hot sterilized jars and seal.

---

2 qts.	finely chopped large cucumbers	2 L
2 qts.	finely chopped onions	2 L
1	large cauliflower, finely chopped	1
3	green peppers, finely chopped	3
1	red pepper, finely chopped	1

MUSTARD VEGETABLE RELISH

A Rotary favorite.

1 cup	pickling salt	250 mL
9 cups	water	2.25 L

BRINE

2 cups	brown sugar	500 mL
1 qt.	cider vinegar, divided	1 L
¼ lb.	white mustard seed	125 g
½ oz.	celery seed	15 g
¾ cup	flour	175 mL
¼ cup	dry mustard	50 mL
½ oz.	turmeric	15 g

SEASONINGS

Cover chopped vegetables with brine and let stand overnight. • Drain well; add brown sugar, 2 cups (500 mL) cider vinegar, white mustard seed and celery seed and let come to a boil. Boil 10 minutes. • Make a paste of flour, mustard and turmeric with 2 cups (500 mL) reserved cider vinegar. Stir into relish. • Boil slowly for 30 minutes. • Bottle while hot and seal.

FREEZING TOMATOES: Wash, dry off and put in freezer bags. Freeze and when ready to use, run hot water over them for a few seconds. Skin will peel right off. These tomatoes are good for casseroles, stews, chili and spaghetti sauce.

DILL PICKLES

	cucumbers	
	dill	
6 tsp.	mustard seed	30 mL
6	pieces green pepper, 1" (2.5 cm)	6
6	garlic cloves	6
1 cup	pickling salt	250 mL
4 cups	pickling vinegar	1 L
12 cups	distilled water	3 L

Use only fresh cucumbers which are free of any markings. Clean cucumbers thoroughly in several different baths, removing all traces of stem and blossom ends. • Wash and sterilize jars. Prepare lids according to instructions. • Inspect dill for aphids which are very common and not easy to detect. Wash in hot water, if necessary, to clean and soak in salt water for an hour or so. • Prick cucumber skins at 1" (2.5 cm) intervals with sharp fork. Pack in jars. • Pack dill in jars and divide mustard seed, green pepper and garlic between jars. • Add salt and vinegar to water and boil until salt dissolves. Keep boiling while filling jars to within ¼" (.6 cm) of top. Immediately put lids in place and tighten completely. • Store 2 weeks, then enjoy. • This recipe is detailed, but cleanliness makes the difference in success in the quality and keeping of dills. • Makes about 6 quarts (6L).

PICKLED MIXED VEGETABLES

	small green tomatoes OR wedges	
	cucumber chunks	
	zucchini chunks	
	carrot chunks	
	green beans	
	celery pieces	
8	dill heads	8
2 tsp.	mustard seed	10 mL
4	cloves garlic	4
4	1" (2.5 cm) segments hot pepper OR 2 tsp. (10 mL) cayenne pepper	4
2 cups	white vinegar	500 mL
6 cups	water	1.5 L
6 tbsp.	salt	90 mL
	dill stalks	

Pack mixed vegetables in warm, sterilized 1-quart (1 L) jars. Add 2 dill heads, ½ tsp. (2 mL) mustard seed and 1 clove garlic per quart (L). Add a segment of hot pepper or ½ tsp. (2 mL) cayenne to each quart (L). • Combine vinegar, water, salt and dill stalks and bring to a boil. Remove dill stalks and pour hot brine over vegetables, leaving ½" (1.25 cm) head space. • Process for 10 minutes in a steam canner, or boiling water bath. • Let rest for 4 weeks before using. • Makes 4 quarts (4 L). • Variation: Add 1 tbsp. (15 mL) pickling spices to each quart (L). Omit hot pepper.

12	cucumbers, chopped	12
10	onions, chopped	10
10	large ripe tomatoes, finely chopped	10
1	green pepper, finely chopped	1
1	red pepper, chopped	1
	coarse pickling salt	
3 cups	vinegar	750 mL
1 cup	water	250 mL
6 cups	sugar	1.5 L
1 tbsp.	each curry powder turmeric, mustard	15 mL
½ cup	flour	125 mL

RIPE TOMATO CHOP SUEY PICKLES

Sprinkle vegetables with pickling salt and let stand overnight. • Drain thoroughly; add vinegar, water, sugar, curry powder, turmeric and mustard. • Cook 30 minutes, thicken with flour mixed with water. • Pour into hot jars. Seal.

---

4 lbs.	green tomatoes	2 kg
4 lbs.	apples	2 kg
4 cups	seedless raisins	1 L
3 cups	currants	750 mL
½ cup	mixed peel	125 mL
4 cups	sugar	1 L
4 tsp.	salt	20 mL
¾ cup	vinegar	175 mL
1 cup	chopped suet	250 mL
2 tbsp.	cinnamon	30 mL
1 tsp.	cloves	5 mL
1 tsp.	nutmeg	5 mL

GREEN TOMATO MINCEMEAT

Wash tomatoes, remove cores and put through coarse blade of a food chopper. • Wash, peel and core apples. Chop finely. • Combine all ingredients in a very large pot. Bring to a boil. • Boil uncovered for 30-40 minutes, stirring occasionally. • Pour into hot, sterilized jars. Seal. • Makes 14 cups (3.5 L).

---

1 cup	currants, plumped	250 mL
2	oranges, peeled and chopped	2
1	apple, chopped	1
1	peach, chopped	1
2 tbsp.	apricot jam	30 mL
1 tsp.	lemon juice	5 mL
pinch	salt	pinch
1 tsp.	cornstarch	5 mL

HOT FRUIT RELISH

Delicious with spareribs and chicken!

Stir all ingredients together and cook until mixture starts to thicken. • Serve hot. • Other fruits may be added for variety.

PLUM-TOMATO CHUTNEY

Serve with roast beef, lamb curries, etc. It has a rich deep-red color.

2 lbs.	freestone blue plums	1 kg
1 lb.	red tomatoes	500 g
½ cup	seedless raisins	125 mL
4	medium onions	4
2 tsp.	salt	10 mL
2 tbsp.	curry powder	30 mL
1 tbsp.	ground ginger	15 mL
¼ tsp.	cayenne pepper	1 mL
1 tsp.	allspice	5 mL
1½ cups	white vinegar	375 mL
2 cups	brown sugar	500 mL

Chop plums coarsely, discarding pits. • Scald and skin the tomatoes; cool and chop. • Place fruit, with remaining ingredients, in large stainless steel pan and bring to a full boil while stirring. Lower heat and simmer gently for about 1¼ hours, or until mixture is thickened. • Pour into sterilized jars, seal and cool. • This may be kept in the freezer — allow headspace. • Yields 2 quarts (2 L).

FRUIT CHILI SAUCE

30	ripe tomatoes	30
6	large onions	6
3	red peppers	3
6	ripe peaches	6
6	ripe pears	6
4 cups	white sugar	1 L
4 cups	white wine vinegar	1 L
3 tbsp.	salt	45 mL
	mixed spices (remove some red peppers for less heat)	

Peel tomatoes and cut into chunks. • Put onions and peppers through food chopper. • Combine tomatoes, onions and peppers and boil for awhile. • Add chopped peaches and pears. • When tomato mixture has thickened, add sugar, vinegar, salt and spices, tied in a bag. • Boil about 2 hours, or until it thickens slightly. • Seal in sterile jars. • Makes about 6 quarts (6 L).

WATERMELON RIND PICKLE

This is just like Mango Chutney!

5 qts.	1" (2.5 cm) cubes of watermelon rind (white part only)	5 L
7 cups	sugar	1.75 L
2 cups	vinegar	500 mL
¼ tsp.	cloves	1 mL
½ tsp.	cinnamon	2 mL

Blanch rind in boiling water and drain. • Combine the remaining ingredients and boil to make syrup. • Pour over rind and let stand overnight. • Remove rind and reboil syrup. • Pack rind in sterilized jars and cover with hot syrup. • Seal and store in cool place. • Makes about 4 quarts (4 L).

16	small crab apples	16
½ cup	sugar	125 mL
½ cup	cold water	125 mL
6	whole cloves	6
10	coriander seeds	10
pinch	salt	pinch
3	strips lemon peel	3

SPECIAL SPICED CRAB APPLES

Use firm crab apples. Wash, remove blossom ends, but leave on stems. • Place the remaining ingredients in a saucepan. Stir until the sugar is well mixed. Bring to a boil. • Prick each apple in several places with a skewer and place upright in the saucepan, 1 next to the other. Cover and cook 10 minutes over low heat. Do not stir or uncover. If the heat is low, the apples will be tender, but won't burst. • Remove from heat and cool. Do not disturb the apples. • When cold, pick up apples by the stems, pack in a freezer container, stagger them so that the second layer fits between the first. Strain juice over apples. Seal and freeze. • To serve, let thaw 1 to 2 hours. • Yields 2 cups (500 mL).

4 lbs.	ripe tomatoes, peel, seed and chop	2 kg
4	garlic cloves, minced	4
2	medium onions, chopped	2
⅔ cup	apple cider vinegar	150 mL
3-4 tsp.	oregano	15-20 mL
pinch	cayenne pepper	pinch
2 tbsp.	tomato paste	30 mL
5-8	jalapeño chilies, sliced, some seeds	5-8

SALSA SAUCE

Combine all ingredients, except chilies and simmer for 10 minutes to reduce some of the excess liquid from tomatoes. Add chilies and simmer 10-15 minutes more. Use a 5-quart (5 L) open sauté pan, as it allows the liquid to reduce quickly without over-cooking. • This is an all-purpose easy-to-make, medium-hot salsa. Keeps refrigerated for a month. • Makes 1 quart (1 L).

1 tbsp.	sugar	15 mL
1 tsp.	salt	5 mL
1 tbsp.	dry mustard	15 mL
½ cup	vinegar	125 mL
3	egg yolks, beaten	3
1 cup	whipped cream	250 mL

MUSTARD SAUCE

Mix first 3 ingredients; add vinegar to make paste. Mix into the beaten egg yolks. • Cook in double boiler until thick. • Cool, add whipped cream. • Mustard mixture may be cooked in microwave, on defrost. Whip until thick.

Brown-shelled eggs have the same nutritional value as white.

SUPERB MUSTARD SAUCE

3 tbsp.	white vinegar	45 mL
3 tbsp.	salad oil	45 mL
3 tbsp.	prepared mustard	45 mL
2 tbsp.	sugar	30 mL
pinch	EACH salt and pepper	pinch
	lots of fresh dill	

Combine all ingredients. • Adjust to your own taste. • Particularly good on fish. • Serves 10.

SAUCE BÉARNAISE

To crown your best steak.

2 tbsp.	white wine	30 mL
1 tbsp.	vinegar	15 mL
1 tsp.	dried tarragon	5 mL
2 tsp.	finely chopped onion	10 mL
¼ tsp.	pepper	1 mL
½ tsp.	salt	2 mL
3	egg yolks	3
dash	cayenne pepper	dash
½ cup	melted butter	125 mL

Bring first 5 ingredients to a boil and cook until almost all the liquid evaporates. • Place onion mixture in a blender container and add salt, egg yolks and cayenne pepper, cover and mix at high speed. Remove cover, gradually pour in melted butter, blending at low speed to mix. • This sauce is excellent served with bacon-wrapped fillets or any other cut of steak and is even tasty with hamburgers.

HALIFAX MARINADE

½ cup	soy sauce	125 mL
¼ cup	consommé	50 mL
2	onions, sliced	2
1	garlic clove, crushed	1
2 tbsp.	sugar	30 mL
	pepper, to taste	
¼ cup	salad oil (if barbecuing)	50 mL

Combine all ingredients. • Enough to marinate 8 steaks.

PEPPER MARINADE

4 tsp.	lemon juice	20 mL
2 tsp.	Dijon mustard	10 mL
½-1 tsp.	pepper	2-5 mL
½ tsp.	oregano	2 mL
¼ tsp.	cloves	1 mL

Rub lemon juice and Dijon mustard into steaks. Sprinkle on combined seasonings. • Enough to marinate 4 steaks.

When using wooden skewers for shish kabobs, soak skewers in water 2 hours before use.

PORK
Flamed Pork Fillets with Apricots, page 115
French-Style Rice Pilaf with Herbs, page 89
Fresh Spinach Salad, page 70

¾ cup	vinegar	175 mL
2 tsp.	chili powder	10 mL
½ tsp.	pepper	2 mL
2 cups	tomato juice	500 mL
2 tbsp.	sugar	30 mL
1 tsp.	salt	5 mL
½ tsp.	allspice	2 mL
2 tbsp.	cooking oil	30 mL

TEXAS MARINADE

Combine all ingredients. • Enough for 3-4 lbs. (1.5-2 kg) of roast or steaks.

---

1 tsp.	black peppercorns	5 mL
1½ tsp.	whole cumin	7 mL
1½ tsp.	whole coriander	7 mL
3	garlic cloves, finely chopped	3
1 tbsp.	paprika	15 mL
1	bunch fresh coriander OR parsley	1
3 tbsp.	olive oil	45 mL
4 tbsp.	water	60 mL

MOROCCAN MARINADE

Grind together in a mortar, or in the coffee grinder, the peppercorns, cumin and coriander. Add garlic and paprika, then the water and crush together with the pestle. Chop the coriander leaves finely, (if unavailable, use parsley) and stir into the mixture, together with the oil. • The result should be a thick paste. • Rub all over the meat, filling every crevice and leave to marinate for 3-5 hours, turning once. • Marinade will cover a minimum of 2 lbs. (1 kg) of any meat.

---

3 tbsp.	salad oil	50 mL
½ cup	lemon juice	125 mL
¼ cup	ketchup	75 mL
½ tsp.	Worcestershire sauce	2 mL
3 tbsp.	finely chopped onion	50 mL
2 tbsp.	chopped green pepper	30 mL
¼ cup	finely chopped celery	50 mL
½ tsp.	salt	2 mL
⅛ tsp.	pepper	0.5 mL
½ tsp.	MSG (optional)	2 mL
½	garlic clove	½
2½-3 lb.	chicken	1.25-1.5 kg

CHICKEN BARBECUE SAUCE

Easy and very good!

Throw all ingredients, except chicken, into blender or combine first 4 ingredients in a 2-cup (500 mL) jar. Prepare rest of ingredients except garlic, add and shake well. Place garlic on toothpick, drop in jar and let stand several hours. Remove garlic before using marinade. • Marinate chicken and then barbecue.

BARBECUE SAUCE

2 x 14 oz.	bottles ketchup	2 x 398 mL
12 oz.	bottle chili sauce	341 mL
¼ cup	prepared mustard	75 mL
1½ cups	firmly packed brown sugar	375 mL
2 tbsp.	coarsely ground pepper	30 mL
1½ cups	wine vinegar	375 mL
1 cup	fresh lemon juice	250 mL
1½ cups	bottled, thick steak sauce	375 mL
dash	Tabasco sauce	dash
¼ cup	Worcestershire sauce	50 mL
1 tbsp.	soy sauce	15 mL
2 tbsp.	salad oil	25 mL
12 oz.	beer	341 mL
	garlic, to taste (optional)	

Combine all ingredients. ● Pour over uncooked steaks and marinate, preferably overnight. ● Will marinate 8-12 steaks. ● If refrigerated, it can be used again and again.

SHAKE-AND-BAKE OR PANFRY MIXTURE

Excellent for coating chicken, fish & wild game!

2 cups	flour	500 mL
2 tbsp.	salt	30 mL
1 tbsp.	celery salt	15 mL
1 tbsp.	pepper	15 mL
2 tbsp.	dry mustard	30 mL
4 tbsp.	paprika	60 mL
1 tbsp.	onion OR garlic salt	15 mL
3 tbsp.	monosodium glutamate	45 mL
1 tsp.	ginger	5 mL
½ tsp.	thyme	2 mL
½ tsp.	basil	2 mL
½ tsp.	oregano	2 mL

Combine and mix all ingredients thoroughly. Sift to a fine even mixture and store in a tight container. ● For a crumb coating, combine 1½- 2 tbsp. (22-25 mL) of the seasoned flour with 1 cup (250 mL) of bread crumbs.

CRANBERRY SAUCE (RAW)

2	apples, cored	2
1	orange	1
1 lb.	cranberries	500 g
2 cups	sugar (OR less)	500 mL

Do not peel apples or orange. Put all ingredients through mincer. Stir. Leave overnight, then bottle in the morning.

5 cups	grated zucchini	1.25 L
2	oranges, finely chopped	2
2 tbsp.	lemon juice	30 mL
5 cups	sugar	1.25 L
1	box Certo	1
½ cup	crushed pineapple (optional)	125 mL

ZUCCHINI MARMALADE

Microwave Method:

Mix the first 3 ingredients in a large bowl; cover. Bring to a rolling boil, on HIGH power, for 9-10 minutes. ● Remove from microwave, add sugar and Certo. Leave uncovered and boil hard for 1 minute. ● Pour into sterilized jars, seal.

Stove Method:

Bring the first 3 ingredients to a boil and simmer, covered, for approximately 20 minutes. Add sugar and Certo. Leave uncovered and boil hard for an additional minute. ● Pour into sterilized jars and seal.

6	oranges	6
3	lemons	3
2¼ cups	water	550 mL
2¼ cups	preserved ginger	550 mL
1	box powdered fruit pectin	1
6¾ cups	white sugar	1.75 L

GINGER MARMALADE

Peel fruit. Slice peel very thinly. Add water. Simmer 30 minutes. ● Chop peeled fruit, discarding seeds. Add fruit to cooked rind. ● Measure 6¾ cups (1.75 L) of mixture. Add finely chopped ginger. ● Add pectin and mix well. ● Place over high heat. Stir until mixture comes to hard boil. ● Cook gently 1 minute. Add sugar. Bring to full rolling boil; boil hard for 1 minute. ● Skim. Stir for 5 minutes. ● Bottle as for jelly. ● Makes 2½ quarts (2.6 L). Recipe may be halved.

10 cups	ripe raspberries OR strawberries	2.5 L
2 oz.	Certo Light Crystals	49 g
3¼ cups	sugar	800 mL

LOW-SUGAR FREEZER JAM

Wash enough jars and lids to hold 6 cups (1.5 L) jam. ● Thoroughly crush raspberries, 1 layer at a time. Sieve half the pulp to remove some seeds, if you wish. ● Measure 4 cups (1 L) crushed berries into large bowl. Combine pectin crystals with ¼ cup (50 mL) sugar. Stir into crushed fruit until evenly blended. Set aside for 30 minutes, stirring occasionally. ● Then gently stir in remaining 3 cups (750 mL) sugar and stir for 3 more minutes. A few sugar crystals will remain. Do not stir too vigorously or you may create air bubbles. ● Pour into cooled, clean jars leaving ¼" (.6 cm) headspace and cover. ● Let stand at room temperature until set, about 24 hours. ● Store in freezer, or refrigerate if using within 3 weeks. ● 44 calories per tablespoon (15 mL). ● Makes 6 cups (1.5 L).

RHUBARB JAM

5 cups	finely chopped rhubarb	1.25 L
5 cups	white sugar	1.25 L
19 oz.	crushed pineapple	540 mL
6 oz.	strawberry gelatin	170 g

Combine first 3 ingredients and boil for 20 minutes, or a few minutes longer if it seems runny. • Remove from heat and stir in strawberry gelatin until dissolved. • Pour into jars and seal with a double layer of melted wax.

CHOKE-CHERRY JELLY

1	box Certo powder	1
3 cups	chokecherry juice	750 mL
3 cups	crab apple juice	750 mL
1 tbsp.	lemon juice (optional)	15 mL
8 cups	sugar	2 L

Mix Certo crystals with juices in a large pan. Pan should only be half full to allow for expansion. • Place over high heat and stir until mixture comes to a hard boil. At once stir in measured sugar. Bring to full rolling boil, one that cannot be stirred down. Boil hard for 1 minute, stirring constantly. • Remove jelly from heat and skim off foam with metal spoon. • Pour at once into sterilized jars and cover, while hot, with melted paraffin. • Tastes like chokecherries.

STRAWBERRY JAM

1 cup	water	250 mL
2 cups	sugar	500 mL
2 cups	strawberries*	500 mL
2 cups	sugar	500 mL
2 cups	strawberries*	500 mL

Boil water and 2 cups (500 mL) of sugar until it threads. Add 2 cups (500 mL) of strawberries and simmer for 3 minutes. • Add 2 cups (500 mL) of sugar and 2 cups (500 mL) of strawberries, boil (not rolling) for 10 minutes. • Pour on shallow pans. • Let stand in the sun, or a quiet room. • Over 2 or 3 days, spoon the syrup from the outside edge back over the berries. • When jam is set, bottle and seal with wax. • Do not double this recipe. • This can be used as a topping for ice cream. • * Be generous with strawberries.

APRICOT-RASPBERRY

2 lbs.	ripe fresh apricots	1 kg
2 cups	fresh raspberries	500 mL
2¼ lbs.	sugar	1.15 kg
¼ cup	water	50 mL
1 tbsp.	lemon juice	15 mL

Wash, peel and pit the apricots. • Wash raspberries. • Mix the fruits, sugar and water. • Cook slowly, stirring occasionally, until thick. Test by putting a little on a cold plate. When the syrup stiffens as soon it is cool, the jam is done. • Add the lemon juice. Stir a few seconds. • Pour into hot sterilized jars. Seal with paraffin. • Serve with hot, flaky, buttered biscuits, and tea, scented with a rose petal floated in each cup. • Yields 4 x 6 oz. (170 mL) jelly glasses.

Entrées

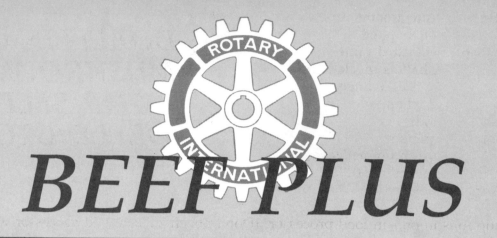

BEEF PLUS

INDIVIDUAL BEEF WELLINGTON

6 x ½ lb.	beef tenderloin, cut from middle, 8 oz. (250 g) per person	6 x 250 kg
	salt	
	freshly ground pepper	
2-3 tbsp.	unsalted butter	30-50 mL
1 tbsp.	oil	15 mL
	feuilletage (puff pastry)	
	duxelles, see page 103	
	truffle pâté de foie gras	
	egg wash (see below)	

Ask butcher to clean and trim meat. Cut 1½" (3.8 cm) slice for rare, 1" (2.5 cm) slice for medium, and ¾" (1.9 cm) slice for well-done. Sprinkle with salt and freshly ground pepper. In heavy-bottomed frying pan, over high heat, with 2-3 tbsp. (30-50 mL) unsalted butter and 1 tbsp. (15 mL) oil, brown and quickly fry each slice to sear both sides and give them a brown crust. Set aside to cool completely.
• Prepare duxelles. • Have enough feuilletage (puff pastry — packaged available) to thoroughly cover each tenderloin. Roll it out fairly thin. • Smear duxelles on both sides of each slice of meat, or for a more exciting taste, cover 1 side of the meat with truffle pâté de foie gras (available in specialty shops). • Lay 1 slice meat in middle of rolled-out dough. Wet edges, envelope the meat with dough and close edges. Leave the edges on the underside so that the juice won't run out. • You can, if preferred, decorate top with puff pastry cut-outs. • To prepare egg wash, combine 1 egg yolk with 1-2 tbsp. (15-30 mL) water or milk. Egg wash tops and lay them, not touching each other, on baking sheet. • Let rest at least 45 minutes in cool place. • Bake in 400°F (200°C) oven for 20 minutes, or until puff pastry is colored light brown. • If you have cut the meat according to your needs, rare, medium or well-done, the time of cooking will be the same for all. • Can be served with Maderia sauce. • Serves 6.

Why is it that our neighbor's barbecue always smells better than ours tastes?

¾ lb.	mushrooms, finely chopped	365 g	
1-2 tbsp.	unsalted butter	15-30 mL	
2	shallots, peeled and VERY finely chopped	2	
dash	salt	dash	
dash	pepper	dash	
	fresh thyme leaves (optional)		
1 tbsp.	cognac	15 mL	

DUXELLES OF MUSHROOMS FOR BEEF WELLINGTON

Chop mushrooms in food processor. (Don't put them into food processor whole, cut them into coarse chunks, turn machine rapidly on and off). • Melt butter in a skillet, add shallots and cook over medium heat for about ½ minute. • Add chopped mushrooms, salt and pepper and, if desired, the thyme. Cook, mixing occasionally with a wooden spoon, for about 10 minutes or until all juices have evaporated and the mixture is dry and starts to sizzle. • At this point, add 1 tbsp. (15 mL) cognac. • Transfer to a bowl, cover with waxed paper and refrigerate until needed.

6	large fresh mushroom crowns	6
6	beef fillets, cut 1-1½" (2.5-3.8 cm) thick	6
2 tbsp.	butter	30 mL
½ cup	chopped onion	125 mL
6	fresh mushroom stems, chopped	6
¼ cup	chopped green onion	50 mL
4 tsp.	cornstarch	20 mL
dash	pepper	dash
1 cup	Burgundy	250 mL
¼ cup	water	50 mL
2 tbsp.	snipped parsley	30 mL
1 tsp.	salt	5 mL

PAMPERED BEEF FILLETS

Flute mushroom crowns. • Brown steaks in butter over high heat, 1 minute per side. Place steaks on squares of heavy foil. • Prepare Mushroom Sauce; adding chopped mushrooms and onions to pan drippings and cook until tender. Add cornstarch. Add remaining ingredients. Cook and stir until thick and bubbly; continue to cook for 1 minute. Spoon 3 tbsp. (45 mL) sauce over each fillet. Top with a mushroom crown. • Bring corners of foil up over steak. Twist gently and seal. • Refrigerate. • These can be prepared ahead of time. • Bake in 500°F (260°C) oven for 14-15 minutes with tops of packets slightly open.

A woman's way to a man's heart is through his stomach, but not by jumping down his throat.

BEEF STRIPS IN RED WINE WITH THYME

2 lbs.	steak, cut in strips	1 kg
2 tbsp.	butter	30 mL
1	small onion, chopped	1
1 tbsp.	tomato paste	15 mL
1 tbsp.	flour	15 mL
½ cup	beef broth	125 mL
½ cup	red wine	125 mL
½	lemon, juice of	½
¼ tsp.	ground OR crushed thyme	1 mL
	salt and pepper	
	parsley for garnish	

Sauté the strips of steak in foaming butter over high heat. • Add chopped onion and cook together until onion is soft. Stir constantly to prevent burning. • Lower heat, add tomato paste and flour. Cook for 1 minute. • Add beef stock and wine, stirring to make a smooth paste. • Add lemon juice, thyme, salt and pepper. Continue to cook 5 minutes, or until beef is tender. • Serve on rice.

BEEF AND BURGUNDY CASSEROLE

4 tbsp.	butter	60 mL
2 tbsp.	bacon fat	30 mL
3 lbs.	round steak, cubed	1.5 kg
1 tbsp.	flour	15 mL
2 tsp.	salt	10 mL
½ tsp.	pepper	2 mL
1	bay leaf	1
½ tsp.	sweet basil	2 mL
½ tsp.	oregano	2 mL
1	garlic clove, minced	1
16 oz.	can tiny white onions	500 g
1 cup	Burgundy OR red wine	250 mL
2 lbs.	frozen carrots	1 kg
1 tbsp.	sugar	15 mL
¾ cup	Madeira wine	175 mL
¼ cup	brandy	50 mL

Heat 2 tbsp. (30 mL) each of butter and bacon fat in a heavy skillet. Brown beef well. Arrange in large casserole. • To fat in skillet, add flour, salt, pepper, bay leaf, basil, oregano, and garlic. Stir until flour is browned. This recipe can be prepared to this stage, the day ahead, and refrigerated. • Strain liquid from onions, add water to make scant 2 cups (500 mL), add to skillet, stirring until thickened. • Add Burgundy to skillet. Stir until smooth and thickened. Pour over meat in casserole. Cover and bake about 3 hours in a 300°F (150°C) oven.
• Heat remaining 2 tbsp. (30 mL) butter in skillet, stir in sugar. Add drained vegetables, stir-fry until slightly browned. Add vegetables and Madeira to casserole and continue to cook, covered, 30 minutes longer. • Stir in brandy just before serving. • Serve with Gourmet Wild Rice, page 89, green salad and garlic bread. • Serves 8. • See photograph on front cover.

4 lbs.	rump OR round beef pot roast	2 kg
2	large onions, peeled and sliced	2
1	carrot, sliced	1
1 tbsp.	pickling spice	15 mL
6	whole cloves	6
1 tbsp.	dry mustard	15 mL
½ tsp.	sage	2 mL
½ tsp.	thyme	2 mL
1 tbsp.	salt	15 mL
2 cups	dry, red wine	500 mL
2 cups	apple cider vinegar	500 mL
2 cups	water	500 mL
3 tbsp.	bacon fat	50 mL
2 tbsp.	flour	30 mL
1 cup	sour cream	250 mL
3 tbsp.	Madeira	50 mL
	salt and pepper	

SAUERBRATEN

This famous pot roast is a specialty in good German restaurants!

Put the meat into a large enamel, earthenware or glass container. • Mix together next 11 ingredients and pour over the meat. Cover and let marinate for 4 days in a cool place. Turn the meat once each day. • Melt the bacon fat in a large heavy pot or kettle. Brown the meat on all sides. Remove to a platter. • Blend the flour with the bacon fat. Gradually pour in the marinade and cook until thickened. • Return the meat to the gravy, cover and simmer slowly until the meat is tender; approximately 3 hours. Add more red wine if necessary. • Before serving, stir in the sour cream and the Madeira. • The aroma that will spread throughout the house makes the waiting worthwhile. Don't forget to whet your appetite by finishing the bottle of red wine! • Serve with noodles, potatoes or potato dumplings, carrots, beans or zucchini. • Serves 6.

2 lbs.	round steak, cubed	1 kg
¼ cup	flour	50 mL
1 tsp.	salt	5 mL
¼ cup	shortening	50 mL
1 cup	water	250 mL
½ cup	ketchup	125 mL
¼ cup	brown sugar	50 mL
¼ cup	vinegar	50 mL
1 tbsp.	Worcestershire sauce	15 mL
1 cup	chopped onion	250 mL
3 cups	chopped carrots, in ½" (1.3 cm) pieces	750 mL

SWEET-SOUR STEW

Coat meat cubes in a mixture of the flour and salt. • In a large skillet, brown meat well in hot shortening. • Combine next 5 ingredients and add to the meat. Add onions. • Cover and cook over low heat for 1 hour. • Add carrots and continue cooking until meat is tender, about 1 hour. • Serves 6-8.

STEAK AND KIDNEY PIE WITH MUSHROOMS

1	pkg. frozen puff pastry	1
1-1½ lbs.	round steak	500-750 g
2	lamb's OR sheep's kidneys	2
4 oz.	ox OR beef kidney	115 g
	salt and pepper, to taste	
4 oz.	button mushrooms	115 g
½-1 oz.	flour	15-30 g
10 oz.	beef stock	284 mL
1	egg, beaten with	1
1 tbsp.	milk OR water	15 mL

Prepare pastry as directed on package. • Cut steak and kidneys into small pieces and roll in seasoned flour. • Center a ceramic pie support, or an egg-cup, in a deep pie dish, to support the pastry. Add meat and mushrooms. Pour enough stock to come half-way over the meat mixture. Do not use more as the liquid may boil over. • Roll out pastry and cover pie. Use scraps to decorate top of pie with leaves and/or pastry rose. Brush the top of pie with the beaten egg and milk mixture. Press rose and leaves into position. Make tiny slit in the pastry cover over the pie support, to allow steam to escape. • Stand pie dish on baking sheet. Bake in center of hot oven, 450-475°F (230-240°C), for 15 minutes to give pastry a chance to rise. Put piece of parchment paper or foil over top of pie. Lower heat to moderate, 325-350°F (160-180°C). Bake for 1½ hours until meat is cooked.

FRAN'S STEW

6	slices bacon, diced	6
2-2½ lbs.	beef chuck	1-1.25 kg
10	pearl onions	10
2 tbsp.	butter (if needed)	30 mL
3 tbsp.	flour	45 mL
1½ cups	red wine	375 mL
1 cup	beef broth	250 mL
3 tbsp.	brandy	50 mL
1 tsp.	grated orange peel	15 mL
2	garlic cloves, crushed	2
½ tsp.	thyme	2 mL
1 tsp.	salt	5 mL
½ tsp.	pepper	2 mL
1	medium whole onion	1
7	whole cloves	7
2-3 tbsp.	butter	30-50 mL
½ lb.	mushrooms, sliced	250 g
3-4	large carrots, sliced	3-4
	chopped parsley	

FRAN'S STEW (continued)

Brown bacon pieces. Remove from pan to covered casserole, leaving the fat in the pan. • In the same skillet, brown the beef; remove to casserole. • Brown the pearl onions and remove to casserole. • If there is no fat left in skillet, add the 2 tbsp., (30 mL) butter; add the flour to make a roux. • Slowly whisk in the wine; add the beef broth, brandy, orange peel, crushed garlic, thyme, salt and pepper and cook until thickened. Pour gravy over beef, bacon, and onions in casserole. • Place the whole onion, studded with cloves, in the middle of the casserole. Cover and bake at 325°F (160°C) for 2½ hours. • Brown in 2-3 tbsp. (30-50 mL) butter the sliced mushrooms and carrots. • Add to meat, cover, bake 15-20 minutes. • To serve, remove whole onion, adjust seasoning, and sprinkle with chopped parsley.

BRAISED SHORT RIBS

2 lbs.	short ribs	1 kg
4	whole allspice	4
4	whole cloves	4
4	peppercorns	4
1½ tsp.	salt	7 mL
¼ tsp.	pepper	1 mL
1"	piece of bay leaf	2.5 cm
4	small potatoes	4
4	small onions	4
4	medium carrots	4
6	2" (5 cm) pieces celery	6

Brown meat. • Add seasonings; cover and cook slowly on low heat for about 1 hour. • Add vegetables and cook for another 45 minutes or until meat is done. • Remove to platter and serve with Horseradish Sauce.

HORSERADISH SAUCE

2 tbsp.	butter	30 mL
2 tbsp.	flour	30 mL
1 cup	milk	250 mL
½ tsp.	salt	2 mL
dash	pepper	dash
¼ cup	horseradish	75 mL
½ tsp.	dry mustard	2 mL
few drops	Tabasco sauce	few drops

Melt butter in saucepan, add flour, cook until bubbly. Add milk, cook until thick, stirring constantly. Stir in salt, pepper, horseradish, mustard and Tabasco sauce. • Reduce to very low heat and cook 10 more minutes. • Makes approximately 1½ cups (375 mL).

For great French fries, soak the cut potatoes in a bowl of cold water for 20 minutes or more, before frying. Dry potatoes thoroughly then cook them for a few minutes. Remove potatoes from pan and blot off the grease, then fry them a second time until golden brown.

RANCH-STYLE BEEF RIBS

4-5 lbs.	beef short ribs	2-2.5 kg
dash	salt & pepper	dash
1 tbsp.	butter OR margarine	15 mL
¾ cup	minced onion	175 mL
1 cup	ketchup	250 mL
1 cup	boiling water	250 mL
1	beef bouillon cube	1
½ cup	molasses	125 mL
¼ cup	brown sugar	50 mL
⅔ cup	vinegar	150 mL
2 tsp.	dry mustard	10 mL
	salt and pepper	
dash	cayenne pepper	dash

Preheat oven to 325°F (160°C). • Cut up ribs, season and place in a large roasting pan. • Bake ribs for 40 minutes. • Remove from oven and drain off grease. • In a saucepan, combine remaining ingredients and stir over low heat until all ingredients have dissolved. Pour over ribs, and bake at 350°F (180°C) for 1 hour.

KOREAN RIBS

3 lbs.	thick-cut beef ribs	1.5 kg
¾ cup	soy sauce	175 mL
2 tbsp.	water	30 mL
4 tsp.	sherry	20 mL
½ tsp.	sesame oil	2 mL
1 tbsp.	brown sugar	15 mL
2	garlic cloves, minced	2
¼ tsp.	powdered ginger	1 mL
2 tbsp.	chopped green onion	30 mL
1 tbsp.	sesame seeds	15 mL

Combine all ingredients. • Marinate ribs for 1 hour. • Barbecue or broil.

UPSIDE-DOWN BEEF PIE

1½ cups	flour	375 mL
1 tbsp.	baking powder	15 mL
½ tsp.	salt	2 mL
1 tsp.	paprika	5 mL
1 tsp.	celery salt	5 mL
3 tbsp.	shortening	45 mL
¾ cup	milk	175 mL
1 tbsp.	shortening	15 mL
¼ cup	chopped onion	50 mL
10 oz.	can tomato soup	284 mL
½ lb.	ground beef	250 g

Mix flour, baking powder and spices; cut in shortening then add milk. (Or add spices to biscuit mix and prepare according to package). Mix until consistency of biscuit dough. • In cast-iron frying pan, melt 1 tbsp. (15 mL) shortening, add onion. Cook until soft. Add soup and beef. Cook about 5 minutes. • Spread biscuit mixture on top of meat in a pie plate. Bake in hot oven, 475°F (240°C), for at least 20 minutes. • Turn upside-down on plate. • Serves 4-6.

2 lbs.	stewing beef	1 kg
1 cup	yogurt	250 mL
¾ tsp.	turmeric	3 mL
	salt, to taste	
1 tbsp.	chili powder, OR to taste	15 mL
1½ tsp.	saffron	7 mL
1 tsp.	EACH crushed garlic and ginger	5 mL
1½ lbs.	onions, thinly sliced	750 g
1½ tbsp.	oil OR butter	22 mL
2	tomatoes, sliced in ⅛'s	2
1 lb.	rice*	500 g
	yellow food color	
¼ cup	milk	50 mL
½ cup	butter	125 mL

BIRYANI

Savory rice and meat curry!

MIXTURE I

5	cinnamon sticks	5
10	whole cloves	10
10	peppercorns	10
5	cardamom pods OR 1 tsp. (5 mL) ground cardamom	5

MIXTURE II

3	cinnamon sticks	3
5	whole cloves	5
5	peppercorns	5
1½ tbsp.	black cumin seeds	22 mL

Marinate beef with yogurt, turmeric, salt, chili powder, 1 tsp saffron, garlic, ginger and Mixture I for 1 hour. ● Brown onions in oil or butter until crispy. Remove onions, cool slightly. Pureé onions in blender. Cook the marinated beef in oil for a few minutes. Add pureéd onions. tomatoes and water to beef. Cook beef in this gravy mixture. ● Cook rice in lots of water. When rice is half cooked, drain. ● Mix ½ tsp. (2 mL) saffron and yellow color to the warm milk and let stand. ● Use a large heavy saucepan, or Dutch oven, with tight lid that will hold both the rice and meat. Add ½ cup (125 mL) rice to pan. Pour in the meat mixture. Add Mixture II to the remaining rice and mix with a fork, being careful not to break the rice. Layer this rice on the meat mixture. Add the saffron milk and with a fork spread over top of rice mixture evenly. ● Heat ½ cup (125 mL) butter, pour over the rice and cover. Place a metal ring between the pan and range. Turn up heat until steam starts to escape from lid edges. Turn heat to low and allow flavor of the meat curry to steam up and seep into the rice and cook for approximately 1 hour. ● Chicken can be substituted for the beef. ● * Try Basmati rice for an authentic flavor. It is available at specialty stores.

To avoid the unpleasant odor of cabbage being cooked, add a stalk of celery to the water in which the cabbage is cooking.

MOUSSAKA

A Middle-Eastern specialty, simple and delicious.

2 lbs.	eggplant	1 kg
1	large onion, chopped	1
2	garlic cloves, crushed	2
2 tbsp.	vegetable oil	30 mL
2 lbs.	ground beef OR lamb	1 kg
1 cup	chopped, peeled tomatoes	250 mL
2 tbsp.	tomato paste	30 mL
½ cup	white wine	125 mL
2 tbsp.	chopped parsley	30mL
1 tsp.	sugar	5 mL
¼ tsp.	cinnamon	1 mL
	salt and pepper, to taste	

CREAM SAUCE

¼ cup	butter	50 mL
¼ cup	flour	75 mL
2 cups	milk	500 mL
⅛ tsp.	nutmeg OR cinnamon	0.5 mL
¼ cup	grated Kefalotiri OR Parmesan cheese	50 mL
	salt and pepper, to taste	
1	egg, slightly beaten	1

Cut eggplant into 5 x ¼" (0.6 cm) slices, unpeeled. Sprinkle slices with salt and leave for 1 hour. ● Dry with paper towel. ● Oil the base of a baking dish, add a layer of eggplant and brush with oil. Lightly brown under a hot grill, turn, brush again with oil and brown other side. (Eggplant may be pan-fried in oil and stacked on a plate when cooked). ● Gently fry onion and garlic in oil for 10 minutes; add meat and brown over high heat, stirring well. ● Add remaining meat sauce ingredients, season to taste. Cover and simmer gently for 30 minutes. ● To make cream sauce, melt butter in saucepan, stir in flour and cook gently for 2 minutes. Add milk all at once and bring to a boil, stirring constantly. Let sauce bubble gently for 1 minute. Remove from heat, stir in nutmeg or cinnamon, 1 tbsp. (15 mL) of the cheese, salt and pepper to taste. Cover top of sauce with buttered paper, if not required immediately. ● Grease a 13" x 9" (4 L) oven dish and place a layer of eggplant slices in the bottom, top with half of the meat sauce, add another layer of eggplant, remainder of meat and finish with eggplant. ● Stir beaten egg into cream sauce and spread on top. Sprinkle with remaining cheese. ● Bake in a 350°F (180°C) oven for 1 hour. Let stand 20 minutes before cutting into squares to serve. ● Serves 6-8.

SUCCESS

Once upon a time I planned to be an artist of celebrity,
A song I thought to write one day, and all the world would homage pay.
I longed to write a noted book. But what I did was learn to cook.
For life with single tasks is filled and I have done not what I willed,
Yet when I see boys' hungry eyes, I'm glad I make good apple pies.

1 lb.	lean ground beef	500 g
8	green onions, including tops	8
12	sprigs fresh mint OR coriander leaves	12
1	green chili OR ¼ tsp. (1 mL) chili powder	1
¼ tsp.	ginger powder	1 mL
⅛ tsp.	garlic powder	0.5 mL
1 tsp.	coriander powder	5 mL
dash	EACH ground cinnamon and cloves	dash
½ tsp.	salt, or to taste	2 mL
½ cup	bread crumbs	125 mL
¼ cup	barbecue sauce	50 mL
3 tbsp.	shortening, for frying	45 mL
1	medium onion	1
2 x 14 oz.	cans baked beans	2 x 398 mL

MEAT KABOBS WITH BAKED BEANS

Put ground meat in a large bowl. Chop green onions, mint and green chili and add to meat. • Add and mix remaining ingredients, except shortening, onion, and beans. Let stand for 1 hour. • Shape into 24 meatballs. • Heat shortening in frying pan and fry meatballs until brown. • Chop onion as finely as possible. • Remove meatballs and keep warm. • In the same pan, fry onions until light brown. Add beans and cook for 5 minutes. Add meatballs. • Serve with bread rolls and a green salad. • Serves about 6.

1	small head cabbage, shredded*	1
2 tsp.	salt	10 mL
2 tbsp.	butter	30 mL
1 tbsp.	dark corn syrup	15 mL
¼ tsp.	marjoram	1 mL
¼ tsp.	salt	1 mL
1 lb.	lean ground beef	500 g
1 cup	bread crumbs	250 mL
½ cup	milk	125 mL
2	eggs, beaten	2
1 tbsp.	salt	15 mL
1 tsp.	pepper	5 mL

MEAT-CABBAGE CASSEROLE

LIHAKAALILAATIKKO — as the Finns would call it — the lazy (wo)man's cabbage rolls!

Cook the cabbage in enough boiling water, with 2 tsp. (10 mL) salt, to cover for about 5 minutes or until tender-crisp. Drain. Add the butter, syrup, marjoram and a pinch of salt. • In another bowl, mix the beef, bread crumbs, milk, eggs, salt and pepper. • Butter a 2-quart (2 L) casserole and layer the cabbage and meat mixture into it, beginning and ending with cabbage. • Bake in moderate oven, 350°F (180°C), for 1 hour or until the meat is done. • Serves 4-6. • * Frozen or fresh cabbage works equally well.

VEAL BIRDS

2 lbs.	veal steak, cut ¼″ (0.6 cm) thick	1 kg
2 cups	bread crumbs	500 mL
1 tbsp.	minced parsley	15 mL
2 tbsp.	minced green onions	30 mL
¼ cup	minced fresh mushrooms	50 mL
¼ cup	butter	50 mL
1 tsp.	salt	5 mL
⅛ tsp.	pepper	0.5 mL
¼ cup	minced stuffed olives	50 mL
¼ cup	flour	50 mL
1 tsp.	paprika	5 mL
¼ cup	butter	50 mL
½ cup	water	125 mL
1	garlic clove	1
10 oz.	beef broth	284 mL

Cut steak into 6 serving pieces. Pound with mallet. • Combine bread crumbs, parsley, onions and mushrooms. • Heat ¼ cup (50 mL) butter in skillet; add bread crumb mixture and cook gently, stirring until crumbs are golden brown. Remove from heat and mix in salt, pepper and olives. • Spread steak with dressing mixture and roll up tightly, tying with string. • Combine flour and paprika; dip rolls in this to coat all sides. • Heat oven to 350°F (180°C). • Heat ¼ cup (50 mL) butter in heavy skillet; add floured rolls and brown well on all sides. • Rub shallow baking dish with cut sides of garlic clove and put rolls in dish as they are browned. • Add water to drippings in pan and stir, scraping up any browned bits. Pour over rolls. Add beef broth. • Bake about 1 hour, or until veal is very tender, turning once. • Serve with noodles.

FRENCH LAMB STEW

12	lamb shoulder chops*	12
2 tbsp.	vegetable oil	30 mL
4	large onions	4
6	garlic cloves	6
2½ lbs.	tomatoes	1.25 kg
3	large apples, Granny Smith OR Golden Delicious	3
3 oz.	tomato paste	85 g
6 tbsp.	raisins	90 mL
	salt and pepper	

Remove as much fat from chops as possible and brown in oil in large heavy casserole. • Cut onions in wedges; finely chop garlic; peel, seed and quarter tomatoes. Peel apples and cut in wedges. • When all chops are browned, return to casserole and add fruits and vegetables, tomato paste, salt and pepper. Cover casserole and shake a few times to distribute vegetables. • Simmer over low heat for 1½ hours. • No liquid is required, it makes its own sauce. • * Boned lamb leg, cut in 2″ (5 cm) pieces can be substituted.

2-3 lbs.	moose steak, cubed	1-1.5 kg
	butter	
1	small onion, chopped	1
28 oz.	can tomatoes	796 mL
12 oz.	beer	341 mL
1	pkg. onion soup mix	1
6-8	carrots, sliced	6-8
3	celery stalks, sliced	3

FORT MCMURRAY STEW

Brown cubed steak in butter. Remove meat to roaster. • Sauté onion in same frying pan. Add tomatoes and boil 1 minute to loosen bits and brown a little. Add to meat. Add beer, soup mix and vegetables. • Bake, covered, for 2 hours at 325°F (160°C). Remove lid and bake ½ hour more. • Can also be done in a slow cooker. • This recipe can be doubled, or tripled, for large groups. • Serves 10.

1½ lbs.	moose steak	750 g
1 tbsp.	dry mustard	15 mL
4 tbsp.	cornstarch	60 mL
½ tsp.	salt	2 mL
⅛ tsp.	pepper	0.5 mL
1 cup	sliced onion	250 mL
1	carrot, diced	1
1½ cups	tomatoes	375 mL

SAVORY MOOSE STEAKS

Nick edges of steaks. • Mix dry ingredients, pound into steaks on both sides. Sear steak, cover with onions, carrots, and tomatoes. • Bake, covered, for 1½ hours in a moderate oven, 350°F (180°C). • Serve with oven-browned potatoes and baked apples.

ABOUT REINDEER AND CARIBOU

Reindeer and caribou are clean animals who tromp through clean snow, drink clean water, breathe clean air and eat clean lichen.

Caribou meat has a delicate flavor and fine texture. It is lean, containing less than 4% fat, and is rich in protein, iron and B vitamins. The liver and kidneys of caribou can be prepared in the same way as that of other animals.

One outstanding feature of caribou meat is that it retains its quality and taste, when frozen, for longer periods than most meat.

There are many ways of preparing caribou meat and its unique flavor is greatly complemented by red currant jelly or jam, or rowan (mountain ash) jelly.

Especially suited to caribou meat are such vegetables as cauliflower, carrots, broccoli, mushrooms, fried tomatoes and shallots.

If brown sugar has hardened, put in freezer for a couple of days. It will be soft after it has thawed out.

REINDEER OR CARIBOU WITH BEER

1 lb.	reindeer OR caribou meat, in small cubes	500 g
2-3 tbsp.	butter	30-45 mL
1 tsp.	salt	5 mL
¾-1 cup	lager beer	175-250 mL
½ cup	cleaned red currants	125 mL
2 tbsp.	sour cream, mixed with 2 tsp. (10 mL) cornstarch, blended with water	30 mL
	salt and pepper, to taste	

Brown half-thawed meat over medium heat with a little butter. Fry small portions at a time. Clean the pan between each frying. Put meat in a casserole and sprinkle with salt. • Pour beer over meat and add red currants and sour cream which is blended with cornstarch and a little water. • Let this simmer until everything is tender, about 20 minutes. Add salt and pepper to taste. • Serve with mashed potatoes and a fresh salad. • Serves 4.

FILLET OF REINDEER WITH MUSHROOMS

½ lb.	reindeer fillet, per serving	250 g
	good red wine	
	juniper berries	
	bay leaf	
	butter	
	salt	
	coarsely chopped onion	
	pepper	
	mushrooms	

Preheat oven to 440°F (225°C). • Bone, roll and tie fillet with string to hold an even shape. Keep bone for later use. • Marinate 6-8 hours in wine, juniper berries*, and bay leaf. • Dry the fillet and brown in butter. Sprinkle with salt. • Crack bone and put in roasting pan with coarsely chopped onion and pepper. Pour the marinade over all. • Put the fillet over the bone and roast for 30 minutes, or until the meat thermometer reaches 142-150°F (62-65°C). • Brown mushrooms in butter and season with salt and pepper. • Slice the meat and serve with mushrooms, roasting juices, fried, or baked, potatoes and mountain ash jelly, or currant jelly. • * Juniper berries are available in Health Food Stores.

It is better to live in the corner of an attic than with a crabby woman in a lovely home.

PORK

4 oz.	dried apricots	115 g
2 tbsp.	dry sherry	30 mL
1¼ lbs.	pork fillet	625 g
	seasoned flour (garlic salt, pepper, flour)	
1 oz.	unsalted butter	30 g
2 tbsp.	brandy	30 mL
¼ cup	sour cream	75 mL
	salt and pepper	
	lemon juice	

FLAMED PORK FILLET WITH APRICOTS

Soak apricots in water 3-4 hours prior to preparing rest of dish.   •   Place apricots and soaking water into saucepan; add sherry. Cook for 15 minutes on low heat. Reserve liquid.   •   Trim fat from pork. Cut into 1½'' (3.8 cm) thick slices, pound flat and toss in seasoned flour.   •   Heat butter in frying pan on medium heat and fry pork on both sides until gold and tender. Turn only once. Pour off surplus fat.   •   Heat brandy, light brandy and pour over pork.   •   Add drained apricots and stir until brandy flames have burnt out.   •   Mix sour cream with apricot liquid and pour into pan. Simmer for a few minutes, season with salt, freshly ground pepper and lemon juice. Pour over pork.   •   Serve with fluffy boiled rice.   •   Serves 4.   •   See photograph page 96A.

	pork roast	
	salt	
3 tbsp.	bean sauce	45 mL
3 tbsp.	hoi sin sauce	45 mL
2 tsp.	sugar	10 mL
2 tbsp.	oyster sauce	30 mL
½ tsp.	Chinese spice OR 5-flavor spice	2 mL
	M.S.G. (optional)	

BARBECUED OR CHINESE-STYLE ROAST PORK

Score roast 1'' (2.5 cm) apart, all across roast.   •   Sprinkle salt on all sides.   •   Mix remaining ingredients and put on roast.   •   Bake in open pan or on rack, uncovered, for 1½ hours at 350°F (180°C).

SPECIAL OCCASION PORK TENDERLOIN

2½ lbs.	pork tenderloin, cut into 4-5 slices 1-1½" (3-4 cm) thick	1.25 kg
	salt and pepper	
	butter OR oil for frying	
2	medium onions	2
1 tbsp.	chopped parsley	15 mL
1 tsp.	paprika	5 mL
1 lb.	mushrooms, chopped	500 g
1 lb.	tomatoes	500 g
3 cups	whipping cream	750 mL
few drops	browning base for gravy	few drops

Cut tenderloin into slices as indicated above and pound to flatten. Salt and pepper both sides. Brown in butter or oil. Put the slices into a large heavy saucepan. • Chop onions, sauté in butter, then add to the meat. • Sauté parsley and add to meat. • Sauté paprika and mushrooms, add to meat. • Peel tomatoes (blanch in boiling water to do this), and chop into small pieces. Sauté tomatoes in butter in frying pan. • Add enough whipping cream to make a smooth paste. Add tomato mixture to meat. • Heat remaining whipping cream in frying pan and add to meat. • Simmer until meat is tender. Add a bit of browning base to give a rich color to the sauce. • Serves 8.

TENDERLOIN DIANA

¾ lb.	pork tenderloin	365 g
2 tbsp.	clarified butter	30 mL
8	medium mushrooms, sliced	8
4	green onions, chopped	4
2 tsp.	chopped parsley	10 mL
½ tsp.	dried basil	2 mL
¼ cup	brandy	50 mL
1 tsp.	beef bouillon mix, OR 1 cube	5 mL
¼ cup	water	50 mL
2 tbsp.	dry sherry	30 mL
¼ tsp.	Worcestershire sauce	1 mL
½ tsp.	salt	2 mL
¼ tsp.	pepper	1 mL

Cut tenderloin crosswise into 4 slices. Place each between 2 sheets of plastic wrap and pound gently to flatten to about ¼" (0.6 cm). • Heat butter in frying pan. Stir in mushrooms, onions, parsley and basil. Cook 2 minutes, stirring constantly. • Add pork and cook about 3 minutes each side. • Pour in brandy, heat until warm, then ignite carefully. • Add beef bouillon, water, sherry, Worcestershire sauce, salt and pepper. • Stir and scrape up brown bits from bottom of pan. • Continue cooking 3-4 minutes longer until tenderloin is done. • Serve immediately. • Serves 2.

8	pork chops (boneless preferred)	8
2 tbsp.	butter	30 mL
2 tbsp.	flour	30 mL
½ tsp.	salt	2 mL
2 tbsp.	curry powder, OR to taste	30 mL
2 cups	milk	500 mL
½ cup	tomato paste	125 mL
½ cup	drained canned apricots	125 mL
½ lb.	mushrooms	250 g
½ cup	seedless raisins, soaked in sherry	125 mL
2 tbsp.	sherry	30 mL

CURRIED PORK MEXICANO

Brown chops and place in baking dish. • Melt butter; blend in flour, salt and curry. Add the milk slowly. Stir until smooth. Add tomato paste. • Mash the apricots, slice the mushrooms, and add apricots and mushrooms to sauce. • Add raisins and sherry and pour over the chops. • Bake covered at 350°F (180°C) for approximately 1 hour. • Serve with steamed rice, or a mixture of long-grain and wild rice. • Serves 8.

½ lb.	ground pork, pork butt OR chicken	250 g
	oil	
1	slice ginger	1
1	garlic clove, crushed	1
1 tsp.	curry powder	5 mL
3-4	carrots, shredded	3-4
3-4	celery stalks, finely shredded	3-4
1	medium onion, finely shredded	1
5 oz.	can water chestnuts, finely chopped	150 g
1 tbsp.	cornstarch	15 mL
¼ cup	water	50 mL
1 tsp.	soy sauce	5 mL
	salt and pepper	
1	head lettuce, washed, drained	1

PORK WITH VEGETABLES

Chop meat, unless using ground pork. • Heat some oil in skillet or wok. • Add pork, ginger, garlic and curry. Cook about 1 minute. Remove pork. • Add vegetables and cook for a few minutes. • Mix pork in with vegetables. • Thicken with cornstarch mixed in water. • Add soy sauce. • To eat, wrap portions of the vegetables in lettuce leaves. Each diner can roll up his own or the cook can prepare all of the rolls before serving.

OVEN-BARBECUED SPARERIBS

3 lbs.	spareribs	1.5 kg
1	lemon OR 2 tbsp. (30 mL) lemon juice	1
1	medium onion	1
	salt and pepper, to taste	
10 oz.	can tomato soup	284 mL
½	soup can water	½
½	soup can vinegar	½
¾ cup	brown sugar	175 mL
2 tsp.	dry mustard	10 mL
¼ tsp.	cayenne	1 mL
¼ tsp.	chili powder	1 mL
	garlic powder (optional)	

In broiler pan, place spareribs, cut either individually or in serving-sized pieces). • Top with slices of lemon and onion, salt and pepper. • Bake at 450°F (230°C) for ½ hour. • Pour off fat. • Lower oven temperature to 375°F (190°C). • Combine remaining ingredients, heat and pour over the ribs and cook, basting often, for 1 hour. • Makes enough sauce for 8-10 servings. Keeps in refrigerator. • Serves 4-6.

SPARERIBS FOR EIGHT

6 lbs.	spareribs	3 kg
1 cup	ketchup	250 mL
2 tbsp.	vinegar	30 mL
2 tbsp.	lemon juice	30 mL
4 tbsp.	Worcestershire sauce	60 mL
2 tsp.	salt	10 mL
½ tsp.	pepper	2 mL
2 tsp.	dry mustard	10 mL
2 tbsp.	brown sugar	30 mL
2 tbsp.	honey	30 mL
2 tbsp.	chili relish	30 mL
2 tbsp.	chopped onion	30 mL
1 tbsp.	marmalade	15 mL
1 tbsp.	apricot jam	15 mL
2 tsp.	cornstarch	10 mL
pinch	garlic salt	pinch
	hickory salt (optional)	

Separate ribs into serving-sized pieces. • Mix the remaining ingredients to make a sauce. • Cover ribs with the sauce and bake at 300°F (150°C) for 1½ to 2 hours. • Drain off fat. • Serves 8.

Most women enjoy good cooking, especially when it is done by the chef of a good restaurant.

4 lbs.	spareribs	2 kg
1 cup	brown sugar	250 mL
½ cup	chili sauce	125 mL
¼ cup	ketchup	50 mL
½ cup	dark rum	125 mL
¼ cup	soy sauce	50 mL
1 tbsp.	Worcestershire sauce	15 mL
1 tsp.	dry mustard	5 mL
2	garlic cloves, crushed	2
⅛ tsp.	pepper	0.5 mL

RUM RIBS

Cut ribs into bite-sized pieces. Line roasting pan with a double thickness of aluminum foil. Place ribs in pan and seal ribs tightly in foil. ● Bake 1 hour at 350°F (180°C). ● Unwrap ribs and pour off drippings. ● Combine remaining ingredients to make a marinade and pour half of marinade over ribs. ● Continue baking for 1½ to 2 hours. ● Lay ribs on barbecue or broiler pan 6" (15 cm) from heat. Broil or barbecue for 15-20 minutes. ● Baste ribs with remaining marinade several times while cooking. ● Serves 6-8.

1 lb.	pork shoulder	500 g
2	eggs	2
¼ cup	flour	50 mL
	salt, to taste	
¼ tsp.	pepper	1 mL
½ cup	salad oil	125 mL
3	green peppers	3
4	celery stalks, sliced	4
2	cubes chicken bouillon, in 1 cup (250 mL) hot water	2
½ cup	drained pineapple chunks	125 mL
½ cup	pineapple juice	125 mL
3 tbsp.	cornstarch	45 mL
½ cup	sugar	125 mL
3 tbsp.	soy sauce	45 mL
½ cup	vinegar	125 mL
	cooked rice	

HAWAIIAN PORK

Cut pork in 1" (2.5 cm) cubes. ● Beat together eggs, flour, salt and pepper to make a batter. ● Heat oil in heavy skillet. ● Dip pork cubes into batter and drop into hot oil. Fry slowly to brown. Drain off excess oil. ● Cut peppers into 1" (2.5 cm) pieces. ● Add vegetables to meat. ● Add ¼ cup (50 mL) of chicken bouillon-water mixture, pineapple and pineapple juice. ● Cover and simmer 10-15 minutes, until vegetables are tender-crisp. ● Combine cornstarch and sugar in saucepan. ● Blend in soy sauce, vinegar and remaining chicken bouillon. ● Cook over medium heat, stirring until thick and clear. Pour over meat, cover and simmer 5 minutes. ● Serve over hot rice. ● Serves 6.

SWEET AND SOUR PORK

1 lb.	lean pork	500 g
2 tbsp.	dry sherry	30 mL
1	egg	1
3 tbsp.	flour	45 mL
3 tbsp.	oil	45 mL
2	medium carrots	2
3	medium onions	3
1	medium cucumber	1
1	garlic clove	1
4 tbsp.	tomato ketchup	60 mL
2 tsp.	soy sauce	10 mL
2 tbsp.	vinegar	30 mL
1 tbsp.	brown sugar	15 mL
1 tbsp.	cornstarch	15 mL
2 cups	water	500 mL

Cut meat into ½" (1.3 cm) cubes. Marinate for 30 minutes in sherry. • Dip cubes into lightly beaten egg and coat with flour. • Fry pork in hot oil until golden brown. • Remove from pan. • Peel and chop carrots, onions and cucumbers. • Peel and crush garlic. • Stir-fry vegetables and garlic. • Combine and add remaining ingredients to sherry, from marinade. • Boil 3 minutes, stirring. • Return pork to pan and heat. • Serves 4.

JANE'S FEAST FOR TARZAN

4	ripe bananas	4
½ lb.	thinly sliced boiled ham	250 g
8 oz.	can pineapple chunks	250 mL
1 tbsp.	vinegar, malt	15 mL
5 oz.	brown sugar	140 g
1 tsp.	cinnamon	5 mL
1 tbsp.	cornstarch	15 mL
1 cup	cold black coffee	250 mL
1-2 tsp.	rum OR rum extract	5-10 mL
	parsley	

Peel bananas and halve lengthwise. Roll each piece in a slice of ham. Place rolls close together in a shallow greased ovenproof dish and bake at 350°F (180°C) for 30 minutes. • To make sauce, drain pineapple juice into heavy saucepan, reserving fruit. Add vinegar and 4 oz. (115 g) of brown sugar to juice. Bring to a boil and boil for 5 minutes. Mix cinnamon and cornstarch and gradually blend in coffee. Add this mixture to saucepan and boil until it thickens and becomes transparent. Add pineapple chunks and rum; heat through gently. • Remove ham and banana rolls from oven and spoon sauce over them. Sprinkle with remaining sugar, return to oven and continue cooking for the remainder of 30 minutes. • Remove and allow to cool for a few seconds before serving. • Garnish with parsley. • Serve with boiled rice which has been tossed in fried diced onions and tomatoes. Accompany with tossed green salad and an oil and vinegar dressing. • Try swinging from tree to tree after that! • Serves 4 — 2 apes and 2 jungle bunnies.

3 tbsp.	vegetable oil	45 mL
2	finely chopped onions	2
2	green peppers, cut in strips	2
1 cup	long-grain rice	250 mL
2	garlic cloves, minced	2
28 oz.	can tomatoes, drained, chopped	796 mL
½ tsp.	thyme	2 mL
1½ tsp.	chili powder	7 mL
1 tsp.	salt	5 mL
	ground pepper	
1½ cups	chicken stock	375 mL
¼ tsp.	powdered saffron, if available	1 mL
2 cups	diced cooked ham	500 mL
	freshly chopped parsley	

JAMBALAYA

Heat oil in a heavy casserole, or Dutch oven, and cook onions until limp; add green pepper strips and stir for a few minutes. • Add rice and stir again until rice grains glisten and turn slightly opaque. • Add garlic, tomatoes, thyme, chili powder, salt and black pepper. • Add chicken broth and saffron, if you are using it. • Stir again, and bring slowly to a boil. • Stir in ham. • Reduce heat and cover. Cook at a bare simmer for 20 minutes, without stirring. • If rice is cooked, but mixture is too soupy, simmer longer. • Sprinkle with fresh parsley before serving. • Serves 4.

2 cups	long-grain rice	500 mL
½ lb.	ham	250 g
3	eggs, separated	3
2 cups	peas	500 mL
1 cup	grated Parmesan cheese	250 mL
	salt, to taste	
4 cups	hot water (If using canned peas, use liquid as part of water)	1 L
3½ oz.	butter OR margarine	100 g

ARROZ DE FORNO

This is rice in the oven — from Brazil. Delicious!

Put rice in bottom of 9″ x 12″ (4 L) glass baking dish. • Cut ham into cubes and mix with the beaten egg yolks, peas, cheese and salt. • Pour water over the rice and dot with butter. • Beat egg whites until stiff, like meringue, and cover the top of the casserole. • Bake at 350°F (180°C) until meringue is brown, approximately 1 hour.

Of many kinds of remote control, a man's control of his wife is by far the remotest.

TOURTIÈRE

*My mother's recipe.
Enjoy this typical
French Canadian dish.*

1½ lbs.	ground lean pork	750 g
1½ lbs.	ground lean beef	750 g
1½ cups	finely chopped onion	375 mL
1 tbsp.	cinnamon	15 mL
1½ tsp.	cloves	7 mL
2 tsp.	allspice	10 mL
2 tsp.	salt	10 mL
1 tsp.	nutmeg	5 mL
	pepper, to taste	
	water to cover meat	
3	medium potatoes, mashed	3
	pastry for 3 x 2 crust, 9" (23 cm) pies	

Brown meat in large frying pan. Drain off excess fat and place meat in large saucepan. • Add onions, spices, salt, pepper and enough water to cover mixture. Mix well. Place over high heat and bring to a boil. Reduce heat, cover and simmer 45 minutes, stirring frequently. • Add mashed potatoes to meat mixture, blending well. • Fill pie shells with meat mixture. • Roll out remainder of pastry, cut several slits or a fancy design near center, place on top of meat mixture, seal and flute edges. • Bake at 425°F (220°C) for 15 minutes. Reduce oven heat to 350°F (180°C) and bake 45 minutes longer. • A tasty variation uses all ground pork and includes 1 tsp. (5 mL) each of thyme, sage and dry mustard, plus 2 minced cloves of garlic instead of the cinnamon, allspice and nutmeg.

SAUSAGE AND ONION ROLY-POLY

SUET PASTRY

3	medium onions	3
½ oz.	lard	15 g
½ lb.	pork sausage meat	250 g
8 oz.	self-raising flour	250 g
2 oz.	shredded suet	55 g
1 tsp.	salt	5 mL
¼ tsp.	pepper	1 mL
½ tsp.	mixed dried herbs	2 mL
	cold water	

Gently fry chopped onions in lard until soft, but not brown. • Place sausage meat in bowl, add onions and mix well. • Mix flour, suet, salt, pepper and mixed herbs in another bowl. Add about ½ cup (125 mL) cold water and mix with fork to form soft, but not sticky, dough. Turn out on floured board, knead lightly and roll out to a 9" (23 cm) square. • Spread sausage meat mixture over dough and roll up Swiss-roll style. Place roll, seam down, on greased foil. Fold edges of foil together loosely on top of roll. Place in a roasting pan and cook in center of 350°F (180°C) oven for about 1½ hours. • Remove foil, place roly-poly on warm serving dish and serve with green vegetables and tomato sauce or ketchup, if desired. • Serves 4.

CHICKEN

4	boneless, skinless chicken breast halves	4
1½ cups	grated Jack OR mild Cheddar cheese	375 mL
¼ cup	mayonnaise	50 mL
2 tsp.	chopped green onion	10 mL
2 tsp.	dried parsley flakes	10 mL
½ tsp.	Dijon mustard	2 mL
6 oz.	jar marinated artichoke hearts, drained	170 mL
½ cup	flour	125 mL
½ tsp.	salt	2 mL
pinch	pepper	pinch
1	egg	1
1 tbsp.	water	15 mL
½ cup	seasoned dry bread crumbs	125 mL
¼ cup	vegetable oil	75 mL

CHICKEN BREASTS WITH ARTICHOKE CHEESE STUFFING

Pound chicken breasts until ¼" (0.6 cm) thick. Set aside. • Mix cheese, mayonnaise, onion, parsley and mustard in small mixing bowl. • Cut artichoke hearts into bite-sized pieces; stir into cheese mixture. • Place ¼ of artichoke-cheese mixture at end of each chicken breast. Roll, folding sides. • Mix flour, salt and pepper in a shallow dish. • Combine egg and water in shallow dish. • Place bread crumbs in a shallow dish. • Dip chicken rolls in flour mixture to coat, then in egg mixture, then in bread crumbs. • Cover and refrigerate for 1 hour. • Preheat oven to 350°F (180°C). • Place oil in 13" x 9" (4 L) baking pan and heat in oven 10 minutes. • Remove pan from oven. • Carefully roll coated chicken breasts in hot oil, using tongs. Arrange chicken in pan. • Bake at 350°F (180°C) 35 minutes, or until golden brown. • Serves 4.

CHICKEN BREASTS IN SOUR CREAM

6	whole chicken breasts, halved	6
2 cups	sour cream	500 mL
¼ cup	lemon juice	50 mL
4 tsp.	Worcestershire sauce	20 mL
4 tsp.	celery salt	20 mL
2 tsp.	paprika	10 mL
4	garlic cloves, finely chopped	4
4 tsp.	salt	20 mL
½ tsp.	pepper	2 mL
1¾ cups	bread crumbs	425 mL
½ cup	melted shortening	125 mL
½ cup	melted butter	125 mL

Combine first 9 ingredients and coat breasts in mixture. • Place coated breasts into dish, cover and refrigerate overnight. • Roll chicken in bread crumbs and arrange on cookie sheet. • Pour the shortening and half the butter over chicken. • Bake at 350°F (180°C) for 45 minutes. • Pour rest of butter over and bake 15 minutes longer. • Serves 6 or more.

CHICKEN BREASTS BORDELAISE

4	whole chicken breasts, skinned and boned	4
1	lemon, juice of	1
½ tsp.	salt	2 mL
¼ tsp.	pepper	1 mL
⅛ tsp.	thyme	0.5 mL
3 tbsp.	peanut oil	45 mL
3 tbsp.	butter	45 mL
½-1 lb.	fresh mushrooms, sliced	250-500 g
4 tbsp.	flour	60 mL
2 cups	chicken stock OR bouillon cubes	500 mL
½ cup	dry white wine	125 mL
⅛ tsp.	tarragon OR	0.5 mL
1	bay leaf	1

In the morning, or the previous evening, split breasts; rub with lemon juice. • Mix salt, pepper and thyme together on a plate. Roll the breasts in the spices; put in a bowl, cover and refrigerate. • Heat peanut oil in frying pan over medium heat and fry breasts until golden on both sides. Remove and place in a deep casserole. • After all chicken is brown, use same frying pan (do not wash) and add butter. When hot, add mushrooms and stir; cook 1 minute over high heat. • Add flour and stir until well mixed. • Add stock and wine; cook over medium heat until creamy stirring constantly. • Add tarragon, or bay leaf, taste for seasoning. • Pour sauce over chicken. • Cover and bake for 1 hour at 300°F (150°C). • Serves 6-8.

4-5	whole chicken breasts, boned	45
1 cup	orange juice	250 mL
½ cup	chili sauce	125 mL
¼	green pepper, chopped	¼
1 tsp.	prepared mustard	5 mL
1½ tsp.	garin salt	7 mL
2 tbsp.	soy sauce	30 mL
1 tbsp.	molasses	15 mL
10 oz.	can mandarin oranges	284 mL

CHICKEN À L'ORANGE

Bake chicken in roasting pan, or casserole dish, until cooked. • Mix all remaining ingredients for sauce. • Pour sauce over cooked chicken and bake an additional ½ hour. • Excellent served with rice and stir-fried vegetables. • Serves 4-6.

---

	chicken breasts, skinned and boned	
	Swiss cheese	
1	slice thinly sliced ham per chicken breast	
	flour	
1	egg white	1
1 tbsp.	water	15 mL
	finely crushed dry bread crumbs	
	seasoning to taste	
	paprika	

CHICKEN CORDON BLEU

A microwave specialty.

Pound chicken pieces between wax paper until quite thin. • Place cheese and 1 slice of ham on each chicken breast. Fold over. • Dip breast into flour, then into egg white beaten with water, then into the seasoned bread crumbs. • Arrange chicken breasts on a plate; sprinkle with paprika. • Cover with waxed paper. • Cook on HIGH power 4 minutes per chicken breast. • Let stand 5 minutes before serving. • Serve with mushroom sauce.

½ cup	mirim*	125 mL
10 tbsp.	soy sauce	150 mL
½ cup	melted honey	125 mL
2 tsp.	ground fresh ginger root	10 mL
2	garlic cloves, minced	2
24	chicken pieces	24

CHICKEN TERIYAKI

Combine all ingredients except chicken until well mixed. • Marinate the chicken in the sauce for 1-2 hours. • Bake in 375°F (190°C) oven for 30 minutes or until chicken is done. • Serves 8-12. • * Mirim is available at oriental food stores.

For fluffier omelets, add a pinch of cornstarch before beating.

CHICKEN ELEGANTÉ

8	slices corned beef (not canned)	8
4	whole chicken breasts, boned and halved	4
10 oz.	can cream of mushroom soup	284 mL
1 cup	dairy sour cream	250 mL
½ cup	slivered almonds	125 mL
¼ cup	cooked, crumbled bacon	75 mL

Preheat oven at 325°F (160°C). • Roll slice of beef around each half of chicken breast. Arrange in 13" x 9" (4 L) baking pan, or 3-quart (3 L) casserole. • In small bowl, combine soup and sour cream; pour over chicken. • *Sprinkle with almonds and bacon bits. • Bake, covered, for 1¼ to 1½ hours, or until chicken is tender. • To make ahead, prepare to *, cover and refrigerate up to 1 day; continue as directed. • Serves 6-8.

CHICKEN SUPREME

4 cups	cubed cooked chicken	1 L
¾ cup	mayonnaise	175 mL
¾ cup	sour cream	175 mL
10 oz.	cream of chicken OR mushroom soup	284 mL
1 tbsp.	lemon juice	15 mL
1 tsp.	salt	5 mL
10 oz.	can mushrooms, diced	284 mL
5 oz.	can water chestnuts	150 g
1 cup	grated Cheddar cheese	250 mL
1	can French-fried onions*(optional)	1

Combine all ingredients, except cheese and onions, and spread in a 9" x 13" (4 L) pan. • Sprinkle cheese on top and bake at 350°F (180°C) for 30 minutes. • Sprinkle can of French-fried onions on top, if desired, and bake an additional 15 minutes. • * Found in specialty area of your supermarket.

WINDOW CLEANER

½ cup	sudsey amonia (drug store)	125 mL
2 cups	70% isopropyl rubbing alcohol	500 mL
½ tsp.	liquid dish detergent	2 mL
3¾ quarts	water	3.75 L

Combine ingredients in 1 gallon (4 L) plastic or glass container with closeable lid or top. Yields 1 gallon (4 L).

1	broiler chicken, quartered	1	
½ tsp.	dried thyme	2 mL	
¼ tsp.	paprika	1 mL	
¼ tsp.	onion powder	1 mL	
3 tbsp.	frozen orange juice concentrate	45 mL	
½ tsp.	honey	2 mL	
1 tsp.	dried parsley	5 mL	

BROILED CHICKEN À L'ORANGE

Sprinkle chicken with thyme, paprika and onion powder; arrange, skin side down, in pan and broil 10 mintues. • In small saucepan, combine orange juice, honey and parsley. Heat and stir until melted. • Brush chicken lightly with half of the mixture during first 10 minutes of broiling, then turn and broil other side about 10 minutes or until done. Brush with remaining mixture about 3 minutes before removing from broiler. • Serves 4 (143 calories per serving).

4	chicken breasts, skinned and boned	4
¾ cup	flour	175 mL
2 tsp.	salt	10 mL
½ tsp.	pepper	2 mL
1 tsp.	paprika	5 mL
½ cup	butter	125 mL
2 oz.	slivered almonds	55 g
1¼ cups	water	300 mL
10 oz.	can beef consommé	284 mL
3 tbsp.	ketchup	50 mL
¾ cup	sour cream	175 mL
28 oz.	can peach halves	796 mL
½ cup	Parmesan cheese	125 mL

CHICKEN AND PEACHES

Cut chicken into bite-sized pieces; dredge in a mixture of flour, salt, pepper and paprika; brown in butter. Remove to a 9″ x 13″ (4 L) baking dish. • Brown almonds lightly in remaining butter and then add flour left from dredging. Stir in water, beef consommé and ketchup. • Remove from heat and add sour cream. • Pour over chicken and bake, covered, at 350°F (180°C) for 40 minutes. • Place peach halves on top, sprinkle with Parmesan and bake for 15 minutes, uncovered. • Serves 4-6.

FURNITURE POLISH

4 oz.	lemon oil	125 mL
4 oz.	white table vinegar	125 mL
1 tsp.	rubbing alcohol	5 mL

Combine all ingredients. Rub on furniture (finish will turn foggy). This is to clean really dirty furniture. For continuing use, make-up a batch without the rubbing alcohol.

127

PEACH BARBECUED CHICKEN

1	fryer chicken, cut-up OR 12 thighs	1
¼ cup	flour	50 mL
¼ tsp.	salt	1 mL
¼ tsp.	pepper	1 mL
½ tsp.	seasoned salt	2 mL
2 tbsp.	oil OR butter	30 mL
1 cup	pure peach jam	250 mL
½ cup	regular barbecue sauce	125 mL
1	medium onion, thinly sliced	1
2 tbsp.	soy sauce	30 mL
1	green pepper, sliced in thin rings	1
½ cup	canned water chestnuts, drained and sliced	125 mL

Coat the chicken with seasoned flour and brown in oil or butter. • Combine the jam, barbecue sauce, onion and soy sauce; pour over the chicken. • Cover and simmer for 40 minutes or put into the oven and bake at 350°F (180°C) until chicken is tender. • Add the green peppers and water chestnuts during the last 10 minutes of cooking. • Serve on a bed of rice. • Serves 4.

PINEAPPLE CHICKEN

3 lb.	frying chicken	1.5 kg
1	egg, beaten	1
1 tbsp.	flour	15 mL
½ tsp.	salt	2 mL
¼ cup	salad oil	75 mL
⅔ cup	water	150 mL
1	garlic clove, minced	1
½ cup	fresh OR canned pineapple chunks	125 mL
¼ cup	sliced celery	75 mL
1 tbsp.	cornstarch	15 mL
¼ cup	honey	50 mL
¼ tsp.	ground ginger	1 mL
¼ cup	corn syrup OR pineapple syrup	75 mL
1 tbsp.	soy sauce	15 mL
1 tbsp.	sherry	15 mL

Cut chicken into individual pieces. Mix together in a bowl, the egg, flour, and salt. Dip the chicken pieces in this mixture and fry in salad oil until well-browned. • Add the water, garlic, pineapple chunks and celery. Cover and simmer 45 minutes, or until the chicken is tender. • Blend, in a small bowl, the cornstarch, honey and ginger. • Add the corn syrup, or pineapple syrup, soy sauce and sherry. • Pour into the chicken sauce and stir over medium heat until smooth and creamy. • Serve with boiled rice.

POULTRY
Cornish Hens in Honey, page 134
Crusty Pecan Squash, page 82

1 lb.	chicken breasts	500 g
	green onions	
7 oz.	soy sauce	189 mL
3 tbsp.	sugar	50 mL
2	garlic cloves, grated	2
¼ oz.	fresh ginger root, grated	7 g
1	small cucumber	1
1	tomato	1

CHICKEN KABOBS

Remove skin and bones from chicken and cut into cubes l" x l" (2.5 x 2.5 cm). • Cut white part of the green onions into 1¼" (3.2 cm) lengths. • Skewer chicken alternately with onions. • To make marinade, combine soy sauce, sugar, garlic and ginger root in a shallow dish. Marinate the kabobs for 1 hour, turning them once or twice. • Broil, or charcoal grill, 20 to 25 minutes basting occasionally with marinade. • Garnish with cucumber slices and tomato wedges. • Serves 4.

2	whole chicken breasts, skinned and boned	2
8 oz.	can sliced mushrooms	250 mL
3 cups	hot cooked rice	750 mL
1½ tsp.	salt	7 mL
¼ tsp.	pepper	1 mL
2 tbsp.	butter OR margarine	30 mL
1 cup	sliced green onions, including tops (optional)	250 mL
½ cup	dry sherry	125 mL
1 cup	fresh OR frozen green peas	250 mL
1½ cups	chicken broth	375 mL
3	fresh tomatoes, peeled and cut in ⅛ths	3
2 tbsp.	cornstarch	30 mL
	parsley	

CHICKEN À LA FRANÇAISE

Great company fare.

Cut chicken into ¼" (0.6 cm) strips. • Drain mushrooms, reserve liquid. • While rice is cooking, season chicken with salt and pepper. • Sauté chicken strips in butter until brown. Add onions and mushrooms; continue cooking 2 minutes longer. Stir in sherry, peas and chicken broth. Cover and simmer 20 minutes. Add tomatoes. • Dissolve cornstarch in mushroom liquid and stir into chicken mixture. Cook, stirring constantly, approximately 5 minutes longer, until thickened. • Serve over bed of rice; garnish with fresh parsley. • Preparation time: ½ to ¾ hour. • Serves 6.

Drop a copper penny in the water with tulips, and they will stand erect and not open wide.

CHICKEN ALMOND CURRY

1 tsp.	curry powder	5 mL
½ cup	yogurt	125 mL
2 lbs.	chicken parts	1 kg
3	medium onions	3
2 tsp.	grated ginger	10 mL
3-4	cloves	3-4
½ tsp.	cinnamon	2 mL
2 tsp.	salad oil	10 mL
12-15	almonds	12-15
1 cup	tomato paste	250 mL
1 tsp.	salt	5 mL
2	medium potatoes, cut up	2
1 tsp.	shredded coconut	5 mL

Mix curry powder into the yogurt. Coat chicken pieces with yogurt paste. Let stand for 2-3 hours. Then bake in 350°F (180°C) oven for 20 minutes. ● Place onions, ginger, cloves and cinnamon into blender and make a paste. ● Heat oil in a large pan and fry almonds for about 2 minutes. Add the onion paste and fry for 10 minutes. Add the tomato paste and salt and cook the mixture for another 5 minutes. Add the chicken and potatoes and mix well. ● Cover the pan and cook, at low heat, for 20-30 minutes. ● Garnish with shredded coconut and serve with fried rice or rice pilaf. ● Serves 4-6.

MUSHROOM VELVET CHICKEN

1 lb.	chicken breasts	500 g
	salt and pepper	
2 tbsp.	soy sauce	30 mL
¼ cup	peanut oil	50 mL
½ tsp.	sesame oil	2 mL
⅛ tsp.	Accent	0.5 mL
½ cup	chopped celery	125 mL
½ cup	chopped green onion	125 mL
3 cups	sliced fresh mushrooms	750 mL
¼ cup	water	50 mL
1 tsp.	cornstarch, in ½ cup (125 mL) water	5 mL
¼ tsp.	grated fresh ginger	1 mL

Slice chicken extremely thin and marinate at least 10 minutes in a mixture of a little salt and pepper, 1 tsp. (5 mL) soy sauce, 1 tsp. (5 mL) peanut oil, sesame oil and Accent. ● Heat 2 tbsp. (25 mL) peanut oil in wok, or pan, until it smokes.
● Add a little salt, celery and onions and stir for 30 seconds. Add mushrooms, ¼ cup (50 mL) water and remaining soy sauce, and cover for 30 seconds. Add enough of the cornstarch solution to thicken like a gravy. Remove from the wok. ● Clean and dry wok, add 1 tbsp. (15 mL) peanut oil and heat until it smokes. Add a little salt, add the chicken and stir-fry until done. Add the ginger and stir for 5 seconds. Add the cooked vegetables and stir for another 30 seconds. ● Serves 4.

130

1 lb.	chicken, in strips	500 g
6 cups	cooked rice	1.5 L
1 tbsp.	vegetable oil	15 mL
1	large onion, chopped	1
2	garlic cloves, minced	2
3	bacon strips, chopped	3
2 cups	chopped mixed vegetables	500 mL
1 cup	diced celery	250 mL
2 tbsp.	soy sauce	30 mL
1 tbsp.	teriyaki sauce	15 mL
1 tsp.	salt	5 mL
1 tsp.	Chinese spice	5 mL
1 tbsp.	sugar	15 mL
4 oz.	can shrimp	113 g

CHICKEN-FRIED RICE

Sauté chicken quickly until browned. • Prepare rice. • Heat oil in a large skillet; add onion and garlic. Stir-fry for 2 minutes. • Add chicken, bacon and vegetables. Stir-fry for 5 minutes. • Add rice and all other ingredients. Stir until well mixed. • Serve hot. • Serves 4.

3	medium onions, sliced OR chopped	3
½ cup	vegetable oil	125 mL
2¼ lbs.	chicken pieces, skinned	1 kg
1½ tsp.	crushed garlic	7 mL
1 tsp.	crushed ginger	5 mL
¼ tsp.	crushed hot pepper	1 mL
½ tsp.	coriander powder	2 mL
½ tsp.	cumin powder	2 mL
¼ tsp.	turmeric powder	1 mL
¼ tsp.	hot chili powder OR cayenne, to taste	1 mL
2	medium tomatoes, chopped	2
2 tsp.	tomato paste	10 mL
1 tsp.	salt OR to taste	5 mL
1 tbsp.	coriander leaves	15 mL
4	small potatoes	4
	hot water	

CHICKEN CURRY

Sauté onions in oil over medium heat until golden brown. • Add chicken and sauté for further 3-4 minutes. • Add tomatoes, tomato paste, all the spices and coriander leaves and cook until chicken is half done. • Add potatoes; again cook for a few minutes and add hot water to desired consistency. • Cook until chicken and potatoes are cooked. • For stronger or milder curry, add or reduce spices to your personal taste. • For best results, cook curries ahead of time and reheat thoroughly before serving. • Serve with rice or pita bread. • Serves 4.

TANDOORI-STYLE CHICKEN

2½ lbs.	chicken pieces, skinned	1.25 kg
1 tsp.	salt	5 mL
1	lemon, juice of	1
2 cups	plain yogurt	500 mL
½	medium onion, peeled and quartered	½
1	garlic clove, peeled	1
¾″	cube fresh ginger, peeled and quartered	2 cm
½	fresh hot green chili, sliced	½
2 tsp.	garam masala (see below)	10 mL
3 tbsp.	liquid yellow food coloring, mixed with ½-1½ tbsp. (7-22 mL) liquid red food coloring	45 mL
	few wedges lime (optional)	

Spread chicken pieces on large platter. Sprinkle with ½ tsp. (2 mL) salt and squeeze half of lemon juice over them. Turn pieces and do the same with remaining salt and lemon juice. Set aside for 20 minutes. • Combine yogurt, onion, garlic, ginger, green chili, and garam masala. Blend until smooth paste is achieved. • Combine food coloring to make a deep orange color. Paint chicken pieces with food coloring. • Pour yogurt paste over the pieces of chicken and marinate for 6-24 hours in refrigerator. • Preheat oven to maximum temperature. • Shake off as much marinade as possible and arrange chicken pieces in a shallow dish in a single layer. • Bake 20-25 minutes. • Leftover marinade may be frozen, or boiled until thickened and use it as a dip or on steamed Basmati rice or pita bread. • Serves 4.

GARAM MASALA

1 tsp.	nutmeg powder	5 mL
1 tbsp.	cardamom powder	15 mL
1 tsp.	cinnamon powder	5 mL
1 tsp.	black cumin powder	5 mL
1 tsp.	clove powder	5 mL
1 tsp.	black pepper powder	5 mL

Mix together and store for future use.

A discarded quilted robe or housecoat will make a number of good potholders or oven mitts.

3-4 lb.	chicken	1.5-2 kg
1½ cups	white vinegar	375 mL
1 tbsp.	saffron	15 mL
1 cup	yogurt	250 mL
1½	onions, coarsely chopped	1½
1	garlic clove	1
2 tsp.	cumin	10 mL
½ tsp.	salt	2 mL
½ cup	cream	125 mL
5 tbsp.	chopped coriander leaves	75 mL

CHICKEN ANGAR

Cut chicken into 16 pieces. • In a large bowl, mix together remaining ingredients, except for cream and coriander. • Place chicken pieces in marinade for 6-8 hours, turning occasionally. • Remove chicken and grill slowly under broiler or on barbecue. • Place marinade in a saucepan and boil gently until reduced by half. • Add cream and heat without boiling. • Place chicken on a large platter. • Top with sauce and sprinkle with chopped coriander. • Serves 4.

3-4 lb.	chicken	1.5-2 kg
½ tsp.	EACH minced garlic and ginger root	2 mL
1	small onion, chopped	1
1	medium tomato	1
	salt	
1¾ oz.	pkg. coconut cream	50 mL
1½ cups	milk	375 mL
¼ tsp.	turmeric	1 mL
½ tsp.	hot red chili powder OR cayenne	2 mL
1 tbsp.	butter	15 mL
1 tbsp.	lemon juice	15 mL
5	potatoes, halved	5
5	hard-boiled eggs	5
	saffron	

CHICKEN PAKA

This chicken in coconut sauce is delicious!

Boil chicken, in water to cover, with garlic and ginger until tender. Drain, save stock. • Combine onion, tomato and salt. • Melt coconut and milk over low heat. Add turmeric and red chili. Stir occasionally until thick. • Add chicken and ½ cup (125 mL) chicken stock to the coconut milk and stir. • Add tomato mixture and 1 tbsp. (15 mL) of butter and lemon juice. • Add potatoes and eggs. • Cook over moderate heat until potatoes are cooked. • Sprinkle with saffron. • Serve with rice. • Serves 4.

Spray your children's tennis shoes with spray starch after washing them. The starch will help resist soil.

CORNISH HENS IN HONEY

4	Cornish hens	4
	salt and pepper	
	oil	
¾ cup	soy sauce	175 mL
¼ cup	honey	75 mL
1 tbsp.	grated fresh ginger	15 mL
2	cloves garlic, mashed	2
¼ cup	melted butter	50 mL

Season hens with salt and pepper; rub on a little oil and roast in 400°F (200°C) oven for 15 minutes. • Heat together remaining ingredients. • Remove hens from oven and baste with the sauce. • Lower the temperature to 350°F (180°C), return hens and continue roasting until tender, about 1 hour, basting occasionally with the sauce. • Split each hen in half and serve 1 half per person. • Best eaten with the fingers, and very good served cold. • Serves 6-8. • See photograph page 128A.

CHICKEN LIVERS WITH MADEIRA SAUCE

1	small onion, chopped	1
3 tbsp.	butter	45 mL
1 lb.	chicken livers	500 g
1 tsp.	paprika	5 mL
½ cup	beef broth	125 mL
2 tbsp.	Madeira	30 mL
1 tbsp.	flour, in a little water	15 mL
¼ cup	whipping cream	50 mL
	salt and pepper	

Sauté chopped onion in butter. • Add halved chicken livers. • Cook for 8 minutes over high heat. • Add paprika, beef broth and Madeira. • Bring to a boil, stirring in flour mixed with water. • Add cream, salt and pepper. • Serve on rice, pasta, toast or use as an omelet or crêpe filling. • Serves 4.

WILD GOOSE AU BIÈRE

1	wild goose	1
¼ cup	canola oil	50 mL
2	onions, chopped	2
2	green peppers, chopped	2
1 cup	sliced mushrooms	250 mL
1 tsp.	sage	5 mL
1 tsp.	thyme	5 mL
1 tsp.	rosemary	5 mL
1 tsp.	salt	5 mL
12 oz.	beer	341 mL
	cornstarch	

Remove meat from bones and cut into pieces 4" x 2" (10 cm x 5 cm). Cut across the breast. • Heat oil in Dutch oven and brown goose. • Remove and set aside. • Brown onions and return goose to pan along with green pepper, mushrooms, spices and beer. • Bring to a boil, reduce heat, simmer for 1-1½ hours over low heat. • Thicken gravy with cornstarch. • Serve with wild rice.

FISH

15	prawns, deveined	15
½ tsp.	salt	2 mL
1 tsp.	cornstarch	5 mL
½ tsp.	minced ginger	2 mL
¼ tsp.	minced garlic	1 mL
1 tbsp.	cooking wine (rice wine)	15 mL
1 cup	broccoli florets	250 mL
½ cup	sliced carrots	125 mL
½ cup	sliced mushrooms	125 mL
½ cup	canned baby corn cobs	125 mL
½ tsp.	salt	2 mL
¼ tsp.	Accent (M.S.G.)	1 mL
1 tsp.	sugar	5 mL
¼ tsp.	sesame seed oil	1 mL
1 tbsp.	cornstarch	15 mL
¼ cup	water	50 mL

PRAWNS WITH BROCCOLI

SAUCE

Coat prawns with a mixture of salt and cornstarch. • Brown ginger and garlic in wok. Sauté the prawns for 2 minutes on medium heat. • Add cooking wine (rice wine). • Remove prawns and set aside. • Stir-fry the vegetables; do not overcook. • Return prawns to wok. • Mix the sauce ingredients together and add to the prawns. • Bring to a boil. • Serve immediately.

MEASURES:

If you get very old recipes.
Dash, pinch, few grains, speck = 1/16 tsp. (0.25 mL)
Size of a nut = 1 tsp. (5 mL)
Size of an egg = ¼ cup (50 mL)
3 tsp. (15 mL) = 1 tbsp. (15 mL) — not measuring spoons
1 tbsp. (15 mL) averages 1 oz. (30 g) or 2 fl. oz. (56 mL)
16 tbsp. (240 mL) = 1 cup (250 mL)

TEMPURA

1 cup	flour	250 mL
1 cup	ice-cold water	250 mL
1	egg	1
2 lbs.	large shrimp	1 kg
	flour	
	carrots	
	green beans	
	potatoes	
	asparagus	
	broccoli	
	onions	
	eggplant	
	yams	

Mix first 3 ingredients to make the tempura batter. • Shell shrimp, leaving tail fins attached to the flesh. Remove black veins. Slit intersection of shrimp diagonally to prevent curling. Wash and dry. • Measure oil to a depth of about 3" (7.5 cm) in a large pan and heat. • Flour the shrimp with a little dry flour, dip in batter, holding it by the tail, slide it into the hot oil. When shrimp floats sizzling to the surface, turn it over. Fry until light brown. Drain on paper towel. • Vegetables can be cut into bite-sized pieces, dried with paper towels and dipped into the batter. Fry until light brown.

CURRIED SHRIMP À LA CEYLON

2 tbsp.	butter OR margarine	30 mL
1 cup	chopped onion	250 mL
½ cup	chopped green pepper	125 mL
½ cup	chopped celery	125 mL
4 tbsp.	flour	60 mL
2 tsp.	curry powder, OR more	10 mL
3 tbsp.	soy sauce	45 mL
1 cup	water	250 mL
14 oz.	can tomatoes	398 mL
1 tsp.	salt	5 mL
10 oz.	shrimp, cooked OR canned	285 g

Melt butter in saucepan; add onions, green peppers and celery. Cook until tender. • Blend in flour, curry and soy sauce. • Stir in water and tomatoes. • Cover and simmer 20 minutes. • Add shrimp and heat 5 minutes. • Serve over cooked rice.

When you peel potatoes, leave a little potato on the skins and then deep fry them. Great homemade potato chips and very nutritious.

1	garlic clove, minced	1
2 tbsp.	butter	30 mL
½	pkg. chopped frozen okra	½
14 oz.	can stewed tomatoes	398 mL
1 tbsp.	cornstarch	15 mL
1½-2 cups	shrimp, fresh, frozen OR canned	375-500 mL
1 tbsp.	creole seasoning, OR Tabasco, to taste	15 mL

SHRIMP CREOLE

Sauté garlic in 1 tbsp. (15 mL) butter until golden. • Simmer okra in garlic butter plus 1 tbsp. (15 mL) butter until the okra is tender, about 5 minutes. • Add tomatoes and simmer for 30 minutes. • Thicken sauce slightly with cornstarch mixed with a little juice from the tomatoes. • Add shrimp to tomato mixture. • Season with creole seasoning or Tabasco. • Bring to simmer 5 minutes, stirring from time to time. • Cooking time: approximately 1 hour. • Serve over steamed rice, accompanied with cold asparagus salad and hot buttered French bread. • Serves 4.

---

	butter	
2 x 4.5 oz.	cans crab meat	2 x 127 g
½ cup	mayonnaise	125 mL
1 cup	minced celery	250 mL
½ cup	chopped green pepper	125 mL
½ cup	chopped green onion	125 mL
8	slices day-old white bread	8
4	large eggs	4
3 cups	milk	750 mL
10 oz.	can cream of mushroom soup	284 mL
1 cup	grated Cheddar cheese	250 mL

OVERNIGHT CRAB SOUFFLÉ

Easy and delicious.

Butter a casserole large enough that the soufflé will not spill over. • Mix the crab meat, mayonnaise, celery, green pepper and green onion. • Remove the crusts from the bread and cut 4 of the slices into cubes. Arrange these cubes in the bottom of the casserole and top with the crab meat mixture. • Lay the remaining 4 slices of bread on top. • Beat the eggs slightly and mix with the milk. Pour this over the mixture in the casserole and refrigerate overnight. • The next day, bake in a 350°F (180°C) oven for 20 minutes. (Put the casserole into a pan of hot water for baking, if desired). • Remove and spread mushroom soup over casserole. • Sprinkle with the grated cheese and return the casserole to the oven for 1 hour. • Serves 8.

Thaw frozen fish in milk to give it a fresh-caught flavor. Drain before cooking.

RICH MAN'S DELIGHT

2 lbs.	halibut	1 kg
2 lbs.	scallops	1 kg
	soft bread crumbs	
10 oz.	can creamed corn	284 mL
2 cups	sliced mushrooms	500 mL
3 x 4.5 oz.	cans lobster	3 x 127 g
	pepper	
	seasoned salt	
¼ tsp.	nutmeg	1 mL

SAUCE		
4 tbsp.	butter	60 mL
4 tbsp.	flour	60 mL
2 cups	cereal cream	500 mL
1 cup	milk	250 mL
4 oz.	sherry	113 mL

Cook the halibut and scallops separately for approximately 5 minutes. • Line buttered casserole with soft bread crumbs. • Place layers of halibut, corn, (optional), scallops, mushrooms and lobster on top. • Sprinkle with pepper, salt and nutmeg. • Cover with sauce. • If desired, sprinkle bread crumbs on top. • Bake in 375°F (190°C) oven for 30 minutes. • Serves 12.

SCALLOP AND MUSHROOM PIE

8	scallops	8
1 cup	milk	250 mL
	salt and pepper	
1 tbsp.	butter, OR more	15 mL
1 tbsp.	flour	15 mL
¼ lb.	mushrooms, sliced	125 g
4 tbsp.	sweet sherry	60 mL
3 cups	cold mashed potatoes	750 mL
1 tbsp.	chopped parsley	15 mL

Cut scallops in half. Simmer in milk with salt and pepper for 15 minutes; strain. Reserve milk. • Melt butter in saucepan. Add flour. Mix well, gradually stir in warm milk. Add sliced mushrooms, sherry and scallops. • Place in ovenproof dish and cover with mashed potatoes. Dot with butter. • Bake at 350°F (180°C) for 20-30 minutes until gently browned. • Garnish with parsley.

CHINESE SALMON

¼ cup	sliced ginger root	50 mL
1	whole salmon	1
¼ cup	vegetable oil	75 mL
	soy sauce	
	green onions	
1-2 tbsp.	sliced ginger root	15-30 mL

Put ¼ cup (50 mL) sliced ginger root into salted water in large roasting pan. • Poach whole salmon for approximately 20 minutes, or until not quite done. • Take out and remove skin and bones. • Lay fillets on a platter. • Meanwhile, heat oil with 1-2 tbsp. (15-30 mL) ginger root until spitting hot. • Pour hot oil over salmon and sprinkle with soy sauce and green onions. • Serve.

4	trout, heads and tails on, cleaned seasoned flour	4
5 tbsp.	butter	75 mL
1 cup	sliced mushrooms, fresh OR canned	250 mL
2 tbsp.	lemon juice	30 mL

MUSHROOMS AND TROUT

Roll trout in seasoned flour; fry in butter until meat flakes and skin is golden. ● Remove to a platter and keep hot. ● Sauté mushrooms in butter until tender. ● Add lemon juice and pour over trout. ● Serves 4.

2 lbs.	white fish OR cod steaks	1 kg
1¼ tsp.	salt	6 mL
½ tsp.	cayenne pepper	2 mL
¼ tsp.	ground turmeric	1 mL
9 tbsp.	vegetable oil	150 mL
1 tsp.	EACH whole mustard seeds, whole fennel seeds	5 mL
¾ cup	finely chopped onions	175 mL
2	garlic cloves, finely chopped	2
2 tsp.	ground cumin seeds	10 mL
14 oz.	can tomatoes, chopped	398 mL
½ tsp.	ground roasted cumin seeds, (optional)	2 mL
¼ tsp.	garam masala*	1 mL

WHITE FISH IN A SPICY TOMATO SAUCE

Pat fish steaks dry. ● Rub with ¼ tsp. (1 mL) salt, ¼ tsp. (1 mL) cayenne and turmeric. Set aside for 30 minutes. ● Heat 4 tbsp. (60 mL) oil in saucepan over medium heat. ● Add mustard seeds and fennel seeds. As soon as mustard seeds pop, add onions and garlic. Stir-fry onions until slightly brown. ● Add cumin powder, 1 tsp. (5 mL) salt and ¼ tsp. (1 mL) cayenne. ● Add chopped tomatoes with liquid, roasted cumin seeds and garam masala. Bring to a boil. ● Cover, cook on low heat, simmer for 15 minutes. ● Preheat oven to 350°F (180°C).
● Put remaining 5 tbsp. (75 mL) oil in large skillet. Heat over medium heat. When hot, cook fish steaks; brown both sides. Partially cook only. ● Place steaks in baking dish, pour tomato sauce over the fish. Bake uncovered for 15 minutes or until done. ● Serve with rice, peas pilaf and spinach. ● * Garam masala is available in the specialty section of your grocery store, or make your own as on page 132.

Add lemon juice to shortening when frying fish. This eliminates smoke and odor.

PACIFIC SALMON WELLINGTON

2 lbs.	salmon fillets	1 kg
¼ cup	whipping cream	75 mL
½ tsp.	salt	2 mL
⅛ tsp.	pepper	0.5 mL
2 drops	Tabasco sauce	2 drops
1 tbsp.	butter	15 mL
½ cup	minced onions	125 mL
1 tbsp.	flour	15 mL
1 tbsp.	unsalted butter, softened	15 mL
¼ tsp.	salt	1 mL
pinch	freshly ground pepper	pinch
1 tbsp.	butter	15 mL
½ cup	sliced mushrooms	125 mL
½ cup	whipping cream	125 mL
2 tsp.	lemon juice	10 mL
	salt and pepper, to taste	
2 x 7 oz.	pkgs. puff pastry, enough for 2-crust pie	2 x 215 g
5	hard-cooked eggs, halved lengthwise	5
1	egg, beaten	1

Divide salmon into 2 portions of 1½ and ½ lbs. (750 and 250 g). Put smaller portion through a meat grinder, or chop finely, then blend with whipping cream, salt and pepper and Tabasco. Cut the larger portion into very thin slices. • Melt butter in a frying pan and sauté onion until soft, but not brown. Remove from heat and set aside. • Prepare beurre mani by combining flour, butter, salt and pepper. Blend well. • Melt butter in frying pan and sauté mushrooms. Add whipping cream and cook over medium heat, stirring constantly until the liquid is reduced by half. Stir in the beurre mani and simmer for 5 minutes. Add lemon juice. Season with salt and pepper. Remove from heat and set aside. • Roll out puff pastry into 2 pieces, 12″ x 6″ (30 x 15 cm). Place 1 piece on a buttered baking sheet. Along the center of the pastry, arrange a layer of half the salmon slices. Top with sautéed onions, then with half the mushroom mixture. Cover with the remaining salmon slices. Top with 2 rows of hard-cooked egg halves. Spread with remaining mushroom mixture. Cover with minced salmon mixture. • Place second piece of pastry over the layers. Brush the edges with beaten egg and seal well. Brush the top of the pastry with beaten egg and use a fork to punch several holes in pastry in a decorative manner. Preheat oven to 400°F (200°C) and bake 25 minutes. • Serve with Sherry Mushroom Cream Sauce page 141. • Serves 8-10.

A cut lemon may be kept longer by smearing the cut surface with the white of an egg.

2 tbsp.	butter	30 mL
1½ cups	sliced mushrooms	375 mL
2 tbsp.	flour	30 mL
1 cup	light cream	250 mL
2 tbsp.	whipping cream	30 mL
2 tbsp.	sherry	30 mL
	salt and pepper	

SHERRY MUSHROOM CREAM SAUCE

Melt butter in a saucepan and sauté mushrooms for 2-3 minutes. • Stir in flour, then gradually pour in light cream, stirring continuously over medium heat until thickened. • Stir in whipping cream and sherry, then season with salt and pepper. • Serve hot with Pacific Salmon Wellington. • Makes about 2½ cups (675 mL).

3-4 lb.	whole pink salmon	1.5-2 kg
1	onion in rings	1
1	green pepper, sliced	1
2	tomatoes, sliced	2
1	lemon, sliced	1
3	strips side bacon	3

WHOLE SALMON

Rinse and dry salmon. Place salmon on a sheet of foil. Put a layer of sliced onion, green pepper, tomato, and lemon in cavity of salmon. Place a layer of each on top of salmon. • Place strips of side bacon over top. • Fold up foil at top. Leave a small opening to let out steam. • Place in roasting pan. Do not cover the roasting pan. • Bake in 375°F (190°C) oven for 1 hour. Allow 15 to 20 minutes extra for salmon, if it's partly frozen. • We enjoy this salmon served with rice, mixed vegetables and salad greens. • Serves 4-6.

2	herrings per person	2
	oatmeal	
	salt and pepper	
1-2 oz.	butter	30-55 g
1 tbsp.	vegetable oil	15 mL
1	small onion	1
1 oz.	butter	30 g
½ oz.	flour	15 g
1 tsp.	dry mustard	5 mL
1-2 tbsp.	vinegar	15-25 mL
½ cup	water	125 mL

HERRINGS IN OATMEAL

MUSTARD SAUCE
(Enough for 4 herrings)

Sprinkle herrings with salt and pepper, then dip into oatmeal until well coated. Press oatmeal into the flesh to make it stick. • Meanwhile, heat butter and oil gently. Fry herrings, split side down until well browned; then turn and fry the other side, about 8 minutes altogether. Do not allow pan to get too hot, otherwise oatmeal will burn and fish will become too dry. The oatmeal should be crisp and the flesh moist and succulent. • To prepare Mustard Sauce, chop onion finely and fry in butter until lightly browned. Add flour and mustard, then vinegar and water. Bring to a boil and simmer gently for 3 minutes, stirring constantly.

PASTA

NO-BOIL LASAGNE

1	medium onion, chopped	1
1	garlic clove, minced	1
1 tbsp.	vegetable oil	15 mL
1 lb.	ground beef	500 g
2 x 14 oz.	cans tomato sauce	2 x 398 mL
1 x 10 oz.	can sliced mushrooms	1 x 284 mL
½ cup	water	125 mL
1 tsp.	oregano	5 mL
1 cup	creamed cottage cheese	250 mL
¼ cup	grated Parmesan	75 mL
10 oz.	pkg. frozen chopped spinach, (optional)	283 g
1	egg, slightly beaten	1
2 tsp.	vegetable oil	10 mL
1 tsp.	salt	5 mL
12 oz.	lasagne noodles, uncooked (enough for 3 layers)	375 g
6 oz.	mozzarella cheese, sliced	170 g

Sauté onion and garlic in oil. Add ground beef and brown. Remove excess fat.
● Stir in tomato sauce, mushrooms with their liquid, water and oregano; bring to a boil and remove from heat. ● Combine cottage cheese, Parmesan cheese, well-drained spinach, egg, oil and salt. ● Spoon ¼ of meat sauce into a 9″ x 13″ (22 cm x 33 cm) baking dish. Cover with ¼ of lasagne. Spread another ¼ of sauce over and cover with another ¼ of lasagne. Spread cheese and spinach mixture over and cover with remaining lasagne and sauce. Top with cheese slices. ● Cover with foil paper and bake at 375°F (190°C) for 45 minutes. ● Uncover and bake until cheese starts to brown, about 15 minutes. ● IF USING HOMEMADE SPA-GHETTI SAUCE: make sauce thinner than usual, or thin with water, otherwise lasagne will be dry. If omitting spinach, add 1 cup (250 mL) more cottage cheese. ● Serves 8.

1 lb.	ground beef	500 g
1	garlic clove	1
1 tsp.	dried parsley flakes	5 mL
1 tbsp.	basil	15 mL
1 tsp.	salt	5 mL
2 cups	canned tomatoes	500 mL
2 x 5½ oz.	cans tomato paste	2 x 156 mL
8	wide lasagne noodles	8
3 cups	cream-style cottage cheese OR ricotta	750 mL
2	eggs, beaten	2
1 tsp.	salt	5 mL
⅛ tsp.	pepper	0.5 mL
2 tsp.	parsley flakes	10 mL
½ cup	grated Parmesan	125 mL
1 lb.	mozzarella cheese slices	500 g

LASAGNE

Brown meat slowly, spoon off excess fat. Add next 6 ingredients. Simmer uncovered 30 minutes to blend flavors, stirring occasionally. • Cook noodles in boiling salted water until tender; drain; rinse in cold water. • Combine cottage cheese with eggs, seasonings and Parmesan cheese. • Place half the noodles in 13" x 9" x 2" (4L) baking pan, spread half the cottage cheese mixture over noodles. Next add half the mozzarella cheese slices and half the meat mixture. Repeat layers. • Bake at 375°F (190°C) for 30 minutes. Let stand 10 minutes before cutting into squares. Filling will then be slightly set. • Serves 12.

1 lb.	hamburger	500 g
¼ cup	chopped onion	75 mL
2 tbsp.	vegetable oil	30 mL
14 oz.	can tomato sauce	398 mL
1 tsp.	oregano	5 mL
½ tsp.	pepper	2 mL
3-4 lbs.	zucchini	1.5-2 kg
2 tbsp.	flour	30 mL
½ cup	creamed cottage cheese	125 mL
1	egg	1
1½ cups	shredded mozzarella cheese	375 mL

ZUCCHINI LASAGNE

Brown and cook meat and onions in oil. Drain off excess fat. • Add tomato sauce and spices. Heat to a boil and simmer 5 minutes. Stir. • Meanwhile, slice zucchini lengthwise into ¼" (0.6 cm) thick slices. • In a small bowl, combine cottage cheese with egg and mix well. • Arrange half of zucchini on bottom of 13" x 9" (4 L) pan and sprinkle with 1 tbsp. (15 mL) flour. • Top with cottage cheese mixture, and half the meat mixture, then the other half of cheese mixture. Repeat zucchini, flour and meat sauce layers. Top with shredded mozzarella. • Bake at 375°F (190°C) for 40 minutes.

CHICKEN LASAGNE

3 cups	sliced fresh mushrooms	750 mL
2 cups	chopped onions	500 mL
2 pkg.	Knorr Swiss Hollandaise Sauce, prepared	2 pkg.
1 lb.	lasagne noodles, cooked	500 g
2 lbs.	chicken OR turkey breast, cooked and thinly sliced	1 kg
3 cups	shredded mozzarella cheese	750 mL
1 cup	grated Parmesan	250 mL
2 x 12 oz.	cans asparagus tips, drained	2 x 341 mL
1 tsp.	dried basil	5 mL
1 tsp.	dried oregano	5 mL
	salt and pepper	

Sauté mushrooms and onions until soft. • Using 2, 9" x 13" (4 L) pans. In each pan, spread a small amount of hollandaise on the bottom and place a layer of noodles on top, *then cover each pan with ¼ of the chicken and sprinkle with salt and pepper. Top each pan with ¼ of the mushroom mixture, then ¼ of the remaining hollandaise and sprinkle ¼ of the basil and oregano. Top this with ¼ of the mozzarella and Parmesan cheese*. • Place ½ of the asparagus tips neatly in a layer over the cheese, in each pan • Repeat from * to *. • Cook uncovered in a 340°F (170°C) oven for 35 minutes, or until hot and bubbly.

TAGLIATELLE PORTOFINO

Delicious Italian shrimp/clam sauce for pasta.

2 tbsp.	butter	30 mL
¼ cup	olive oil	50 mL
½ lb.	raw shrimp	250 g
½ lb.	fresh scallops	250 g
5 oz.	can clams	142 g
¾ cup	minced onion	175 mL
3	garlic cloves, crushed	3
¼ tsp.	dry basil	1 mL
2 tsp.	salt	10 mL
½ tsp.	pepper	2 mL
16 oz.	can Italian peeled tomatoes	500 mL
¾ cup	chopped fresh basil (use less if dried)	175 mL

Sauté shrimp and scallops in butter for 3 minutes and remove from heat. • Sauté onion and garlic in oil and add tomatoes, clams and seasoning. Cook until thickened. • Add shrimp and scallops to heated mixture. • Serve with your favorite pasta.

PASTA
Elegant Up-To-Date Macaroni and Cheese, page 145

3½ cups	large bow-tie pasta	875 mL
3 tbsp.	butter	45 mL
2 tbsp.	flour	30 mL
1 cup	chicken broth	250 mL
¾ cup	milk	175 mL
¾ cup	grated sharp Cheddar cheese	175 mL
¼ cup	grated Parmesan cheese	75 mL
¼ tsp.	salt	1 mL
⅛ tsp.	paprika	0.5 mL
pinch	black pepper	pinch
2 cups	broccoli florets	500 mL
1 cup	diced sweet red pepper	250 mL
1 cup	sliced mushrooms	250 mL
¾ cup	sliced green onion	175 mL

ELEGANT UP-TO-DATE MACARONI AND CHEESE

Cook bow-tie pasta and drain. • As bow-ties cook, melt 2 tbsp. (25 mL) butter in medium saucepan. Add flour and stir until blended. Add chicken broth and milk, stir over medium heat until mixture comes to a boil and thickens. Reduce heat to low. Stir in cheeses, salt, paprika and pepper. Stir until cheese is melted. • In a large skillet, melt remaining 1 tbsp. (15 mL) butter over medium heat. Add broccoli, red pepper, mushrooms and onion. • Cook, stirring constantly for 2 minutes. Reduce heat to low. • Stir in drained pasta and sauce. • Serves 4-6. • For presentation, see photograph page 144A.

1 lb.	fettuccini	500 g
1 lb.	hot Italian sausage (6-8)	500 g
2 tbsp.	vegetable oil	30 mL
1	large onion, coarsely chopped	1
1 cup	sliced fresh mushrooms	250 mL
28 oz.	can Italian plum tomatoes	796 mL
2 tbsp.	fresh sage OR ½ tsp. (2 mL) dried sage	25 mL
½ tsp.	sugar	2 mL
½ tsp.	basil	2 mL
	salt, to taste	
	cayenne pepper	

ITALIAN SAUSAGE AND FRESH SAGE WITH PASTA

Cook pasta. • Remove casing from sausage. Heat oil, add sausage and cook until lightly browned, working with forks to keep meat separated. • Add onion, mushrooms and juice from tomatoes. • Chop tomatoes and add, along with seasonings and sugar. • Boil gently, uncovered, reduce to desired thickness.

CANNELLONI

4	eggs	4
1 cup	flour	250 mL
½ tsp.	salt	2 mL
1½ cups	milk	375 mL
3 tbsp.	butter OR margarine, melted	45 mL

FILLING

1 lb.	ground beef	500 g
1	large onion, chopped (1 cup [250 mL])	1
2	slices white bread, crumbled (1 cup [250 mL])	2
1	egg, beaten	1
½ cup	parsley flakes	125 mL
1 tsp.	basil flakes	5 mL
1 tsp.	salt	5 mL
¼ tsp.	pepper	1 mL

Crêpes: Combine first 5 ingredients in order, in blender, and blend until smooth. Refrigerate at least 2 hours. Heat 8″ (20 cm) skillet or crêpe pan. Grease pan lightly with butter or margarine. Pour batter, scant ¼ cup (50 mL) at a time, into pan. Cook 1-2 minutes. Layer between wax paper to prevent sticking. Makes 12 x 8″ (20 cm) crêpes.

Filling: Shape ground beef into a large patty in bottom of a large skillet, brown 5 minutes. Cut into quarters and turn, brown 5 minutes longer. Break into small pieces. Remove with slotted spoon and drain on paper towel. Sauté onions and garlic until soft in drippings. Remove from heat, add cooked meat with bread crumbs, egg, parsley, basil, salt and pepper to skillet and mix well. Spread ¼ cup (50 mL) of filling on each crêpe and roll up crêpes.

TOMATO SAUCE FOR CANNELLONI

1	large onion, chopped	1
1	garlic clove, minced	1
	oil	
28 oz.	can tomatoes	796 mL
5½ oz.	can tomato paste	156 mL
2 tsp.	crushed leaf basil	10 mL
1 tsp.	crumbled leaf rosemary	5 mL
	salt, to taste	
1 cup	dry red wine OR beef broth	250 mL

Sauté onions and garlic in oil in large saucepan until soft. • Stir in tomatoes, tomato paste, basil, rosemary, salt and beef broth. • Bring to a bubbling boil, reduce heat and simmer, uncovered, 1 hour or until sauce thickens. • Cool, cover and refrigerate. • Use within 2 weeks.

---

3 cups	light cream OR milk	750 mL
1	bay leaf	1
¼ cup	butter OR margarine	75 mL
¼ cup	flour	75 mL
2 tsp.	instant chicken broth mix	10 mL
1 tsp.	salt	5 mL
¼ tsp.	white pepper	1.5 mL
dash	ground nutmeg	dash

BECHAMEL SAUCE FOR CANNELLONI

Combine above ingredients and cook until thickened.

TO ASSEMBLE CANNELLONI:
Spoon Tomato Sauce into bottom of 9" x 8" (2.5 L) casserole dish. • Place stuffed crêpes on top of Tomato Sauce. • Cover with Bechamel Sauce and bake at 350°F (180°C) for 45 minutes.

½ lb.	ground beef	250 g
¼ cup	minced onion	75 mL
¼ cup	chopped green pepper	50 mL
5½ oz.	can tomato paste	156 mL
2 cups	water	500 mL
½ tsp.	pepper	2 mL
1½ tsp.	salt	7 mL
1 tsp.	sugar	5 mL
1½ tsp.	Italian seasoning	7 mL
8-9	manicotti shells	8-9
1 cup	ricotta cheese OR dry curd cottage cheese (½ lb. [250 g])	250 mL
½ lb.	mozzarella cheese, shredded	250 g
1	egg	1

MANICOTTI

Sauté meat, onion, and green pepper. Drain off fat. Add tomato paste, water, salt, pepper, sugar and Italian seasoning. Simmer about 2 hours. • Partially boil manicotti shells in salted water for 4 minutes. Drain in colander. • Combine ricotta or cottage cheese, mozzarella cheese and egg. Fill shells, using small spoon. • Place shells in shallow baking dish, 8" x 11" (3 L). Cover with sauce and bake, covered, in 350°F (180°C) oven for 20 minutes. Remove cover and bake additional 20 minutes. • For a very cheesy variation, try 1-2 lbs. (0.5-1 kg) mozzarella cheese.

Add a little cooking oil in the water when boiling macaroni or spaghetti. It will keep the pasta from boiling over and prevent it from sticking together.

VEGETABLE SAUCE FOR PASTA

3	medium onions, coarsely chopped	3
2	large garlic cloves, minced	2
½ cup	olive oil	125 mL
2	large stalks celery, sliced	2
2	green peppers, chopped	2
1	red pepper, chopped	1
1 cup	chopped zucchini	250 mL
1-1½ cups	peeled and diced eggplant (1 small)	250-375 mL
6-8	fresh tomatoes, peeled and chopped OR 14 oz. (398 mL) can peeled plum tomatoes	6-8
1 cup	grated carrots (optional)	250 mL
1 tbsp.	chopped fresh basil OR 1 tsp. (5 mL) dried basil	15 mL
2 tbsp.	chopped parsley	30 mL
2-3 tsp.	sugar	10-15 mL
1-2 tsp.	salt, OR to taste	5-10 mL
	black pepper, to taste	
½-1 tsp.	cinnamon	2-5 mL
½-1 cup	dry red wine OR ½ cup (125 mL) sweet vermouth OR Cinzano, plus ½ cup (125 mL) dry red wine	125-250 mL
	freshly grated Parmesan cheese	

Sauté onion and garlic in oil until clear (don't burn). ● Add celery, peppers, zucchini, eggplant, tomatoes and carrots, if using. Grated carrots add a sweetness, if desired. ● Cook over medium heat until steaming and add basil, parsley and sugar. Add salt, pepper, cinnamon and wine. Cook slowly. ● If too thick, add a little water or tinned tomato juice. Cook until desired thickness. ● Use this sauce with any pasta noodle, preferably flat noodles like fettucine, or small shells. ● Sprinkle with freshly grated Parmesan cheese. ● A chicken baked with Italian spices goes well with this sauce. ● And remember, pasta is good for you! Look what it does for hockey players!

Add ½ tsp. (2 mL) white sugar to the water when cooking frozen peas. The color will be much brighter.

Desserts

CHEESECAKE PLUS

LUSCIOUS LEMON CHEESECAKE

24	slices zwieback OR 2⅔ cups (650 mL) graham crumbs	24
½ cup	icing sugar*	125 mL
1½ tsp.	grated lemon peel	7 mL
½ cup	softened butter	125 mL

FILLING

2½ lbs.	cream cheese	1.25 kg
1¾ cups	sugar	425 mL
3 tbsp.	all-purpose flour	45 mL
1½ tsp.	grated lemon peel	7 mL
½ tsp.	vanilla	2 mL
5	eggs, slightly beaten	5
2	egg yolks, slightly beaten	2
¼ cup	whipping cream	50 mL

To make crust, blend all ingredients with fork. Butter bottom and sides of a 9″ (22 cm) springform pan. Reserve ¾ cup (175 mL) of crumbs. Evenly spread remaining crumbs over sides and bottom of pan. • To make filling, beat first 5 ingredients until smooth and fluffy. Gradually add the slightly beaten eggs and the egg yolks, beating thoroughly. Blend in the whipping cream. Spread evenly in pan. Sprinkle reserved crumb mixture over top. • Bake at 250°F (120°C) for 1 hour. Turn off heat. Let stand in oven 1 hour longer. • Remove to cooling rack to cool for 4-6 hours. • Chill in refrigerator overnight. • Serves 16-20.

NOTE: Icing, confectioner's and powdered sugar are interchangeable.

Egg whites will whip faster and to a greater volume when brought to room temperature before beating.

150

36	chocolate wafers	36
¼ cup	melted butter	75 mL
1	egg, separated	1
1 cup	whipping cream	250 mL
8 oz.	soft cream cheese	250 g
⅔ cup	icing sugar	150 mL
⅔ cup	raspberry juice, undiluted, (other juices may be substituted)	150 mL
1 tsp.	lemon juice	5 mL

FROZEN RASPBERRY CHEESECAKE

Crush wafers to yield about 1½ cups (375 mL) crumbs. Blend in melted butter. Spread with fingers and press into a greased 9" (22 cm) pie plate or 8½" (21 cm) springform pan. Freeze while preparing cheesecake. • Assemble all ingredients before beginning. Beat egg whites until stiff, then beat whipping cream. Set aside. Beat cream cheese, gradually adding sugar, until smooth. Beat in egg yolk, then juices. Fold whipped cream into cheese mixture, then fold in egg white. Pour into crust, freeze until firm, about 4 hours or overnight. • To serve, let sit at room temperature a few minutes before cutting. Garnish with frozen raspberries, chocolate curls or leaves and/or whipped cream. • Serves 8-10. • See photograph page 192A.

1¼ cups	chocolate wafer cookie crumbs (about 24 cookies)	300 mL
¼ cup	sugar	50 mL
¼ cup	butter OR margarine, melted	50 mL
8 oz.	pkg. cream cheese, softened	250 g
10 oz.	can Eagle Brand sweetened, condensed milk (not evaporated)	300 mL
⅔ cup	chocolate syrup	150 mL
2 tbsp.	instant coffee	30 mL
1 tsp.	hot water	5 mL
1 cup	whipping cream, whipped	250 mL

FROZEN MOCHA CHEESECAKE

In small bowl, combine crumbs, sugar and butter. • In buttered 9" (22 cm) springform pan, or 9" x 13" (22 cm x 33 cm) baking dish, pat crumbs firmly on bottom and up sides of pan. • Chill. • In large mixing bowl, beat cheese until fluffy, add Eagle Brand milk and chocolate syrup. • In small bowl dissolve coffee in water. Add to Eagle Brand mixture. Mix well. • Fold in whipped cream. • Pour into prepared pan. Cover. • Freeze for 6 hours, or until firm. • Garnish with additional chocolate crumbs, if desired, or grated chocolate. • Return leftovers to freezer. Very filling! Enjoy! • Serves 12-15.

SINFUL CHOCOLATE CHEESE TORTE

1¼ cups	graham wafer crumbs	325 mL
3 tbsp.	sugar	45 mL
3 tbsp.	cocoa	45 mL
¼ cup	butter, melted	75 mL
12 oz.	cream cheese, softened	350 g
¾ cup	sugar	175 mL
2	eggs	2
1 tbsp.	coffee-flavored liqueur OR rum	15 mL
1 tsp.	vanilla	5 mL
8 oz.	carton sour cream	250 mL
FILLING #1 — 1 oz.	unsweetened chocolate, grated	30 g
1½ tsp.	instant coffee	7 mL
FILLING #2 — 2 tbsp.	boiling water	30 mL
4 oz.	squares semisweet chocolate	115 g
4	eggs, separated	4
¼ cup	sugar	75 mL
1 tbsp.	coffee-flavored liqueur OR rum	15 mL
½ tsp.	vanilla	2 mL
	whipping cream	

To make crust, preheat oven to 350°F (180°C). Blend crumbs, sugar, cocoa and melted butter together. Press firmly on bottom and sides of a 9″ (22 cm) springform pan. Bake 10 minutes. Cool while preparing filling. • To make filling #1, beat softened cream cheese in large bowl with electric mixer at high speed until light and fluffy. Gradually beat in sugar. Add 2 eggs, 1 at a time, beating well after each addition. Add liqueur and vanilla. Turn into baked crust. Bake at 350°F (180°C) for 30 minutes. Cool on wire rack. Gently spread sour cream over baked layer. Sprinkle with grated chocolate. Regrigerate. • To make filling # 2, dissolve coffee in boiling water. Place in double boiler over hot water. Add chocolate squares. Stir until melted. Beat the 4 egg yolks until thick. Gradually beat in sugar and add small amount of chocolate mixture. Beat well. Continue adding chocolate to the egg in small amounts until all has been used. Add liqueur and vanilla. Beat egg whites until fluffy. Gently fold into chocolate mixture. Spread over cooled baked layer, refrigerate until firm. When ready to serve, loosen sides of pan and remove. Decorate with whipped cream. • Serves 12.

To keep cut fruit from turning brown, dip it in a mixture of lemon juice and water. Use the juice of 1 lemon to a quart (litre) of water.

2 cups	crushed chocolate wafers (1 pkg.)	500mL
½ cup	butter, melted	125 mL
1 tbsp.	unflavored gelatin (7 g pkg).	15 mL
¼ cup	cold water	50 mL
¼ cup	white rum	75 mL
6	egg yolks	6
1 cup	white sugar	250 mL
2 cups	whipping cream, whipped	500 mL
	kiwi fruit, peeled and sliced	
	mandarin oranges, drained	
	maraschino cherries, halved	

RUM CREAM TORTE

Combine wafers and butter and press on bottom and sides of a 9″ (22 cm) spring-form pan. • Soak gelatin in water. Bring to a slight boil to dissolve, then cool slightly. • Add rum, set aside. • Beat egg yolks until thick, then slowly add sugar, beating constantly. • Fold in cooled gelatin mixture, then gently fold in whipped cream. • Pour into wafer-lined pan. • Wrap well and freeze. • Can be frozen for several months. • Defrost, garnish and serve.

10 oz.	sweetened condensed milk	300 mL
13 oz.	evaporated milk	369 mL
2 qts.	homogenized milk	2 L
2½ tbsp.	custard powder	37 mL
3 tbsp.	cold milk	45 mL
½ tsp.	ground cardamom	2 mL
½ cup	ground unsalted almonds	125 mL
½ cup	ground pistachio nuts	125 mL

KULFI

A delicious Indian ice cream!

In a heavy saucepan, mix the condensed, evaporated and homogenized milks and bring to a boil. Reduce heat to low and cook for about 30 minutes, stirring occasionally to avoid sticking. • In a cup, mix the custard powder and cold milk. Add this mixture to the hot milk and keep stirring until custard thickens enough to coat the back of a spoon. • Grind the almonds and pistachios; add to the milk and add the ground cardamom. Cook for a couple of minutes. • Cool the mixture and stir occasionally to avoid a skin from forming on the top. • Pour into a glass dish, cover with plastic wrap and foil. • Freeze overnight. • Serves 12.

APRICOTS AND PEACHES ripen best at room temperature. Cherries do not ripen further after being picked.

SPOOM

*A refreshing sorbet, delicious!
A great pallet cleanser before
serving your entrée dish.*

1 cup	sugar	250 mL
½ cup	water	125 mL
4	egg whites, at room temp.	4
1 qt.	lemon sherbet, softened	1 L

Early in day, or up to 1 week before serving, combine in a medium saucepan the sugar and the water. Cook over medium heat just until temperature reaches 238°F (114°C) on candy thermometer, or until syrup forms thin threads when dropped from a spoon onto waxed paper. • Meanwhile, in a large bowl, with mixer at high speed, beat the egg whites until soft peaks form. • Continue beating, pouring hot syrup in a thin thread into whites. • Stir in the lemon sherbet. • Spoon into 12 freezer-proof stemmed glasses, or dessert dishes, to about ¾ full. • Cover and freeze. • To serve, at the table, pour a few tablespoons (30 mL) rosé, white wine, or champagne on top of each serving. • Serves 12.

TANGY FRUIT COMBO

⅔ cup	fresh orange juice	150 mL
2 tbsp.	lemon juice	30 mL
¼ cup	white sugar	75 mL
2 tbsp.	grated orange rind	30 mL
1 tsp.	grated lemon rind	5 mL
⅛ tsp.	salt	0.5 mL
3	peaches	3
3	pears	3
1 cup	blueberries, fresh OR frozen	250 mL

Combine juices, sugar, orange and lemon rind and salt in small saucepan. Bring to a boil. Lower heat and simmer 5 minutes. Pour into shallow metal pan and place in freezer until ice crystals form around the edges. • Peel and slice peaches; peel and cube pears. Combine fruit and orange juice mixture. • Spoon into 6 sherbet glasses and garnish with a sprig of mint. • Serves 6.

SINFUL CHOCOLATE MOUSSE

8 oz.	semisweet chocolate	250 g
½ cup	strong coffee	125 mL
5	eggs, separated	5
5 tbsp.	sugar	75 mL
½ cup	whipping cream	125 mL
4 tbsp.	brandy, rum OR cointreau (or more)	60 mL

Break chocolate into a pan. Place pan over boiling water and melt chocolate. • Stir in coffee. • Remove from heat. • In another bowl, beat together egg yolks and sugar until foamy. • Fold egg mixture into chocolate. • Beat egg whites until stiff. • In a separate bowl, beat cream until stiff. Fold into egg whites. Then fold egg white and cream mixture into chocolate mixture. • Pour into a large serving bowl, or individual serving dishes. • Just before serving, pour brandy, rum or cointreau over finished mousse. • Serves 6.

2 x 10 oz.	pkgs. frozen strawberries, thawed, drained, reserving liquid unflavored gelatin (2 x 7 g pkgs.)	2 x 283 g
2 tbsp.	unflavored gelatin (2 x 7 g pkgs.)	30 mL
4 tbsp.	dark rum OR to taste	60 mL
1½ cups	heavy cream	375 mL

STRAWBERRY MOUSSE

In a food processor, chop the strawberries coarsely. • In a small saucepan, sprinkle the gelatin over the reserved strawberry syrup, combined with the rum. Let it soften for 5 minutes. Heat the mixture over moderate-low heat, stirring until the gelatin is dissolved. • With the processor running, add the gelatin mixture in a stream to the strawberry purée and blend the mixture until it is combined.
• Transfer the strawberry mixture to a metal bowl, set in a larger bowl of ice and cold water, and stir the mixture until it is cold and slightly thickened, but do not let it begin to set. • In a chilled bowl, beat the cream until it holds soft peaks and then fold into the strawberry mixture. • Chill for several hours and decorate with fresh sliced strawberries and whipped cream, if desired, or strawberry syrup made with strawberry juice and cornstarch.

¼ lb.	sugar (10 tbsp. [150 mL])	125 g
6	egg yolks	6
6	sheets husblas (a European sheet gelatin available in most German or Danish deli's)	6
¼ cup	hot water	50 mL
1 cup	rum	250 mL
2 cups	whipping cream	500 mL
28 oz.	can sweet dark pitted cherries	796 L
1 cup	water, mixed with 1-2 tbsp. (15-25 mL) cornstarch OR potato flour	250 mL

RUM FROMAGE WITH HOT CHERRY SAUCE

SAUCE

Beat sugar and egg yolks until pale yellow. • Dissolve husblas in hot water after softening sheets by immersing them in cold water. Add the husblas and the rum to the egg mixture. • Whip the cream until stiff, fold in rum-egg mixture until blended completely. • Pour into decorative bowl, refrigerate until serving time. • To make sauce, heat cherries and juice, add cornstarch mixture to thicken. Cook 2 minutes. Serve hot over Rum Fromage in dessert bowls.

LEMON MOUSSE

Citron fromage.

2	eggs	2
½ cup	white sugar	125 mL
1	lemon, grated rind and juice of	1
2 tbsp.	unflavored gelatin (2 x 7 g pkgs.)	30 mL
1 cup	whipping cream	250 mL

Separate eggs. • Beat yolks with sugar until white. • Add lemon juice and grated lemon rind. • Soak the gelatin in cold water for about 10 minutes. Stir into egg yolks. • Beat the egg whites stiffly. Beat the whipping cream stiffly. Then stir both into the egg yolk mixture as soon as it begins to stiffen. • Pour the mousse into a bowl and let it stand in a cold place for a few hours to set. Decorate with whipped cream before serving, and perhaps a sprinkle of grated lemon rind. • A Danish Christmas treat — light and tangy.

ALMOND APRICOT COFFEE TRIFLE

1	layer sponge cake, about ½ lb. (250 g)	1
6 tbsp.	sherry	90 mL
30	crisp almond macaroons	30
2 x 28 oz.	can apricots	2 x 796 mL
1 cup	whipping cream	250 mL
1 tbsp.	icing sugar	15 mL
1 tsp.	almond extract	5 mL
¼ cup	chopped toasted almonds	50 mL

SOFT CUSTARD SAUCE

4	egg yolks	4
2 cups	light cream	500 mL
4 tbsp.	sugar	60 mL
⅛ tsp.	salt	0.5 mL
1 tsp.	vanilla	5 mL
1½ tsp.	instant coffee	7 mL

Prepare custard by beating together egg yolks, cream, sugar and salt. Cook in double boiler, stirring, until mixture coats spoon. Add vanilla and instant coffee. Cool. • Place cake in bottom of a large, deep glass bowl and sprinkle with 4 tbsp. (60 mL) sherry. Arrange macaroons on top. Sprinkle with 1 tbsp. (15 mL) sherry. Drain apricots and arrange half over macaroons. Repeat another layer of macaroons, sherry and apricots. Arrange leftover macaroons around side of bowl. Pour cooled custard sauce over contents in the bowl and chill covered for at least 4 hours. • To serve, whip the cream until stiff and flavor with icing sugar and almond flavoring. Swirl on top of trifle and garnish with almonds. • Note: Macaroons are available at some Italian bakeries.

To keep meringue from weeping, add 1 tbsp. (15 mL) water per egg before beating.

156

4 tsp.	unflavored gelatin	20 mL
½ cup	cold water	125 mL
1 cup	granulated sugar	250 mL
pinch	salt	pinch
2 cups	hot water	500 mL
1 tbsp.	grated lemon peel	15 mL
½ cup	lemon juice	125 mL
6	egg whites	6
½ cup	granulated sugar	125 mL

CHRISTMAS SNOW

Sprinkle gelatin on cold water in a large bowl. Let soften 5 minutes. • Add 1 cup (250 mL) sugar, salt, hot water and stir until gelatin is dissolved. • Add lemon rind and lemon juice; stir. • Cool until small amount mounds when dropped from a spoon (may take several hours). • Beat egg whites until they form moist peaks. • Add ½ cup (125 mL) sugar slowly, beating until stiff. • Add to gelatin mixture, beating with a hand beater until thoroughly combined. • Pour into a large glass bowl, or 12-15 sherbet dishes. • Cool, lightly covered with waxed paper; may be kept overnight in the refrigerator. • Serve with Custard Sauce, below, and if desired, a drizzle of crème de menthe and a cherry. Pass extra custard sauce. • Our family has preferred this dessert with Christmas dinner for at least 20 years; the steamed pudding is saved for Boxing Day to follow leftovers. • Serves 12-15.

2 cups	milk	500 mL
6	egg yolks	6
3 tbsp.	granulated sugar	45 mL
¼ tsp.	salt	1 mL
1 tsp.	vanilla	5 mL

CUSTARD SAUCE

Preferably cook in a double boiler but a heavy enamelled, glass or ceramic saucepan over low heat will be satisfactory. • Heat milk slowly until tiny bubbles appear around edge. • In medium bowl, beat egg yolks slightly with a fork, then stir in sugar and salt. • Add hot milk slowly, stirring to avoid cooked egg specks. Pour back in saucepan. • Cook over low heat, stirring constantly, until thick enough to coat a spoon with a thin film of custard. • Then remove from heat at once and pour into a chilled bowl. • Let cool, add vanilla, cover and chill thoroughly. • Custard sauce is even more delicous if made the day before serving. • Serve with Christmas Snow, above, or hot puddings, or use to make trifle.

To substitute cocoa for chocolate use 3 tbsp. (45 mL) cocoa in place of each 1 oz. (30 g) square of chocolate called for. If substituting cocoa for chocolate in batter, also add 1 tbsp. (15 mL) shortening for every 3 tbsp. (45 mL) cocoa used.

LEMON CURD

¼ lb.	butter (½ cup [125 mL])	125 g
2 cups	sugar	500 mL
6	egg yolks, beaten	6
4	egg whites, beaten	4
3	lemons, grated rind of 2 and juice of 3	3

Melt the butter slowly in a double boiler. • Add the sugar and the beaten eggs, the rind and the juice of the lemons and cook carefully until thick. • This is delicious as a filling for small tarts and absolutely sinful to put on toast. It is a rich lemon filling not suitable for pie, unless you are really decadent. My grandmother used to make this and my mother made it and so have I. I don't know how old this recipe is, but my grandmother passed away many years ago and my mother is 93 years old. I won't say how many years I have been making it!

PAVLOVA

4	egg whites	4
1 cup	white sugar	250 mL
½ tsp.	vanilla	2 mL
1 tsp.	vinegar	5 mL
2 cups	whipping cream fresh fruit	500 mL
½ cup	toasted slivered almonds	125 mL

Whip egg whites until they form peaks, gradually add sugar, vanilla and vinegar. Continue beating until very stiff. • Spread, on waxed paper or brown paper, on cookie sheet,in a circle slightly smaller than desired size. • Bake 1 hour at 200°F (100°C). Turn off oven and leave meringue in to dry for several hours. • Top with whipped cream, fresh fruit and almonds.

MICROWAVE PAVLOVA

4	egg whites	4
1 cup	berry (castor) sugar	250 mL
½ tsp.	vanilla	2 mL
1 tsp	vinegar	5 mL
1 tbsp.	melted butter	15 mL
	cornstarch	
	whipped cream	
3-4	kiwi fruit	3-4

Beat egg whites until soft peaks form. Add ½ cup (125 mL) berry sugar, beat until dissolved, beat in remaining sugar, add vanilla and vinegar, beating 1 minute. • Grease 9″ (22 cm) or 10″ (25 cm) pie plate, or deep bowl, with melted butter; dust with cornstarch, shake off excess. • Spoon meringue into dish leaving a higher outside edge than center. • Cook 3-4 minutes in microwave oven on HIGH. • Place under preheated grill until pale gold, if desired. • Fill with whipped cream, covering the Pavlova top. • Cover Pavlova with your favorite seasonal fruit, strawberries and kiwi are perfect!

5	egg yolks	5	
1 cup	berry sugar	250 mL	*STRAWBERRIES*
1 cup	liqueur	250 mL	*ROMANOFF*
1 cup	heavy whipping cream, whipped	250 mL	
1 qt.	strawberries, hulled	1 L	*Positively decadent!*

Beat egg yolks until lemon colored. • Slowly beat in the sugar. • Add liqueur of your choice (Grand Marnier, Cointreau, kirsch, brandy, rum or sherry). • Cook until custard coats spoon. Stirring constantly. (I use defrost in microwave oven, stirring every 30 seconds until it thickens.) Cool. Fold into whipped cream. • Fold in, or pour over, the hulled whole strawberries. • This sauce may be kept in the refrigerator for several days if you add 1 tsp. (5 mL) of Whip it. • Variation: Pour sauce over blueberries or Saskatoons. Put under preheated broiler until golden. • See photograph page 160A.

2	firm ripe small bananas, peeled	2	
1 tbsp.	lemon juice	15 mL	*SPECIAL*
¼ cup	brown sugar	50 mL	*BANANAS*
2 tbsp.	butter	30 mL	*FOSTER*
dash	cinnamon	dash	
3 tbsp.	light rum	45 mL	
	vanilla ice cream		

Cut bananas in half lengthwise, then crosswise into quarters. Drizzle with lemon juice. • Heat sugar and butter in a 10″ (25 cm) skillet until sugar is melted and caramelized. • Add bananas and cook slowly 1-2 minutes until heated. Add rum. Ignite. • Serve warm over vanilla ice cream. • Serves 2.

¼ cup	milk	75 mL	
2 tbsp.	vegetable oil	30 mL	*BAKED*
1	egg yolk	1	*APPLE*
2 cups	biscuit mix	500 mL	*DESSERT*
4	medium baking apples, cored	4	
2 tbsp.	raisins	30 mL	
2 tbsp.	chopped walnuts	30 mL	
2 cups	packed brown sugar	500 mL	
1½ cups	apple juice	375 mL	

Beat the milk, oil and egg yolk slightly. • Stir in the biscuit mix. • Knead on floured board until smooth, about 10 times. • Roll dough into 4 squares. • Place 1 apple on each square; fill the center with raisins and nuts. Moisten corners of the squares; bring opposite corners up over apple and press together, folding in sides. • Place apples in ungreased baking dish. • Heat brown sugar and apple juice to boiling, carefully pour around apples. • Bake at 400°F (200°C) for about 40 minutes, until the crusts have browned. Baste apples with syrup 2 or 3 times while baking. • Serve topped with ice cream, or whipping cream.

FLAMING PEACHES

28 oz.	can peach halves	796 mL
½ cup	peach syrup	125 mL
½ cup	brandy	125 mL
	ice cream	

Preheat chafing dish. • Warm peach halves in syrup on stove and then arrange the peaches in a chafing dish. • Bring syrup to boil and reduce slightly and then ladle over peaches. Bring syrup to boil again in chafing dish. • Meanwhile, heat brandy in small pan. • Ignite brandy and pour over peaches. • Serve at the table over ice cream. • Serves 6.

BAKLAVA

20	sheets phyllo pastry	20
¾ cup	melted unsalted butter	175 mL
2 cups	finely chopped walnuts	500 mL
1 cup	finely chopped almonds	250 mL
¼ cup	castor (berry) sugar	50 mL
2 tsp.	ground cinnamon	10 mL
⅛ tsp.	ground cloves	0.5 mL

SYRUP

1½ cups	sugar	375 mL
1½ cups	water	375 mL
¼ cup	honey	50 mL
	thinly peeled strip of lemon rind	
	small piece cinnamon bark	
3	cloves	3
2 tsp.	lemon juice	10 mL

Butter base and sides of 13″ x 9″ x 2″ (22cm x 33 cm) oven dish and place 9 sheets of phyllo separately into dish, brushing each with melted butter. • Mix nuts, sugar and spices and spread half of this mixture over pastry and top with another 2 sheets of phyllo, brushing each with butter. • Spread remaining nuts on top and finish with remaining phyllo, brushing each sheet as before. • Trim edges and brush top with butter. • Cut baklava with a sharp knife into diamond shapes. • Sprinkle lightly with water to prevent top layer curling upward. • Bake on center shelf in a moderately slow oven for 30 minutes, move up 1 shelf and cook for further 30 minutes. • Cover with greased brown paper or foil, if top colors too quickly. Pastry must be allowed to cook thoroughly. • When baklava goes into the oven, make the syrup. Place sugar, water and honey in a heavy pan and stir over medium heat until sugar is dissolved, add remaining syrup ingredients, bring to boil and boil for 15 minutes. Strain and cool. • Spoon syrup evenly over hot baklava. • Leave for several hours before cutting again into serving portions.

160

DESSERT
Profiteroles, page 161
Strawberries Romanoff, page 159

1 cup	water	250 mL
¼ tsp.	salt	1 mL
½ cup	butter OR margarine	125 mL
1 cup	flour	250 mL
4	eggs, at room temperature	4

PROFITEROLES

Cream Puffs.

10 oz.	semisweet chocolate	285 g
½ cup	butter OR margarine	125 mL

GLAZE

Put water, salt, and butter in saucepan; bring to a boil. • When boiling, add flour all at once and stir until it leaves the edges. Remove from heat and let cool about 2 minutes. • Beat in eggs, 1 at a time, beating each time until the dough no longer looks slippery. • Grease a cookie sheet and drop dough in small amounts, about 2 tsp. (10 mL). • Bake in preheated 400°F (200°C) oven for 10 minutes. Lower heat to 350°F (180°C) and bake about 25 minutes longer. • Cool puffs away from draft. • When cream puffs are cool, cut in half horizontally. • Prepare Chocolate Glaze by melting the semisweet chocolate and the butter together. • Fill with ice cream and pour chocolate glaze over. • Superb! • See photograph page 160A.

3 tbsp.	cornstarch	45 mL
1½ cups	milk	375 mL
½ cup	butter	125 mL
½ cup	icing sugar	125 mL
½ tsp.	vanilla	2 mL
1 cup	rice	250 mL
2 cups	boiling water	500 mL
½ cup	raisins	125 mL
1 tsp.	cinnamon	5 mL
½ tsp.	nutmeg	2 mL

MICROWAVE CREAMY RICE PUDDING

Combine cornstarch and milk in microwave bowl. Microwave for 2-3 minutes on HIGH. Add butter, sugar, and vanilla. Beat until creamy. Set aside and prepare rice. • Put rice and boiling water into 3-quart (3 L) casserole. Microwave for 15-18 minutes on medium, covered. Let stand 5 minutes. Add raisins and spices. Stir. Fold cream mixture into rice. Reheat 2-3 minutes on HIGH. Serve warm.

½ cup	short-grain rice	125 mL
½ cup	white sugar	125 mL
½ tsp.	salt	2 mL
3½ cups	milk	875 mL
1 tsp.	vanilla	5 mL
dash	nutmeg	dash
sprinkle	cinnamon	sprinkle
½ cup	raisins (optional)	125 mL

RICE PUDDING

Old-fashioned and delicious!

Mix all ingredients together in a 2½-quart (2.5 L) baking dish. • Bake at 300°F (150°C) for 2¼ hours without stirring.

SAILORS DUFF

1	egg	1
2 tbsp.	sugar	30 mL
½ cup	molasses	125 mL
2 tbsp.	melted butter	30 mL
1 tsp.	baking soda	5 mL
2 tbsp.	hot water	30 mL
1½ cups	flour	375 mL
½ cup	boiling water	125 mL

CARAMEL SAUCE

1¼ cups	brown sugar	300 mL
¾ cup	corn syrup	175 mL
4 tbsp.	butter	60 mL
¾ cup	cream	175 mL

Mix well the egg and sugar. Add the molasses. Beat in the melted butter. • Dissolve the baking soda in the hot water. Combine the soda mixture with the first mixture. Add the flour and boiling water. Beat together. • Steam in the upper part of a 1-quart (1 L) double boiler for 45 minutes. • Prepare sauce by boiling sugar, syrup and butter until soft-ball stage in cold water. Beat in the cream. • Serve warm. • Serves 6.

CARROT HALVA

5 cups	grated carrots	1.25 L
1 qt.	milk	1 L
1 cup	light cream	250 mL
1 cup	dark brown sugar combined with 1 tbsp. (15 mL) dark molasses	250 mL
½ cup	sugar	125 mL
4 oz.	toasted slivered almonds	115 g
¼ cup	butter OR margarine	50 mL
¼ tsp.	nutmeg saffron	1 mL
½ tsp.	cardamom toasted almonds for garnish	2 mL

In a saucepan, combine carrots, milk and cream. Bring to a boil, stirring constantly. • Lower heat and cook for approximately 1 hour, stirring occasionally. • Stir in sugars and continue cooking for about 10 minutes. • Lower heat to simmer, add almonds, butter or margarine, saffron and nutmeg and cook. • Stir in cardamom. • Mound on platter, or serve in bowls, and decorate top with toasted almonds.

Toasting coconut: sprinkle 1 cup (250 mL) flaked coconut in a microproof pie plate. Microwave 2-3 minutes on high, uncovered. Stir in 2 minutes.

PIES

8″	baked pie shell, not pricked	20 cm
sprinkle	icing sugar	sprinkle
4 cups	fresh strawberries OR raspberries	1 L
1 cup	sugar	250 mL
3 tbsp.	cornstarch	45 mL
1 tbsp.	lemon juice	15 mL
	whipping cream	

FRESH STRAWBERRY RASPBERRY PIE

Sprinkle icing sugar over bottom of baked pie shell. • Pick over the berries, picking out 2 cups (500 mL) of the nicest whole berries and hull them all. Arrange the best whole berries in a circle in the bottom of the pie shell, pointed ends up. • Coarsely chop or mash the remaining berries, and put into a small saucepan. • Mix sugar and cornstarch together and add to the chopped berries, cooking slowly until mixture is thick and clear. • Remove from heat and add lemon juice. • Pour this sauce over the berries in the pie shell. • Chill. • Top with whipped cream and a berry slice when ready to serve. • TERRIFIC TASTING PIE!!!

9″	pastry shell, unbaked	22 cm
4-8	apples, depending upon size	4-8
½ cup	sugar	125 mL
2 tbsp.	flour	30 mL
½ tsp.	nutmeg	2 mL
2 tbsp.	lemon juice	30 mL
½ cup	flour	125 mL
½ cup	butter	125 mL
½ cup	sugar OR honey	125 mL

BROWN PAPER BAG APPLE PIE

Prepare your favorite pastry shell. • Peel and quarter apples, cut them into chunks into a bowl with the sugar, flour and nutmeg. Toss and then drizzle lemon juice over them. Place in pastry shell. • Combine flour, butter and sugar, or honey, until well-mixed. Spread on apples. • Slide into paper bag, fold over end twice and fasten with paper clips. • Bake 1 hour at 425°F (220°C).

PEAR AND ALMOND TORTE

	Press-In Lemon Pastry, below	
4	medium, fresh pears OR 19 oz. (540 mL) can pears	4
4 oz.	pkg. cream cheese, softened.	125 g
1 cup	whipping cream	250 mL
¼ cup	powdered sugar	50 mL
2 tsp.	grated lemon peel	10 mL
1 tsp.	lemon juice	5 mL
¼ tsp.	EACH almond and vanilla extract	1 mL
2 tbsp.	Kirsch (optional)	30 mL
1 cup	apricot jam	250 mL
¼ cup	sliced OR slivered almonds, toasted	50 mL

Prepare and bake pastry. This can be done the day before. • To poach fresh pears bring to boil 1½ cups (375 mL) water, ¾ cup (175 mL) sugar and 1 tsp. (5 mL) each of grated lemon peel and vanilla, stirring until sugar dissolves. Peel pears, cut in half and core. Place pear halves in syrup, cover and simmer for 10 minutes, or until fork tender. Drain well. Save syrup to sweeten other fruits. • If using canned pears, just drain well. • Beat cream cheese with electric mixer, slowly add whipping cream. Beat. (Or try whipping the cream first and then beating in the softened cream cheese.) • Add powdered sugar, lemon peel, lemon juice, almond and vanilla extracts and Kirsch. Beat until thick. • Spoon filling into baked, cooled pastry shell and spread evenly. • Cut top off 1 pear half to make the pear round. Place pear in center of torte. • Arrange remaining pear halves, cut side down, around center to make a circle. Gently push pears into filling. • Cover and chill until firm. • Heat apricot jam just to melt. Strain. Lightly drizzle jam over pears and filling, forming a thin glaze over all. • Put almonds around edge and center. Cover with foil tent and refrigerate. • Pastry, or entire dessert, can be made the day before. • Serves 8-10.

PRESS-IN LEMON PASTRY

1¼ cups	flour	325 mL
¼ cup	sugar	50 mL
1 tsp.	grated lemon peel	5 mL
½ cup	cold butter OR margarine	125 mL
2	egg yolks	2

Blend the first 3 ingredients together. Cut in the butter, or margarine, and crumble with your fingers until mixture is mealy. • With fork, stir in egg yolks until blended, then work dough with hands until it holds together as a smooth, non-crumbly, ball. • Press dough evenly into bottom and slightly up sides, about ½-1" (1.3-2.5 cm), of 10" (25 cm) or 11" (27.5 cm) torte pan with removable bottom. • Bake at 300°F (150°C) for 30 minutes, or until golden brown. • Cool and loosen from pan; it can be lifted out carefully with turners.

RHUBARB CUSTARD PIE

	pastry for double-crust, 9″ (22 cm) pie	
1½ cups	white sugar	375 mL
¼ cup	all-purpose flour	50 mL
¼ tsp.	ground nutmeg	1 mL
dash	salt	dash
3	eggs, beaten	3
4 cups	rhubarb, cut in 1″ (2.5 cm) pieces	1 L
2 tbsp.	butter	30 mL

Line a 9″ (22 cm) pie plate with pastry. ● In large mixing bowl, mix remaining ingredients, except butter, well and fill pastry shell. ● Dot with butter. ● Cover top with pastry and seal. ● Bake at 400°F (200°C) for 50 minutes.

FRESH PEACH CREAM PIE

½ cup	butter	125 mL
1½ cups	flour	375 mL
½ tsp.	salt	2 mL
4 cups	sliced fresh peaches	1 L
1 cup	sugar	250 mL
2 tbsp.	flour	30 mL
1	egg	1
¼ tsp.	salt	1 mL
½ tsp.	vanilla	2 mL
1 cup	sour cream	250 mL

TOPPING

¼ cup	sugar	75 mL
¼ cup	butter	50 mL
¼ cup	flour	75 mL
1 tsp.	cinnamon	5 mL

Cut butter into flour and salt. Press dough into a 9″ (22 cm) pie plate. ● Slice peaches into a bowl, sprinkle with ¼ cup (50 mL) sugar. Let stand while preparing rest of filling. ● Combine ¾ cup (175 mL) sugar, flour, egg, salt and vanilla. Fold in sour cream. ● Stir in peaches. ● Pour into crust. ● Bake at 400°F (200°C) for 15 minutes. Lower heat to 350°F (180°C) and bake another 20 minutes. ● Prepare topping by combining sugar, butter, flour and cinnamon until crumbly. After the 20 minute baking period is over, sprinkle the topping crumbs evenly over the top of the pie, or just around the edge if you prefer. Bake again at 400°F (200°C) for 10 minutes. ● Serve slightly warm.

Know how to pick a ripe melon?
1. *Honeydew: If you can hear the seeds and juice sloshing around inside, it's ripe.*
2. *Watermelon: Thump sharply with your knuckle. The most hollow sound will indicate the ripest.*
3. *Cantaloupe: The skin should be tan, not green. Ends soft with plenty of aroma.*

PUMPKIN PIE

A delicious, prize-winning recipe.

1½ cups	pumpkin, cooked OR canned	375 mL
1 tbsp.	flour	15 mL
1 cup	sugar	250 mL
1 tsp.	cinnamon	5 mL
1 tsp.	ginger	5 mL
½ tsp.	nutmeg	2 mL
¼ tsp.	mace	1 mL
¼ tsp.	salt	1 mL
3	eggs	3
½ cup	milk	125 mL
	unbaked pie shell	

Mix pumpkin, flour, sugar, spices and salt together. • Beat eggs, add milk and stir well. • Stir all ingredients together well. • Pour into a deep pie plate lined with a good pastry. • Bake until firm, about 35 minutes, in moderate oven, 350°F (180°C). • This is lovely topped with whipped cream. • Makes 1 pie.

PECAN PIE

	pastry for a single-crust 9″ (22 cm) pie	
¼ cup	butter	50 mL
½ cup	sugar	125 mL
3	eggs	3
1 cup	dark corn syrup	250 mL
1 cup	pecans	250 mL

Cream butter and sugar. • Add eggs, 1 at a time, beating after each addition. • Add corn syrup. • Stir in pecans. • Pour filling into shell and bake at 400°F (200°C) for 15 minutes. • Lower heat to 325°F (160°C) and bake until the filling is set.

PRIZE BUTTER TARTS

	pastry for 24 small tart shells	
1	egg, beaten	1
¼ cup	butter	75 mL
1 cup	brown sugar	250 mL
1 tbsp.	flour	15 mL
2 tbsp.	milk	30 mL
1 tsp.	nutmeg	5 mL
½ cup	raisins	125 mL
1 tsp.	vanilla	5 mL

Prepare pastry and press into small tart pans. • Mix all filling ingredients together and fill tart shells ⅔ full. • Bake in hot oven, 450°F (230°C) for 8 minutes, lower temperature to 350°F (180°C) and bake for 15 to 20 minutes longer. • Makes 24 small tarts or 12-15 medium. • This recipe may be doubled.

Store cottage cheese and sour cream upside-down in refrigerator. They keep much longer.

MINCEMEAT

2 lbs.	lean meat (venison, caribou OR beef)	1 kg
1 lb.	suet	500 g
4 lbs.	apples	2 kg
1	orange	1
1	lemon	1
2 lbs.	brown sugar	1 kg
¼ cup	vinegar	50 mL
1 lb.	currants	500 g
1 tsp.	allspice	5 mL
1 tsp.	cloves	5 mL
1 tsp.	nutmeg	5 mL
¼ tsp.	pepper	1 mL
1 tbsp.	salt	15 mL
1 cup	molasses	250 mL
1½ lbs.	raisins	750 g

Boil meat, in water just to cover, until tender in a large Dutch oven. • Put meat, suet, apples, orange and lemon through food grinder and add to broth from meat. • Add other ingredients. • Cook slowly until apples and suet are cooked. • Put in jars and store in refrigerator. Keeps for several months or can be frozen for longer storage. • Great filling for pies and tarts or as a date-mixture substitute in old-fashioned date squares.

LEMON PIE WITH COCONUT CRUST

¼ cup	butter	50 mL
2 cups	coconut	500 mL
1 tbsp.	unflavored gelatin (7 g pkg.)	15 mL
½ cup	sugar	125 mL
½ tsp.	salt	2 mL
4	eggs, separated	4
¼ cup	lemon juice	75 mL
⅔ cup	water	150 mL
1 tbsp.	grated lemon peel	15 mL
½ cup	whipping cream, whipped	125 mL

Gluten-free.

Melt butter in skillet, add coconut and sauté, stirring constantly until coconut is golden brown, 7-8 minutes. • Pour into an 8" (20 cm) or 9" (22 cm) pie plate. Press firmly to cover bottom and sides of pan. • Cool to room temperature, about 30 minutes. • In saucepan, mix gelatin, sugar and salt. • Beat together egg yolks, lemon juice and water. Stir into gelatin mixture. • Cook and stir over medium heat just until mixture comes to a boil. • Remove from heat and stir in lemon peel. • Chill, stirring occasionally, until partially set. • Beat egg whites until soft peaks form, then gradually add sugar beating until peaks form and sugar has dissolved. Fold in gelatin mixture and then fold in the whipped cream. • Pour into coconut base. • Serves 6.

LEMON PARFAIT PIE

1¼ cups	sugar	325 mL
¼ cup	cornstarch	75 mL
½ tsp.	salt	2 mL
1½ cups	hot water	375 mL
¼ cup	fresh lemon juice	75 mL
2	eggs, separated	2
2 tbsp.	butter	30 mL
1 tsp.	grated lemon peel	5 mL
1 tsp.	vanilla	5 mL
1 tbsp.	unflavored gelatin, (7 g pkg.)	15 mL
¼ cup	cold water	50 mL
½ cup	heavy cream, whipped	125 mL
1	baked 9" (22cm) pie shell	1
	sweetened whipped cream for garnish	
	thin slices of lime and lemon	

In 2-quart (2 L) saucepan, combine sugar, cornstarch and salt. • Stir in hot water and lemon juice. • Cook and stir over medium heat until mixture is thickened and mounds when dropped from a spoon. • Remove from heat; stir small amount of hot mixture into egg yolks, then stir yolks back into remaining hot mixture. • Return to heat and cook 2 minutes, stirring constantly. • Remove from heat. Stir in butter until melted, then stir in lemon peel and vanilla. • Measure out 1 cup (250 mL) and set aside to cool. • Sprinkle gelatin over cold water; let stand 1 minute. • Add to remaining hot lemon mixture and stir until gelatin is completely dissolved. • Refrigerate, stirring occasionally, until mixture is slightly thickened, about 30 mintues. • Meanwhile, beat egg whites until stiff. • Fold whipped cream, then egg whites into cooled lemon mixture. • Pour into pie shell. • Refrigerate 3-4 hours until set. Garnish with whipped cream and slices of lime and lemon. • Serves 8.

TAKE TIME FOR 10 THINGS
1. *TAKE TIME TO WORK, it is the price of success.*
2. *TAKE TIME TO THINK, it is the source of power.*
3. *TAKE TIME TO PLAY, it is the secret of youth.*
4. *TAKE TIME TO READ, it is the foundation of knowledge.*
5. *TAKE TIME TO WORSHIP, it is the highway of reverence and washes the dust of earth from our eyes.*
6. *TAKE TIME TO HELP AND ENJOY FRIENDS, it is the source of happiness.*
7. *TAKE TIME TO LOVE, it is the one sacrament of life.*
8. *TAKE TIME TO DREAM, it hitches the soul to the stars.*
9. *TAKE TIME TO LAUGH, it is the singing that helps with life's loads.*
10. *TAKE TIME TO PLAN, it is the secret of being able to have time, to take time for the first nine things.*

1	baked pie shell	1
1 cup	milk	250 mL
6 tbsp.	sugar	90 mL
1	egg	1
¼ cup	cornstarch	75 mL
dash	vanilla	dash
½ cup	heavy cream	125 mL
2 cups	heavy cream	500 mL
1 tbsp.	unflavored gelatin (7 g pkg.)	15 mL
3 oz.	diced macadamia nuts	85 g

MACADAMIA NUT CREAM PIE

Prepare custard by bringing the milk and sugar to a boil. Combine the egg, cornstarch, vanilla and ½ cup (125 mL) heavy cream and add to the milk mixture. Stir and bring to a quick boil. Remove from heat and allow to cool. • Whip the 2 cups (500 mL) of heavy cream. • Dissolve the gelatin in a little hot water and while still hot, add to the custard stirring with a whisk. • Add ⅔ of the whipped cream and the diced macadamia nuts. Blend until smooth and pour into pie shell. • Decorate pie with remaining whipped cream. • Refrigerate for 2 hours before serving.

1	baked 9" (22cm) pie shell	1
1 tbsp.	unflavored gelatin (7 g pkg.)	15 mL
⅔ cup	granulated sugar	150 mL
½ tsp.	salt	2 mL
3	eggs, separated	3
¼ cup	cold water	50 mL
½ cup	fresh OR bottled lime juice	125 mL
1 tsp.	grated lemon OR lime rind	5 mL
	green food coloring	
¼ cup	light rum	75 mL
¼ cup	granulated sugar	75 mL
½ cup	whipped cream	125 mL

DAIQUIRI PIE

In top of double boiler combine gelatin, ⅔ cup (150 mL) sugar and salt. Add egg yolks, water and lime juice. Beat until blended. • Cook over boiling water, stirring well until mixture coats spoon. Remove from heat, add rind, and tint pale green. Cool mixture slightly, then stir in rum. • Refrigerate mixture until slightly thicker than egg whites. • In large bowl, beat egg whites until they form moist peaks. Add ¼ cup (75 mL) sugar, a teaspoon (5 mL) at a time, beating until stiff. • Fold in gelatin mixture. • Turn into pie shell. • Refrigerate several hours. • To serve, decorate with whipped cream.

IRISH COFFEE CREAM PIE

1½ cups	vanilla wafer crumbs	375 mL
¼ cup	sugar	75 mL
¼ cup	melted butter	75 mL
½ cup	crushed toasted almonds	125 mL

FILLING

1 tbsp.	unflavored gelatin (7 g pkg.)	15 mL
¼ cup	cold water	50 mL
1 tbsp.	instant coffee	15 mL
2	eggs, separated	2
¼ cup	whiskey	50 mL
½ cup	dark brown sugar	125 mL
½ tsp.	vanilla	2 mL
pinch	salt	pinch
1 cup	whipping cream	250 mL

Prepare crust by mixing together the vanilla wafer crumbs and the sugar. Gradually stir in the melted butter until well blended. Stir in the almonds. Press into a 9″ (22cm) pie plate. Bake in preheated oven, 425°F (220°C), for 5-8 minutes, until browned. Cool. • Prepare filling by sprinkling the gelatin over the cold water in a small heavy-bottomed saucepan. Add instant coffee, then stir over low heat until the gelatin and coffee are dissolved, about 1 minute. Run a spatula around the sides of the pan to prevent gelatin clinging to the sides. Remove from heat and cover to keep warm. • Immediately whisk egg yolks in a large bowl with whiskey, sugar, vanilla and salt. Beat until light. Gradually whisk in warm coffee mixture. Beat egg whites until they hold soft peaks. Whip cream until it holds soft peaks. Fold cream into coffee mixture, then fold in egg whites. Pour into cold, prepared crust. Refrigerate until set. • Serves 8-12.

ANGEL PIE WITH CHOCOLATE FILLING

2	egg whites	2
⅛ tsp.	salt	0.5 mL
⅛ tsp.	cream of tartar	0.5 mL
½ cup	sugar	125 mL
½ cup	chopped pecans	125 mL
½ tsp.	vanilla	2 mL
4 oz.	sweet cooking chocolate	115 g
3 tbsp.	water	45 mL
1 tsp.	vanilla	5 mL
1 cup	whipping cream	250 mL

Beat together egg whites, salt and cream of tartar until soft peaks form. • Add sugar slowly and beat after each addition. Continue beating until stiff, then fold in nuts and ½ tsp. (2 mL) vanilla. • Shape the meringue, with a spatula and large spoon, or a pastry bag, into a large nest on a cookie sheet lined with a double-thickness of wax paper. • Bake in slow oven, 300°F (150°C), for 50-55 minutes. • Put chocolate and water in saucepan and melt over low heat. • Add 1 tsp. (5 mL) vanilla. • Whip cream stiff and fold chocolate mixture into whipped cream then pour into meringue.

1 cup	butter	250 mL
¾ cup	sugar	175 mL
1 oz.	unsweetened chocolate, melted	30 g
1 tsp.	vanilla	5 mL
2	eggs, beaten	2
1	baked pie shell	1

FRENCH SILK PIE

Cream butter, gradually adding sugar, chocolate and vanilla. • Beat in eggs, 1 at a time, for 3 minutes each. • Pour into baked pie shell. • Keep refrigerated. • No baking time required. • The secret to this pie is in the beating, the longer you beat (until the sugar granules dissolve) the smoother the filling will be!

1½ cups	flour	375 mL
2 tsp.	sugar	10 mL
1 tsp.	salt	5 mL
2 tbsp.	milk	30 mL
½ cup	vegetable oil	125 mL

PRESS PASTRY

Sift flour, sugar and salt into pie plate. • Whip milk into vegetable oil and pour into flour. • Mix and pat down into pan. • Prick all over. • Cook unfilled (blind), or filled. • Bake at 425°F (220°C) for 10-15 minutes for unfilled crust.

---

2 cups	all-purpose flour, unsifted	500 mL
½ tsp.	double action baking powder	2 mL
¼ tsp.	baking soda	1 mL
1 tsp.	salt	5 mL
½ lb.	lard (out of refrigerator for 6 hrs.)	250 g
1	egg, in a 1 cup (250 mL) measure	1
1 tbsp.	white vinegar	15 mL
½ cup	cold water	125 mL

NEVER-FAIL PASTRY

Mix dry ingredients in a large bowl and cut in lard until mixture is in coarse crumbs. • Blend liquid ingredients in a 1 cup (250 mL) measuring cup with a fork. Add to dry ingredients. • Combine well with mixer (dough will be very soft and sticky). • Put in refrigerator for 20 minutes before rolling out, or will keep for 2 weeks in a well-sealed container in refrigerator. • When rolling, use flour generously (cannot use too much). • To bake a single shell, prick with fork and bake at 450°F (230°C) for 15 minutes. • To bake a 2-crust pie, brush top with milk and sprinkle with white sugar (for browning) and bake at 450°F (230°C) for 15 minutes, then lower heat and continue baking at 350°F (180°C) for 30 minutes or until filling is cooked. • Makes 2, 9″ (22 cm) 2-crust pies.

CAKES

PLUM CAKE

¼ cup	butter	50 mL
1 cup	sugar	250 mL
2	egg yolks, lightly beaten	2
1½ cups	flour	375 mL
½ cup	milk	125 mL
1 tsp.	baking powder	5 mL
2	egg whites, beaten stiff not dry	2
2 cups	prune plums, drained if canned	500 mL

TOPPING

½ cup	brown sugar	125 mL
¼ cup	butter	50 mL
1 tsp.	cinnamon	5 mL

ICING

¾ cup	icing sugar	175 mL
1 tbsp.	milk	15 mL
½ tsp.	almond OR vanilla extract	2 mL

Mix together topping ingredients and set aside. ● To make the cake, cream together butter, sugar and egg yolks, gradually mix in dry ingredients alternately with the milk. ● Gently fold in the beaten egg whites. (Mixture is fairly sticky.) ● Pour into greased 9″ x 9″ (22 cm x 22 cm) pan. ● Halve and pit plums and arrange on top. ● Trail the butter, sugar and cinnamon mixture all over the fruit to the edges of the pan. ● Bake at 350°F (180°C) until the top has risen and is golden, approximately 30 minutes. ● Prepare the icing and drizzle over warm cake. ● For a delicious variation, try peaches instead of plums.

When you want to frost a cake (like birthday cakes, etc.) freeze the cake beforehand, don't defrost. There will be fewer crumbs in icing.

⅔ cup	butter OR margarine	150 mL
⅞ cup	sugar	200 g
3	eggs	3
1 tsp.	vanilla sugar*	5 mL
1¾ cups	flour	425 mL
1 tsp.	baking powder	5 mL
1	lemon, grated rind of and a few drops juice	1
4-6	fairly large apples	4-6
¼ cup	chopped almonds	50 mL
4-5 tsp.	icing sugar	20-25 mL

POLISH APPLECAKE

Whip butter and sugar together thoroughly. • Add eggs, 1 at a time. • Add vanilla sugar, grated lemon rind and lemon juice. • Mix; then add the flour which has been mixed with the baking powder. • Mix everything well. • Put mixture in a 10″ (25 cm) round pie plate which has been greased and floured. • Smooth mixture evenly. • Peel apples and cut each into 4-6 pieces. • Put the pieces over the cake and press them in lightly. • Sprinkle chopped almonds over the apples. • Put the cake on a grill rack on the bottom of the oven • Bake at 350°F (180°C) for 40-45 minutes, until it is a golden brown color. (If you don't have a grill rack, lower temperature a little). • Glaze with a mixture of the icing sugar and a few drops of lemon juice. Spread the glaze evenly over the cake. Don't make the glaze too thin. • * To make vanilla sugar, put 1 or 2 vanilla beans in 2 cups (500 mL) of sugar, and seal in a jar for at least 1 week.

½ cup	butter	125 mL
¼ cup	sugar	75 mL
¼ tsp.	vanilla	1 mL
1 cup	flour	250 mL
8 oz.	cream cheese	250 g
¼ cup	sugar	50 mL
1	egg	1
½ tsp.	vanilla	2 mL
14 oz.	can apple pie filling	398 mL
¼ cup	sliced almonds	50 mL

BAVARIAN APPLE TORTE

Put first 4 ingredients in food processor and process 2 minutes. • Press crumbs into a 9″ (22 cm) springform pan, to form base. • Put cream cheese, sugar, egg and vanilla in processor and process until blended. • Pour over base and bake in 400°F (200°C) for 10 minutes. • Spread apple pie filling over cream cheese mixture and top with almonds. • Bake at 400°F (200°C) for another 20 minutes. • Cool before slicing. • Serves 8.

Before turning out cake onto the serving plate, dust it with icing sugar and the cake won't stick to the plate when serving.

BLUEBERRY UPSIDE-DOWN CAKE

¼ cup	melted butter	50 mL
½ cup	brown sugar	125 mL
2 cups	blueberries, fresh OR frozen	500 mL
1 tbsp.	lemon juice	15 mL
½ cup	butter	125 mL
¾ cup	sugar	175 mL
1	egg	1
1 tsp.	vanilla	5 mL
1¼ cups	all-purpose flour	325 mL
2 tsp.	baking powder	10 mL
¼ tsp.	salt	1 mL
1 tsp.	cinnamon (optional)	5 mL
¾ cup	milk	175 mL

In a 9″ (22 cm) square pan, combine melted butter and brown sugar and spread evenly on bottom. • Spread blueberries evenly over base. • Sprinkle with lemon juice. • Cream butter, gradually adding sugar, beat until light. • Beat in egg and vanilla. • Sift or mix together flour, baking powder, salt and cinnamon, if using. • Add dry ingredients alternately with milk to creamed mixture. • Spread batter evenly over blueberry layer. • Bake in 350°F (180°C) for 45-50 minutes, or until toothpick inserted in center comes out clean. • Let cool 10 minutes in pan, then turn out onto large flat plate.

GÂTEAU REVERSE

A colorful upside-down cake!

2 cups	fresh OR frozen rhubarb, cut in pieces	500 mL
1 cup	sugar	250 mL
3 tbsp.	water	45 mL
15 oz.	frozen strawberries	425 mL
¼ cup	shortening	75 mL
1 cup	brown sugar	250 mL
2	eggs	2
1 cup	milk	250 mL
2 cups	flour	500 mL
2 tsp.	baking powder	10 mL
½ tsp.	salt	2 mL
	vanilla, to taste	

Preheat oven to 350°F (180°C). • Cook rhubarb, 1 cup (250 mL) sugar and water in large saucepan until soft. • Add frozen strawberries and heat until blended. • Pour into well-greased mold and set aside. • In a large mixing bowl, beat shortening, brown sugar and eggs until smooth. • Add milk, a little at a time, until well mixed, followed by flour, baking powder and salt. • Add vanilla to taste. • Spread evenly over rhubarb-strawberry mixture and bake 35-40 minutes. • To serve, turn upside down onto a serving dish. • This is an old Quebec recipe which is quick and easy to make!

2 cups	flour	500 mL
½ cup	butter OR margarine	125 mL
¼ tsp.	salt	1 mL
1 tsp.	baking powder	5 mL
1	egg, beaten	1

RHUBARB CAKE

4 cups	fresh rhubarb, cubed	1 L
1½ cups	sugar	375 mL
½ cup	melted butter OR margarine	125 mL
½ cup	flour	125 mL
2	eggs, beaten	2
	sugar, cinnamon	

TOPPING

To make base, crumble flour, butter, salt and baking powder. Mix egg in with fork. Reserve ¾ cup (175 mL) of this mixture for topping. Press remainder in a greased 9″ x 13″ (22 cm x 33 cm) pan. • Mix topping ingredients and spread on top of base. Cover with reserved crumbs. Sprinkle with sugar and cinnamon. • Bake at 350°F (180°C) for 50 minutes. • Cut into squares and serve hot or cold, with whipped cream or ice cream. • Variation: May substitute peaches, apples, plums or Saskatoons for the rhubarb.

---

1 cup	white sugar	250 mL
1 cup	salad oil	250 mL
3	eggs	3
1¼ cups	flour	325 mL
½ tsp.	salt	2 mL
1½ tsp.	baking soda	7 mL
1¼ tsp.	baking powder	6.5 mL
1½ tsp.	cinnamon	7 mL
2 cups	finely grated carrot	500 mL
1 cup	finely chopped Brazil nuts	250 mL

CARROT CAKE

8 oz.	pkg. cream cheese	250 g
2 cups	icing sugar	500 mL
¼ cup	butter	50 mL
2 tsp.	vanilla	10 mL
sprinkle	chopped Brazil nuts	sprinkle

ICING

Combine sugar and oil. Beat eggs into oil mixture. • Sift flour, salt, baking soda, baking powder and spice and add to first mixture. • Beat until well-blended. • Fold in carrots and nuts (save about 1 tbsp. [15 mL] of nuts for sprinkling on icing). • Bake in 2 greased 9″ (1.5 L) layer pans, or a 9″ x 13″ (22 cm x 33 cm) pan. • Bake at 300°F (150°C) for 1 hour. • Cool cake. • Combine icing ingredients and spread between layers and on top and sides of cake. Sprinkle with reserved nuts.

CARROT-PINEAPPLE CAKE

4 cups	flour	1 L
2 tsp.	baking powder	10 mL
1 tbsp.	baking soda	15 mL
4 tsp.	cinnamon	20 mL
dash	cloves	dash
1 cup	salad oil	250 mL
1½ cups	sugar	375 mL
2 tsp.	salt	10 L
3	large eggs	3
14 oz.	can crushed pineapple	398 mL
3 tbsp.	lemon-orange marmalade	50 mL
3 cups	shredded coconut	750 mL
1½ cups	light raisins	375 mL
3 cups	grated carrots	750 mL

CREAM CHEESE ICING

4 oz.	pkg. cream cheese	125 g
¼ cup	butter	50 mL
½ tsp.	vanilla	2 mL
¾ cup	icing sugar	175 mL

Sift together first 5 ingredients. • Mix together next 9 ingredients. • Combine the 2 mixtures and turn into a greased 10″ x 18″ (25 cm x 45 cm) pan, or 4 loaf pans, and bake at 350°F (180°C) for 1 hour, or until toothpick inserted in center comes out clean. • Cool completely and frost with Cream Cheese Icing, if desired. • Double icing recipe to frost 4 loaves. • To make Cream Cheese Icing, beat first 3 ingredients, then gradually beat in the icing sugar until smooth. Enough for a 6″ x 12″ (3L) cake. • Serves 20 or more.

CARROT CAKE

Gluten-free

2 cups	brown OR white rice flour	500 mL
2 cups	white sugar	500 mL
1 tsp.	baking soda	5 mL
2 tsp.	cinnamon	10 mL
1¼ cups	salad oil	300 mL
4	eggs, well-beaten	4
3 cups	grated carrots	750 mL
1 tsp.	salt	5 mL

FROSTING

8 oz.	pkg. cream cheese	250 g
4 tbsp.	butter	60 mL
1 lb.	icing sugar	500 g
2 tsp.	vanilla	10 mL

Combine flour, sugar, soda and cinnamon. Add oil, eggs and carrots. • Mix well and refrigerate batter for about 30 minutes. • Pour into a greased and floured (with rice flour) 9″ x 13″ (22 cm x 33 cm) pan, or into cupcake pan. • Bake at 350°F (180°C) for 50-60 minutes. Shorter time period is required for cupcakes. • Cream frosting ingredients together and frost cake, or cupcakes, when cool.

1½ cups	dried apricots	375 mL
½ cup	honey	125 mL
2 cups	seedless raisins	500 mL
1 cup	seeded raisins	250 mL
¼ cup	brandy	50 mL
1 cup	diced candied pineapple	250 mL
1 cup	halved candied cherries	250 mL
1½ cups	diced citron peel	375 mL
1 cup	diced orange peel	250 mL
1 cup	sliced dates (optional may substitute equal amount of fruit cake mix)	250 mL
1 cup	slivered blanched almonds	250 mL
1 cup	coarsely chopped pecans	250 mL
1 cup	butter	250 mL
1¼ cups	brown sugar	300 mL
4	eggs	4
2 cups	sifted all-purpose flour	500 mL
1 tsp.	salt	5 mL
¼ tsp.	baking soda	1 mL
1 tsp.	cinnamon	5 mL
½ tsp.	mace	2 mL
¼ tsp.	cloves	1 mL

SUGARPLUM FRUIT CAKE

Rinse apricots, cover with water and boil for 10 minutes. Drain, cool and chop. Combine with honey in small saucepan, heat to boiling, cover, let stand until cool. ● Rinse raisins and drain; chop seeded raisins. ● Turn apricots and honey into large bowl, add raisins and pour brandy over all. Cover and let stand overnight. ● Candied fruits, citron, peel, dates and nuts may be prepared and added to the bowl the same day, but do not mix, to allow dried fruits to soak in honey and brandy. ● The following day, cream butter and sugar thoroughly. Beat in eggs, 1 at a time. Sift together flour, salt, baking soda, and spices; mix thoroughly into creamed mixture. ● Now mix fruits in large bowl by lifting from bottom with large spoon. Pour batter over fruits; mix thoroughly. ● Turn into pans that have been lined with 3 layers of brown paper, greasing the layer next to batter. Pack batter into pans. ● Place shallow pan of water in oven during baking. ● Bake in slow oven, 275°F (140°C), for several hours or, depending on size of pans, until done, when toothpick inserted in center comes out clean. ● Age 3-4 weeks before serving. ● Yields 6½-7 lbs. (3-3.25 kg).

FOOD FOR THOUGHT: *Never miss an opportunity to make others happy — even if you have to let them alone to do it.*

CHRISTMAS CAKE

1 lb.	blanched almonds	500 g
2 lbs.	light sultana raisins	1 kg
1 lb.	candied mixed peel	500 g
8 oz.	glacé cherries, halved	250 g
8 oz.	colored candied pineapple	250 g
26 oz.	inexpensive brandy	750 mL
13 oz.	rum	375 mL
1 lb.	butter	500 g
2 lbs.	brown sugar	1 kg
12	eggs	12
4½ cups	all-purpose flour	1.125 L
1½ tsp.	baking powder	7 mL
1 tsp.	EACH cinnamon, mace, allspice, cloves	5 mL
1½ tsp.	vanilla	7 mL

Soak the 5 fruits in the brandy and rum for 1 week; stir or shake daily. • Cream the butter and sugar. • Separate the eggs. • Add the beaten yolks to the creamed mixture and then add the dry ingredients. • Lightly beat the egg whites and fold into the batter. • Add the soaked fruit, vanilla and marinade. Mix well. • Put into greased pans with foil on the outside. • Bake at 275°F (140°C). Watch carefully! A large cake will take about 4 hours. • When cool, take out of pans, leave uncovered overnight. • Store, wrapped in cheesecloth and foil with extra cheesecloth on top, soaked with rum, and sealed with masking tape. • Will keep for 2 years in a cool place (probably longer, but they have never been given the chance).

ANGEL DELIGHT

A light-tasting dessert after a hefty dinner!

10″	angel cake	25 cm
1 tbsp.	unflavored gelatin (7 g pkg.)	15 mL
¼ cup	cold water	50 mL
6	eggs, separated	6
¾ cup	sugar	175 mL
1½ tsp.	grated lemon peel	7 mL
¾ cup	lemon juice (fresh is best)	175 mL
¾ cup	sugar	175 mL
	whipped cream	

Trim crust from angel cake. Tear cake into medium-sized pieces. • Soften gelatin in cold water. • Combine beaten egg yolks, ¾ cup (175 mL) sugar, lemon peel and lemon juice. Cook over hot water until mixture coats a metal spoon. Remove from heat. • Add softened gelatin, stir. • Chill until partially set. • Beat remaining ¾ cup (175 mL) sugar gradually into stiffly beaten egg whites. Fold into gelatin mixture. • Arrange ¼ of cake pieces loosely in bottom of 10″ (25 cm) tube pan. Pour ¼ lemon mixture over cake so it will run between pieces. Repeat until there are 3 layers of each. • Chill until firm. • Turn out onto cake plate and "ice" with whipped cream. • Serves 12.

2 cups	flour	500 mL
2 tsp.	baking powder	10 mL
1 cup	milk	250 mL
2 tsp.	butter	10 mL
5	eggs, room temperature	5
⅛ tsp.	salt	0.5 mL
2 cups	sugar, scant	500 mL
2½ tsp.	fresh lemon juice	12 mL
1¼ cups	walnuts	325 mL
1 lb.	icing sugar	500 g
2 tsp.	lemon juice	10 mL
	butter OR margarine	

FAMILY TRADITION CAKE

Butter a 9" x 13" (22 cm x 33 cm) cake pan and in it, fit a waxed paper lining. Press wax paper in carefully so as to butter it as well. Remove paper and turn it over and replace so that there is a wax paper lining, buttered on both sides. This is for easy removal after baking. • Preheat oven to 350°F (180°C). • Measure flour, mix in baking powder, sift and set aside. • Rinse saucepan with water to avoid sticking, then pour in milk and 2 tsp. (10 mL) of the butter and place on burner, but heat only just before using. • Beat eggs until thick, beat in salt and continue beating until it looks like whipped cream. Add the sugar a tablespoon (15 mL) at a time. Taste for remaining granules; add the lemon juice slowly as the beater works. Slowly add flour. Slow beaters to avoid splatter and add hot milk ALL AT ONCE. Beat at high speed until well mixed. • Pour batter into cake pan and bake for 25-30 minutes, until cake pulls away from sides of pan. Cool in pan.
• TO MAKE PETIT FOURS: We prefer to use freshly shelled walnuts finely ground in the blender, but packaged ones are fine too. Cut cooled cake into 24 pieces and ice then coat with the nuts, 1 piece at a time (The cut pieces of cake may be frozen at this point as the icing is a little easier to apply to frozen cake.)
• ICING: In large bowl of mixer put icing sugar, 2 tsp. (10 mL) lemon juice and add butter to make a spreadable icing. Beat. • TO ICE: Have a small amount of ground nuts in a small bowl, adding more as needed. Ice each piece of cake around on the cut sides first. Then with bottom on palm of your hand, ice the top side of cake; place this top into the bowl of nuts while you ice the bottom. Roll the piece of completely iced cake around in the nuts. Remove loose nuts and set on a plate so the pieces do not touch. Serve within the next day or two as these get sticky if kept in a closed container. • NOTE: Use separate clean cups and utensils to measure all ingredients. Do not measure sugar with a residue of flour in the cup.

Use bananas as a substitute for whipped cream. Add sliced bananas to the white of an egg and beat with an electric mixer until stiff. A tasty substitute for whipped cream and fewer calories too!

Put a metal jar lid in the bottom of a double boiler, or steamer pan, when in use. When it rattles, the pan needs more water.

POPPY SEED TORTE

¾ cup	poppy seeds	175 mL
¾ cup	milk	175 mL
¾ cup	butter	175 mL
1¼ cups	sugar	300 mL
1 tsp.	vanilla	5 mL
2 cups	sifted cake flour	500 mL
2½ tsp.	baking powder	12 mL
¼ tsp.	salt	1 mL
4	egg whites	4

In a jar, cover poppy seeds with milk and soak overnight in refrigerator. • Cream the butter, add sugar gradually and beat until light. • Stir in poppy seed mixture and vanilla. Beat well. • Sift flour and dry ingrdients, then add to first mixture gradually and blend well. • Beat egg whites until stiff, and fold into batter. • Spoon into oiled and floured cake pan, using 9″ x 12″ (4 L) pan or 2, 8″ (20 cm) square pans or deep round pan. • Bake in 350°F (180°C) oven for about 30 minutes, depending upon pans used. • Remove from pan, cool on rack if cake is to be used immediately. Ice and serve. • For later use as a torte, remove cake from pan, cool and store in freezer, wrapped tightly, on a baking sheet or plate. When ready to use, unfreeze, cut horizontally to make 4 layers, spread with fillings, below, and ice.

CREAM FILLING

Alternate basic cream filling with black currant or apricot jam

1 cup	rich milk OR creamilk	250 mL
¼ cup	sugar	50 mL
1-2 tbsp.	cornstarch	15-30 mL
2-4	egg yolks, as desired for richness	2-4
1-2 tbsp.	butter	15-30 mL
1 tsp.	vanilla	5 mL

Scald milk in double boiler. • Mix together dry ingredients, stirring in a portion of the milk; return mixture to double boiler. • Cook, stirring constantly, until thickened and cooked. • Beat eggs slightly, add some hot sauce, and return to double boiler. • Cook for 1-2 minutes, stirring. • Remove from heat, add butter and vanilla. Cool thoroughly before spreading between bottom and top layer of cake.

ICING FOR TOP AND SIDES

1 cup	whipping cream	250 mL
½ cup	icing sugar	125 mL
¼ cup	cocoa	50 mL
½ tsp.	vanilla	2 mL
	slivered almonds	

Combine cream, sugar and cocoa. • Whip until thick. • Add vanilla. • Spread on cake. • Decorate with almond slivers.

Duty makes us do things well, but love makes us do them beautifully.

1½ cups	all-purpose flour	375 mL
1 tbsp.	baking powder	15 mL
1 tsp.	salt	5 mL
1½ cups	granulated sugar	375 mL
½ cup	vegetable oil	125 mL
7	egg yolks	7
¾ cup	water	175 mL
2 tsp.	vanilla	10 mL
1 cup	egg whites (about 8)	250 mL
½ tsp.	cream of tartar	2 mL

VANILLA CHIFFON CAKE

Sift together first 4 ingredients, add next 4 ingredients; beat until smooth. • Beat egg whites until very stiff, sprinkle with cream of tartar and beat again. • Fold batter into egg whites. • Turn into ungreased 8″ (20 cm) tube pan; cut batter to break large air bubbles. • Bake in 325°F (160°C) oven for 55-60 minutes. • **Variations:** Replace water with orange juice and 2 tbsp. (30 mL) grated orange rind, reduce vanilla to ¼ tsp. (1 mL). Also try apricot nectar.

½ cup	butter	125 mL
1 cup	sugar	250 mL
¼ tsp.	salt	1 mL
1 tsp.	crushed cardamom	5 mL
2	eggs	2
2 tbsp.	cream	30 mL
½ tsp.	vanilla	2 mL
½ tsp.	almond flavoring	2 mL
2 cups	flour	500 mL
2 tsp.	baking powder	10 mL

VINARTERTA

Swedish torte.

Cream butter, sugar and salt. • Sprinkle cardamom over mixture and beat in. • Beat in eggs, 1 at a time, until creamy and light. • Add cream and flavoring, flour and baking powder. • Dough should be soft. • Divide into 4 equal portions. • Roll thin on under side of floured cake pans, 8″ (20 cm) round or square. • Prick with fork. • Bake at 375°F (190°C) until light golden brown, about 10 minutes. • Set aside to cool, while you prepare filling.

2 lbs.	prunes	1 kg
¼ tsp.	salt	1 mL
1 cup	sugar	250 mL
½ tsp.	cinnamon	2 mL
½ tsp.	vanilla	2 mL

VINARTERA FILLING

6 tbsp.	butter	90 mL
1	egg yolk	1
¼ tsp.	almond flavoring	1 mL
1½ cups	icing sugar	375 mL
½ cup	ground almonds	125 mL

ICING

Boil prunes, pit and stone; put through blender. • Add salt, sugar, cinnamon and vanilla. • Heat to dissolved sugar. • Spread between cake layers. • Combine icing ingredients and cover top of cake. • Make 1 day ahead.

WARTIME CAKE

This cake dates back to the First Great War!

1 lb.	raisins	500 g
1¾ cups	sugar	425 mL
½ cup	lard	125 mL
3 cups	cold water	750 mL
4 cups	flour	1 L
1 tbsp.	baking soda	15 mL
¾ tsp.	salt	3 mL
1 tsp.	EACH cinnamon, cloves, and nutmeg	5 mL

Boil raisins in the cold water for 15 minutes. Add lard and sugar, stir to melt lard and dissolve sugar. Cool. • Sift dry ingredients together. Fold into raisin mixture. • Pour into 2 greased loaf pans and bake in a slow oven, 325°F (160°C), until done, about 1 hour and 15 minutes. • Good old recipe!

HOT-WATER GINGER-BREAD

½ cup	butter and lard, mixed	125 mL
½ cup	brown sugar	125 mL
⅔ cup	molasses	150 mL
1	egg	1
2½ cups	flour	625 mL
½ tsp.	salt	2 mL
2 tsp.	baking powder	10 mL
1 tsp.	baking soda	5 mL
1½ tsp.	ginger	7 mL
1½ tsp.	cinnamon	7 mL
½ tsp.	cloves	2 mL
1 cup	boiling water	250 mL

Cream shortening and sugar. Add molasses and egg. Sift dry ingredients and add to creamed mixture. Add boiling water last. • Bake in a 9″ x 12″ (22cm x 30cm) pan for 45-50 minutes at 325°F (160°C). • Serve with lemon sauce and whipped cream.

HAZELNUT CAKE

Gluten-free with no butter or flour.

4	eggs, beaten	4
1 cup	white sugar	250 mL
1 lb.	shelled hazelnuts, finely ground	500 g
1 tsp.	baking powder	5 mL
pinch	salt	pinch

Combine all ingredients and put into a greased 8″ (20 cm) cake pan. • Bake in moderate oven, 350°F (180°C) until cake tester comes out dry. • Ice with chocolate icing.

When God measures a woman, He puts the tape around her heart, not her waist.

¼ cup	salad oil	75 mL
1½ cups	white rice flour	375 mL
¾ cup	sugar	175 mL
4½ tsp.	baking powder	22 mL
1 tsp.	baking soda	5 mL
½ tsp.	salt	2 mL
3	large eggs	3
1 cup	buttermilk OR sour milk	250 mL
2 tsp.	vanilla	10 mL

BASIC WHITE CAKE

Gluten-free.

Place oil in large mixing bowl. Set aside. • Sift all dry ingredients 3 times together, then sift into oil. • Add eggs and half of the milk; mix until flour is moistened. Beat 2 minutes at medium speed. • Add remaining milk and vanilla. Beat 2 minutes longer. • Bake in a greased and lightly floured (with rice flour) 9" x 9" (22 cm x 22 cm) pan at 350°F (180°C) about 35 minutes, or until toothpick inserted in center comes out clean. • Frost with Broiled Frosting. • See variations, below.

VARIATIONS

Reduce buttermilk, or sour milk, to ¾ cup (175 mL) and add 2 x 1 oz. (2 x 30 g) squares melted, unsweetened chocolate when you add the remaining milk and vanilla.

LEMON

Add 1 tbsp. (15 mL) grated lemon rind to the dry ingredients after they have been sifted into the bowl and add 1 tsp. (5 mL) lemon extract in place of the vanilla.

¼ cup	butter OR margarine, melted	50 mL
½ cup	firmly packed brown sugar	125 mL
3 tbsp.	half and half cream	50 mL
¼ cup	chopped nuts	75 mL
¾ cup	shredded coconut	175 mL

BROILED FROSTING

Combine all ingredients. • Spread evenly over baked cake. • Broil until frosting becomes bubbly.

Marriage is the most certain method yet known for determining whom you can't live with.

TURTLE CAKE

Everyone loves this easy-to-make cake! A sure hit!

19 oz	pkg. German Chocolate cake mix	400 g
½ cup	butter OR margarine	125 mL
1½ cups	water	375 mL
½ cup	vegetable oil	125 mL
10 oz.	can Eagle Brand condensed milk	300 mL
2 cups	chopped pecans	500 mL
1 lb.	caramels	500 g

Mix chocolate cake mix, butter, water, oil and half of the condensed milk. • Pour half of mixture into a 9″ x 13″ (22 cm x 33 cm) greased, floured pan. • Bake 20-25 minutes at 350°F (180°C). • Melt caramels and remaining milk until smooth. Pour over baked layer. • Sprinkle generously with pecans. • Pour on the remaining batter. • Bake 30-35 minutes (watch closely until top layer is set). • Frost with your favorite milk chocolate frosting.

DECADENT CHOCOLATE CAKE

Yum!

1 cup	boiling water	250 mL
½ cup	butter	125 mL
3 oz.	unsweetened chocolate, chopped	85 g
1 tsp.	vanilla	5 mL
2 cups	sugar	500 mL
2	eggs, separated	2
1 tsp.	baking soda	5 mL
½ cup	sour cream	125 mL
2 cups	all-purpose flour	500 mL
1 tsp.	baking powder	5 mL

FROSTING

2 tbsp.	unsalted butter	25 mL
¾ cup	semisweet chocolate chips	175 mL
6 tbsp.	whipping cream	90 mL
1¼ cups	icing sugar, sifted	300 mL
1 tsp.	vanilla	5 mL
	flowers, strawberries OR nuts	

Grease and flour a 10″ (3 L) tube pan. • In a large bowl, pour boiling water over butter and chocolate to melt. Stir in vanilla and sugar. Whisk in egg yolks, 1 at a time, and blend well. • Combine baking soda and sour cream and whisk into chocolate mixture. • Sift flour and baking powder together; stir into batter. • In a bowl, beat egg whites until stiff and stir ¼ into batter to lighten. • Fold in remaining egg whites. • Pour batter into prepared pan and bake on middle rack of oven at 350°F (180°C) for 40-50 minutes, until toothpick inserted in center comes out clean. • Cool 10 minutes in pan, then turn cake onto plate to cool completely before frosting. • To make frosting, in a heavy saucepan, combine butter and chocolate chips over low heat. Whisk until melted. Add cream, icing sugar and vanilla. Cool. Frost cake. • Garnish. • Serves 10-12.

1⅔ cups	flour	400 mL
1½ cups	sugar	375 mL
⅔ cup	cocoa	150 mL
1½ tsp.	baking soda	7 mL
1 tsp.	salt	5 mL
1½ cups	buttermilk OR milk plus 1½ tbsp. (22 mL) vinegar	375 mL
½ cup	shortening	125 mL
2	eggs	2
1 tsp.	vanilla	5 mL
½ cup	kirsch, OR cherry brandy	125 mL
½ cup	butter OR margarine	125 mL
3½ cups	icing sugar	875 mL
pinch	salt	pinch
1 tsp.	strong coffee	5 mL
2 x 14 oz.	cans pitted black Bing cherries, drained	2 x 398 mL
2 cups	whipping cream	500 mL
½ tsp.	vanilla	2 mL
1 tbsp.	kirsch	15 mL
	semisweet chocolate square, for garnish	

BLACK FOREST CAKE

Beat first 9 ingredients on low speed for 30 seconds, then turn on high for 3 minutes. • Line 2 round 8″ (20 cm) pans with wax paper circles. • Pour batter in pans and bake at 350°F (180°C) for 35-40 minutes. • Cool completely. • Divide into 2 layers each by carefully cutting cakes. (Remember to remove wax paper). • Sprinkle layers with kirsch. • Combine butter, icing sugar, salt and coffee to make a cream filling. If too thick, add a little half and half cream so that it is easy to spread. • Spread first layer of cake with ¼ of the cream filling. Top with ¼ of the cherries (this should cover the entire cake). • Repeat layers. • Top cake with last layer of cake. • Whip the whipping cream with the ½ tsp. (2 mL) vanilla and the 1 tbsp. (15 mL) kirsch. Use this to frost the cake and sprinkle with chocolate curls made by using potato peeler on semisweet baking chocolate.

COOKIES AND SQUARES

A house should have a cookie jar, for when it's half past three,
And children hurry home from school as hungry as can be,
There's nothing quite so splendid as spicy, fluffy ginger cakes
And sweet milk in a cup.
A house should have a mother waiting with a hug,
No matter what a boy brings home, a puppy or a bug,
For children only loiter when the bell rings to dismiss,
If no one's home to greet them with a cookie and a kiss!

ZUCCHINI CHOCOLATE CAKE

½ cup	margarine	125 mL
½ cup	salad oil	125 mL
1¾ cups	sugar	425 mL
2	eggs	2
2½ cups	flour	625 mL
1 tsp.	baking soda	5 mL
1 tsp.	baking powder	5 mL
1 tsp.	salt	5 mL
4 tbsp.	cocoa	60 mL
½ tsp.	cinnamon	2 mL
½ tsp.	ground cloves	2 mL
½ cup	sour milk	125 mL
2 cups	finely chopped unpeeled zucchini	500 mL
2 tsp.	vanilla	10 mL
¼-½ cup	chocolate chips	50-125 mL
¼ cup	chopped nuts	50 mL

Cream margarine, oil and sugar. • Add eggs, 1 at a time, beating well after each addition. • Add sifted dry ingredients alternately with milk. • Stir in zucchini, vanilla, chocolate chips and nuts. • Pour into a greased and floured 9″ x 13″ (22 cm x 33 cm) pan. • Bake in preheated 350°F (180°C) oven for 45-55 minutes.

CAKE DOUGHNUTS

3 tbsp.	butter OR margarine	45 mL
¾ cup	white sugar	175 mL
½ tsp.	salt	2 mL
2	eggs	2
1 cup	sour milk	250 mL
½ tsp.	baking soda	2 mL
½ tsp.	nutmeg	2 mL
4 cups	flour, approximately lard and oil for frying	1 L

Cream together the butter and sugar. • Beat in eggs and salt. • Add sour milk, baking soda, nutmeg and enough flour to make dough easy to roll. • Cut with doughnut cutter. • Heat lard and oil mixture, deep enough to let doughnuts come to the top and float free of the bottom, to 375°F (190°C). • Fry doughnuts, turn and brown underside. • (Test heat of oil with a few doughnut centers.)

To glaze the top of rolls, cookies or pies, brush the top before baking with 1 egg white slightly beaten with 1 tbsp. (15 mL) milk, then bake.

If you are bothered by the smell of oil base paint, try adding 1 tbsp. (15 mL) of vanilla extract to a gallon (4 L) of paint.

SQUARES

9 tbsp.	butter	135 mL	
¼ cup	granulated sugar	50 mL	**CARAMEL**
1¼ cups	all-purpose flour	300 mL	**TOFFEE**
½ cup	butter	125 mL	**SQUARES**
½ cup	brown sugar	125 mL	
2 tbsp.	corn syrup	30 mL	
½ cup	sweetened condensed milk (not evaporated)	125 mL	
12 oz.	pkg. semisweet chocolate chips	340 g	

For the bottom layer, crumble the first 3 ingredients well. Pack into a 9″ x 9″ (22 cm x 22 cm) pan. Bake at 350°F (180°C) oven for 20 minutes.   •   For the second layer, combine butter, sugar, syrup and milk in saucepan. Bring to a boil. Boil 5 minutes; remove from heat. Beat and pour over bottom layer.   •   For the third layer, melt chocolate in saucepan over low heat. Pour over second layer.   •   Chill.   •   Cut into squares.   •   Makes 36 squares.

1 cup	butter OR margarine	250 mL	
2 cups	flour	500 mL	**LEMON**
½ cup	icing sugar	125 mL	**SQUARES**
4	eggs	4	
7 tbsp.	lemon juice	105 mL	
2 cups	white sugar	500 mL	
¼ cup	flour	50 mL	
1 tsp.	baking powder	5 mL	
2 cups	icing sugar	500 mL	
2 tbsp.	butter OR margarine	30 mL	*ICING*
3 tbsp.	lemon juice	50 mL	

Mix first 3 ingredients to cornmeal consistency and pat into a 9″ x 13″ (22 cm x 33 cm) pan. Bake at 350°F (180°C) for 20 minutes.   •   Put the next 5 ingredients in a blender. Blend well. Pour over warm crust and bake for 25 minutes. When just cool, glaze with icing.   •   To make icing, blend icing sugar, butter, add lemon juice to make a thin icing. Spread on cake and let cool.   •   Cut in small squares.

MEXICAN CANDY BARS

A colorful addition to a Christmas plate.

6 oz.	pkg. butterscotch chips	170 g
½ cup	butter	125 mL
½ cup	brown sugar	125 mL
1¼ cups	flour	325 mL
¾ tsp.	salt	3 mL
1 cup	slivered almonds	250 mL
1 cup	chopped candied fruit	250 mL
¼ cup	sliced white raisins	50 mL
1 tbsp.	sugar	15 mL
1 tbsp.	grated orange rind	15 mL
2	eggs, slightly beaten	2

Combine the first 5 ingredients and press into a 9″ x 13″ (22 cm x 33cm) pan. Bake at 350°F (180°C) for 15 minutes. • Combine the remaining ingredients and spread evenly over cooked base. • Return to oven and bake for an additional 20 minutes. Cool. • Yields 50 squares.

MARZIPAN BAR

This is an old English recipe passed down for four generations. Nice for Christmas!

	pastry for bottom of 8″ (20 cm) square pan	
	raspberry jam	
½ cup	butter OR margarine	125 mL
⅔ cup	white sugar	150 mL
2	eggs	2
⅔ cup	rice flour	150 mL
½ tsp.	salt	2 mL
	red and green food colorings	

FROSTING

2 tbsp.	butter OR margarine	30 mL
1½ cups	icing sugar, more if necessary	375 mL
2 tbsp.	warm milk	30 mL
1 tbsp.	almond extract	15 mL

Preheat oven to 375°F (190°C). • Line bottom of 8″ (20 cm) pan with pastry. • Cover pastry with thin layer of raspberry jam. • Prepare filling by blending butter and sugar thoroughly. Add eggs and beat until light and fluffy. Add rice flour and salt, beat well. Color half of this mixture pale pink, the other half pale green. Put in small spoonfuls of mixture alternately to cover pastry. Bake for 35 minutes. Cool. • Mix all frosting ingredients together and beat well. Ice cake and cut into bars. • Yields approximately 64 squares.

Once a woman has forgiven her man, she must not reheat his sins for breakfast.

¾ cup	butter	175 mL
1 ½ cups	flour	375 mL
¼ cup	brown sugar	75 mL
2 tbsp.	gelatin	30 mL
½ cup	cold water	125 mL
2 cups	white sugar	500 mL
½ cup	hot water	125 mL
½ cup	maraschino cherries, chopped	125 mL
¼ cup	toasted sliced almonds	50 mL
1-2 drops	red food coloring	1-2 drops
½ tsp.	almond extract	2 mL
	fine coconut	

MARSH-MALLOW SQUARES

Prepare base by mixing butter, flour and brown sugar together. Press into 9" x 13" (22cm x 33cm) pan. Bake at 325°F (160°C) until brown. • Prepare filling by mixing gelatin and cold water; set aside. Boil white sugar and hot water for 2 minutes. Stir in gelatin, beat until very stiff. Fold in maraschino cherries, almonds, food coloring and almond extract. Spread on top of base. Sprinkle with fine coconut.

1¾ cups	rolled oats	425 mL
1½ cups	flour	375 mL
¾ cup	butter	175 mL
¼ tsp.	baking soda	1 mL
1 cup	brown sugar	250 mL
5	peeled apples, sliced	5
2 tbsp.	butter	30 mL
½ cup	white sugar	125 mL
	cinnamon, to taste	

APPLE BARS

Combine first 5 ingredients. Mix until crumb-like. • Pat ¼ of crumb mixture in a greased 9" (22 cm) square pan. • Combine remaining ingredients. • Spread apple mixture over base. • Pat crumbs on top. • Bake at 350°F (180°C) for 1 hour.

1 cup	butter	250 mL
1 cup	sugar	250 mL
1	egg, separated	1
2 cups	sifted flour	500 mL
1 tsp.	cinnamon	5 mL
1 cup	finely chopped walnuts	250 mL

WALNUT CINNAMON SQUARES

Cream together the butter and sugar; beat in egg yolk and mix thoroughly. • Mix together the flour and cinnamon, stir into creamed mixture. • Spread dough evenly over bottom of lightly greased 15" x 10" (38 cm x 25 cm) jelly roll pan. • Beat egg whites slightly, brush over top of dough. With fingertips smooth surface. • Sprinkle nuts over dough and press in. • Bake at 275°F (140°C) for 1 hour. • While still hot, cut into 1½" (3.8 cm) squares. • Cool in pan. • Makes 5½ dozen squares.

CHOCOLATE CHIP BARS

½ cup	butter OR margarine	125 mL
½ cup	brown sugar	125 mL
½ cup	granulated sugar	125 mL
2	eggs	2
2 tsp.	vanilla	10 mL
1 cup	sifted all-purpose flour	250 mL
1 tsp.	baking powder	5 mL
½ tsp.	salt	2 mL
1 cup	rolled oats	250 mL
6 oz.	pkg. chocolate chips	170 g
½ cup	chopped walnuts	125 mL

CHOCOLATE GLAZE

6 oz.	pkg. chocolate chips	170 g
2 tbsp.	butter	30 mL
3 tbsp.	light cream	50 mL
1 cup	sifted icing sugar	250 mL

Heat oven to 375°F (190°C). ● Grease a 13″ x 9″ (22 cm x 33 cm) baking pan. ● Combine butter, brown sugar, granulated sugar, eggs and vanilla in mixing bowl and beat until well blended and fluffy. ● Sift flour, baking powder and salt together and add to creamed mixture. ● Add rolled oats, chocolate chips and walnuts and stir to blend. ● Turn into prepared pan and bake for 20 minutes or until top springs back when touched lightly. ● Cool to lukewarm in the pan and spread with Chocolate Glaze. To make chocolate glaze, combine chocolate chips, butter and cream in saucepan. Set over low heat and stir just until chocolate is melted. Remove from heat. Stir in icing sugar and beat gently until glossy and of the right consistency for spreading. ● Cut into bars or squares when cool.

SAN FRANCISCO CHOCOLATE FOGGIES

Moist and luscious!

1 lb.	semisweet chocolate	500 g
1 cup	unsalted butter	250 mL
¼ cup	strong brewed coffee	75 mL
4	large eggs, room temperature	4
1½ cups	granulated sugar	375 mL
½ cup	all-purpose flour	125 mL
2 cups	walnut OR pecan halves, coarsely chopped	500 mL

Position rack in center of oven and preheat to 375°F (190°C). ● Line a 9″ x 13″ (22 cm x 33 cm) pan with double thickness of aluminum foil so foil extends 2″ (5 cm) above sides of pan. Butter bottom and sides of foil. ● Over hot water, melt chocolate, butter and coffee. Stir until smooth. Cool the mixture. ● In a large bowl, beat eggs on high, until foamy. Add sugar gradually until mixture is light and fluffy, 2 minutes. Slowly beat in chocolate mixture. With wooden spoon, stir in flour, then walnuts. Pour into pan. ● Bake for 28-30 minutes, or until just firm at edges with center moist. ● Cool for 30 minutes and refrigerate for at least 6 hours, covered tightly. ● Lift onto large plate and peel off foil. ● Cut into squares.

2 cups	flour	500 mL
2 cups	white sugar	500 mL
½ cup	butter OR margarine	125 mL
1 cup	water	250 mL
½ cup	salad oil	125 mL
4 tbsp.	cocoa	60 mL
½ cup	buttermilk	125 mL
1 tsp.	baking soda	5 mL
2	eggs	2
1 tsp.	vanilla	5 mL
	nuts, to taste	

BUTTERMILK BROWNIES

½ cup	butter OR margarine	125 mL
3 tbsp.	cocoa	45 mL
2 tbsp.	buttermilk	30 mL
3 cups	icing sugar	750 mL
1 tsp.	vanilla	5 mL

ICING

Mix together the flour and white sugar. ● In a saucepan, combine margarine, water, oil and cocoa and bring to a boil. Pour over the flour and sugar mixture. ● Add the remaining ingredients. ● Add nuts to taste. ● Pour on a large cookie sheet, or 2, 9″ x 13″ (22 cm x 33 cm) pans. Bake at 375°F (190°C) 20-25 minutes. To make icing, bring first 3 ingredients slowly to a boil, remove from heat. Add icing sugar and vanilla. Pour warm icing over warm cake.

1¼ cups	all-purpose flour	300 mL
¼ tsp.	baking powder	1 mL
½ tsp.	salt	2 mL
½ cup	butter OR margarine	125 mL
¾ cup	brown sugar	175 mL
1	large egg	1
¼ cup	Kahlúa liqueur	50 mL
1 cup	semisweet chocolate pieces	250 mL
¼ cup	chopped walnuts	75 mL
1 tbsp.	Kahlúa, for topping	15 mL

KAHLÚA CHOCOLATE WALNUT SQUARES

2 tbsp.	butter	30 mL
1 tbsp.	Kahlúa	15 mL
2 tsp.	cream	10 mL
1¼ cups	sifted icing sugar	325 mL

BROWN BUTTER ICING

Sift flour with baking powder and salt. ● Cream butter, sugar and egg together. ● Stir in Kahlúa, then flour mixture, blending well. ● Fold in chocolate pieces and walnuts. ● Spread in greased pan, 7″ x 11″ (18 cm x 28 cm). ● Bake at 350°F (180°C) for 30 minutes. ● When cool, brush top with 1 tbsp. (15 mL) Kahlúa. ● When cold spread with Brown Butter Icing. ● To make icing, heat butter until lightly browned. Remove and add Kahlúa, cream and icing sugar. Beat until smooth. Spread on cake. ● Makes 24 squares.

SEX IN A PAN

1 cup	ground pecans	250 mL
1 cup	flour	250 mL
3 tbsp.	sugar	45 mL
½ cup	butter OR margarine	125 mL
8 oz.	cream cheese	250 g
1 cup	icing sugar	250 mL
35 oz.	carton Cool Whip	1 L
6 oz.	pkg. Instant Vanilla Pudding	170 g
6 oz.	pkg. Instant Chocolate Pudding	170 g
2 cups	milk	500 mL

Mix pecans, flour, sugar and butter. Crumble and pat into a greased 9" x 13" (22 cm x 33 cm) pan. Bake at 320°F (155°C) for 25 minutes. Cool. • Mix well the cream cheese, icing sugar and half the Cool Whip. Spread on cooked base. • Beat vanilla pudding with 1 cup (250 mL) milk and spread over last layer. Let set. • When vanilla pudding is set, beat chocolate pudding with 1 cup (250 mL) milk and spread over vanilla pudding. Let set. • Cover with remaining Cool Whip. • Garnish with shaved chocolate. • Can be made ahead and frozen.

BUTTER TART SQUARES

1 ¼ cups	flour	300 mL
½ cup	butter	125 mL
¼ cup	brown sugar	50 mL
¼ cup	butter OR margarine	75 mL
2 tbsp.	cream	30 mL
1 tsp.	vanilla	5 mL
1 cup	raisins OR currants	250 mL
1 cup	brown sugar	250 mL
1	egg, beaten	1
1 tbsp.	flour	15 mL

Prepare base by combining flour, butter and brown sugar. Pack in a 9" (22 cm) square pan. • Combine filling ingredients, spread on base. • Bake at 375°F (190°C) for 20-30 minutes.

PEANUT BUTTER SQUARE

Gluten-free.

½ cup	brown sugar	125 mL
½ cup	corn syrup	125 mL
1 tsp.	vanilla	5 mL
1 cup	peanut butter	250 mL
2 cups	cornflakes	500 mL
1 cup	rice krispies	250 mL
1 cup	brown sugar	250 mL
6 tbsp.	cream	90 mL
2 tsp.	butter	10 mL
	icing sugar	

Heat sugar and syrup to dissolve sugar. Remove from heat and add the remaining ingredients. Press into buttered pan. • Combining icing ingredients. Bring to a boil. Cool. Thicken with icing sugar. • Spread on square.

DESSERT
Frozen Raspberry Cheesecake, page 151

COOKIES

2 cups	brown sugar	500 mL
1 lb.	pkg. frozen puff pastry	500 g

COEURS DE FRANCE

Sprinkle 1 cup (250 mL) sugar over pastry board. Roll out the defrosted pastry, on the sugar, into a rectangle. • Sprinkle the other half of the sugar on top. Roll again. • By hand, roll each short side of the rectangle to the centre. • Slice across the double roll into ½″ (1.3 cm) strips. • Bake at 400°F (200°C) for 15-20 minutes or until golden brown.

½ cup	brown sugar	125 mL
½ cup	white sugar	125 mL
½ cup	butter OR margarine	125 mL
1	egg	1
1 tsp.	vanilla	5 mL
½ cup	flour	125 mL
½ tsp.	salt	2 mL
¼ tsp.	baking soda	1 mL
1 cup	large-flake rolled oats	250 mL
1 cup	cornflakes	250 mL
½ cup	coconut	125 mL
¼ cup	chopped walnuts	50 mL

RANGE COOKIES

Cream sugars and butter. Add egg and vanilla and combine. • Sift flour with salt and baking soda and add rolled oats, cornflakes, coconut and nuts. • Combine all together. • Drop by spoonfuls onto a greased cookie sheet. • Bake in a moderate oven, 350°F (180°C), for 12 minutes or until lightly browned. • This recipe doubles easily. • Yields 3 dozen small cookies.

I'm not overweight, I'm just under tall.

CARROT COOKIES

½ cup	butter	125 mL
1½ cups	brown sugar	375 mL
2	eggs	2
2 cups	flour	500 mL
2 tsp.	baking powder	10 mL
½ tsp.	baking soda	2 mL
1 tsp.	salt	5 mL
½ tsp.	nutmeg	2 mL
1 cup	quick-cooking rolled oats	250 mL
1 cup	chopped dates OR raisins	250 mL
1 cup	finely carrots	250 mL

Cream first 3 ingredients together. • Add sifted dry ingredients and rolled oats, and then the fruit and carrots. • Drop by spoonfuls on greased cookie sheets. • Bake until lightly browned in a 350°F (180°C) oven.

JUMBO RAISIN COOKIES

2 cups	raisins	500 mL
1 cup	water	250 mL
1 cup	shortening	250 mL
1¾ cups	white sugar	425 mL
3	eggs	3
4 cups	flour	1 L
1 tsp.	baking powder	5 mL
1 tsp.	baking soda	5 mL
2 tsp.	salt	10 mL
1½ tsp.	cinnamon	7 mL
½ tsp.	nutmeg	2 mL
¼ tsp.	allspice	1 mL
½ tsp.	cloves	2 mL
2 tsp.	vanilla	10 mL

Boil raisins in the water for 5 minutes. Take off burner and let sit. • Cream shortening and sugar. Add the eggs, 1 at a time; beat well after each. • Sift dry ingredients and add alternately with the liquid from the raisins. • Fold in the raisins and vanilla. • Drop on greased cookie sheets. • Bake in hot oven, 400°F (200°C) for 12-15 minutes. • Yields 6 dozen.

BROWN-EYED SUSANS

¾ cup	butter, creamed	175 mL
½ cup	sugar	125 mL
1½ cups	flour	375 mL
¼ tsp.	salt	1 mL

Mix all ingredients well. • Chill for 1 hour. • Shape into balls, place 2″ (5 cm) apart on an ungreased cookie sheet. • Flatten each by pressing a chocolate wafer into the center. • Bake at 400°F (200°C) for 8-10 minutes. • Remove immediately from pan. • Chocolate mint wafers may also be used. • Yields approximately 3 dozen cookies.

1 cup	butter OR margarine	250 mL
1½ cups	sugar	375 mL
2	eggs	2
2 tsp.	vanilla	10 mL
⅔ cup	cocoa	150 mL
¾ tsp.	baking soda	3 mL
½ tsp.	salt	2 mL
2 cups	flour	500 mL
1-2 cups	raisins	250-500 mL

CHOCOLATE COOKIES

Cream the butter, sugar, eggs and vanilla together. Add dry ingredients until well blended; fold in raisins. • Drop by teaspoonfuls (5 mL) onto greased baking sheet. • Bake in 350°F (180°C) oven for 8-10 minutes.

½ cup	butter	125 mL
1 cup	brown sugar	250 mL
1	egg	1
1¼ cups	flour	325 mL
½ tsp.	baking powder	2 mL
¼ tsp.	salt	1 mL
¼ cup	cocoa	50 mL
1 tsp.	vanilla	5 mL

PEPPERMINT PENNIES

1⅔ cups	icing sugar	400 mL
sprinkle	salt	sprinkle
2-3 tbsp.	milk	30-45 mL
1 tsp.	peppermint extract	5 mL

ICING

Cream butter and sugar. • Add egg and beat well. • Mix dry ingredients and add to creamed mixture. • Blend in vanilla. • Chill batter for 1 hour. • Roll dough, cut into small circles. • Bake on greased cookie sheet at 350°F (180°C) for 12 minutes. • Combine icing ingredients. • When cookies are cool, ice cookie and cover with another.

2	egg whites	2
1 cup	brown sugar	250 mL
¼ tsp.	baking powder	1 mL
½ lb.	pecans, halved	250 g
1 tsp.	vanilla	5 mL

PECAN MACAROONS

Beat egg whites, sugar and baking powder in top of double boiler, over simmering water, until stiff. Add vanilla; fold in pecans. • Drop by teaspoonfuls (5 mL) on greased cookie sheet. • Bake at 250°F (120°C) for 50 minutes. Turn off oven and leave until oven cools down.

One way of getting into debt is to spend what you've led your friends to think you make.

SPECULAAS

A light almond-flavored ice-box cookie, of Danish origin.

2 cups	butter	500 mL
2 cups	sugar	500 mL
4 cups	sifted flour	1 L
4 tsp.	cinnamon	20 mL
½ tsp.	nutmeg	2 mL
½ tsp.	cloves	2 mL
½ tsp.	baking soda	2 mL
¼ tsp.	salt	1 mL
½ cup	sour cream	125 mL
½ cup	chopped almonds	125 mL

Cream butter with sugar. • Sift flour with spices, baking soda and salt. Add, alternating with sour cream, to creamed mixture. • Stir in nuts and knead well. • Shape into 1 or more logs, either round or square. • Wrap in wax paper and refrigerate overnight. • Preheat oven to 400°F (200°C). • Slice and bake on greased cookie sheet until brown, about 8-10 minutes.

CINNAMON TWISTS

5 cups	flour	1.25 L
2 tsp.	baking powder	10 mL
1 lb.	butter OR margarine	500 g
2	eggs	2
1 cup	milk	250 mL
2 cups	white sugar	500 mL
8 tsp.	cinnamon	40 mL

Mix flour and baking powder. Cut butter into flour mixture until the size of peas. • Beat eggs slightly and mix with milk. Mix milk mixture with flour and form into 10 balls. • Mix cinnamon and sugar together. Squeeze mixture into each ball. • Roll out each ball like pastry and cut into small pie wedges. Each should be approximately 1″ (2.5 cm) wide at the widest end. • Roll each wedge up from the wide end to small end, then roll in cinnamon mixture again. • Bake on greased cookie sheet at 375°F (190°C) for 20 minutes. (Watch carefully to be sure the sugar doesn't burn.) • These are very meaty cookies and are much daintier if kept small. • Makes about 1½ ice-cream pails full.

FATTIG MAND

This is a Scandinavian pastry.

2	eggs	2
4	egg yolks	4
½ cup	sugar	125 mL
2 tbsp.	melted butter (not margarine)	30 mL
2 tbsp.	whipping cream	30 mL
1 tsp.	nutmeg (optional)	5 mL
1 tsp.	vanilla (optional)	5 mL
2-2½ cups	flour	500-625 mL

Beat eggs until light and lemon-colored. • Add next 5 ingredients. • Add flour, leaving some for rolling. • Roll to ¼″ (0.6 cm) thickness. • Cut into 4″ x 1½-2″ (10 cm x 3.8-5 cm) strips. Cut a diagonal slit in the center, not cutting through edge. Draw 1 end through the slit to form a bow. • Fry in deep fat until golden brown. • Yields approximately 3-4 dozen.

2⅔ cups	unsifted cake and pastry flour	650 mL
½ tsp.	baking soda	2 mL
¼ tsp.	salt	1 mL
1 tsp.	cinnamon	5 mL
1 cup	butter	250 mL
1 cup	brown sugar	250 mL
1 tsp.	almond extract	5 mL
1	egg, beaten	1
1 tsp.	cold water	5 mL
½ cup	almonds, blanched, flaked OR slivered	125 mL
¼ cup	granulated sugar	50 mL

DUTCH COOKIES

Sift flour, baking soda, salt and cinnamon together. Knead in the butter and brown sugar. Add almond flavoring. • Divide the dough in half and press out thinly right to the edges of 2 ungreased cookie sheets, 10″ x 15″ (25 cm x 38 cm). • Beat the egg and add the water. Brush over cookie dough. Sprinkle with the almonds and sugar. • Bake at 350°F (180°C) for approximately 12 minutes, or until lightly browned. • Cut into rectangles while still warm. • Makes about 5 dozen, 2″ x 3″ (5 cm x 7.5 cm) cookies.

1¼ cups	butter OR margarine	300 mL
1 cup	sugar	250 mL
8 oz.	jar Leyle's Golden Syrup	250 mL
2 tsp.	potash OR baking soda	10 mL
1 tbsp.	water OR rosewater	15 mL
2½ cups	flour	625 mL
3½ oz.	flaked almonds	100 g
	finely grated lemon OR orange rind	
1 tbsp.	ground cloves	15 mL
1 tbsp.	cinnamon	15 mL
1 tsp.	cardamom	5 mL
pinch	ginger	pinch

BRUNEKAGER

Danish gingersnaps.

In large saucepan, heat margarine, sugar and syrup to simmer. • Dissolve the potash, or soda, in the water. Add it to heated mixture and let fizz well. Cool to lukewarm. • Add flour, mixed with spices. • Add the flaked almonds, or save to put a flaked almond on top of each cookie. • Knead mixture thoroughly. Roll in long rolls and chill overnight, or longer. Slice thinly with sharp knife. Place almond flake in center of each cookie if you did not mix them in. • Bake at 350°F (180°C) for about 6 minutes. • These are traditional at Christmas in Denmark, but they go down easily all year round in Canada. Make with butter at Christmas!

197

FAVORITE GINGERSNAPS

2 cups	sifted flour	500 mL
½ tsp.	salt	2 mL
1 tbsp.	baking soda	15 mL
1 tsp.	cloves	5 mL
1 tsp.	ginger	5 mL
1 tsp.	cinnamon	5 mL
¾ cup	shortening	175 mL
1 cup	sugar	250 mL
1	egg, slightly beaten	1
¼ cup	light molasses	50 mL
	granulated sugar	

Sift first 6 ingredients together and set aside. • Cream shortening and gradually add 1 cup (250 mL) sugar. • Blend in egg and molasses; then stir in flour mixture until well blended. • Shape dough in 1" (2.5 cm) balls, roll in granulated sugar and place 2" (5 cm) apart on ungreased cookie sheets. Flatten with fingers and sprinkle with more sugar. • Bake 8-10 minutes at 350°F (180°C). Let stand a minute before removing from pans. • Makes approximately 30 cookies.

WHIPPED SHORTBREAD

1 cup	very soft butter	250 mL
½ cup	icing sugar	125 mL
½ cup	cornstarch	125 mL
1 cup	flour	250 mL
1 tsp.	salt	5 mL

Beat ingredients together until they look like whipped cream. • Drop onto ungreased cookie sheets. • Bake at 325°F (160°C) for 10 minutes, lower heat to 300°F (150°C) and bake 10 minutes longer. • Cool for about 5 minutes on pan for easier handling. • Yields approximately 3 dozen.

JIM'S SHORTBREAD

1 cup	cornstarch	250 mL
3 cups	flour	750 mL
1 cup	icing sugar	250 mL
½ tsp.	cream of tartar	2 mL
¼ tsp.	baking soda	1 mL
1 lb.	butter	500 g

Ingredients can be mixed on virtually any clean surface, or in a mixing bowl. • Mix dry ingredients well, then place the butter on top of the mixture and blend it together manually until you have a large ball of dough. • Preheat oven to 350°F (180°C). • Pinch off about 1 tbsp. (15 mL) of dough per cookie. Roll it into a ball, place it on an ungreased cookie sheet and press flat with a fork. • Decorations can be added, if desired. • Bake for 10 minutes or until the bottom of the cookie is a golden brown. • Ideal for Christmas, or other special occasions, or simply because you are a Cookie Monster! • Yields about 3-4 dozen.

A woman's fondest wish is to be weighed and found wanting.

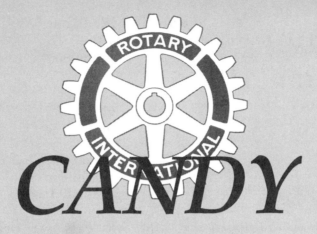

CANDY

1½ cups	salted mixed nuts	375 mL
2 cups	sugar	500 mL
1 cup	packed brown sugar	250 mL
1 cup	corn syrup	250 mL
1 cup	whipping cream	250 mL
1 cup	milk	250 mL
1 cup	butter	250 mL
1 tbsp.	vanilla	15 mL

CHRISTMAS NUT CARAMELS

Butter a 9″ (22 cm) square pan. • Spread nuts in bottom. • Stir sugars, corn syrup, cream, milk and butter in large heavy saucepan. • Set over moderate heat and cook, stirring constantly to 248°F (120°C) on candy thermometer (firm ball in cold water). • Remove from heat and stir in vanilla. • Pour over nuts. • Cool, cut in squares and wrap individually. (Cutting with scissors is easiest.)

1 cup	butter	250 mL
3 cups	brown sugar	750 mL
1 cup	corn syrup	250 mL
10 oz.	can Eagle Brand condensed milk	300 mL
	slivered almonds	

CARAMELS

Heat the sugar, syrup and butter in a heavy saucepan and dissolve, stirring constantly. • Add the milk; cook and stir until syrup cracks in very cold water, about 300°F (150°C). • Stir in the freshly crisped, slivered almonds. • Pour quickly into a well-buttered 9″ x 13″ (22 cm x 33 cm) pan and set to cool. • Turn out onto a board covered with wax paper and cut into squares. • Wrap each in wax paper. • This makes a large quantity of delicious caramels.

Melting chocolate: place chocolate chips or broken pieces in a microproof dish and micro-wave for 2-4 minutes on medium. Stir twice, as chocolate holds its shape.

BRIGADEIRO

2 x 10 oz.	cans Eagle Brand condensed milk	2 x 300 mL
2 tbsp.	cocoa	25 mL
2	egg yolks	2
	chocolate OR colored sprinkles	

In a medium saucepan, heat condensed milk, cocoa and egg yolks, stirring constantly. • When mixture reaches a boil, take off heat. • Transfer the mixture to a buttered plate and let cool for several hours. • With buttered hands, shape into small balls and roll in sprinkles. • Variation: Make balls with a roasted nut inside.

FAVORITE CHOCOLATE FUDGE

1 cup	brown sugar	250 mL
1 cup	white sugar	250 mL
1 cup	cream	250 mL
4 tbsp.	cocoa	60 mL
1 tsp.	salt	5 mL
1 tbsp.	butter	15 mL
1 tsp.	vanilla	5 mL

Combine all ingredients until well-blended. • Boil slowly for 30 minutes, gently stirring occasionally. • Remove from heat. • Beat until smooth and thickened. • Pour into buttered 9" x 9" (22 x 22 cm) pan. Place in refrigerator to set. • Cut into squares. • (Add nuts if you wish before you start beating, or place a nut on each square.) • If you like an orange chocolate flavoring, omit the vanilla and add 1 tsp. (5 mL) Grand Marnier liqueur. Very tasty! • This is a simple fudge recipe, but it does take some patience. Try it, it is so smooth and so delicious, it is worth the time.

CREAMS FOR DIPPING

4 cups	white sugar	1 L
2 tbsp.	butter	30 mL
2 tbsp.	white syrup	30 mL
1 cup	heavy cream	250 mL
½ cup	whole milk, OR if cream isn't really thick, use all cream	125 mL

Stir all ingredients in large heavy saucepan, using only 1 tbsp. (15 mL) butter, over high heat until sugar is dissolved. • Wipe sides of pan with wet paper towelling. • Put lid on pan until it starts to boil hard, then take lid off. • Cook until soft-ball stage. Test with spoon in glass of cold water. Watch closely as it cooks rapidly. • Take off stove, add the other 1 tbsp. (15 mL) of butter and put on the lid. • Cool quickly in snow, or outside where it is cold, or over ice water, until just warm. • Pour out on a buttered board and whip with a paddle until it starts to set, then add flavoring to your taste. • I like grated orange or lemon rind plus a little of the juice. • Roll into balls and dip in light dipping chocolate. • Do not keep in refrigerator.

1¼ cups	sugar, white OR brown	300 mL
1 cup	butter (not margarine)	250 mL
1 tbsp.	corn syrup	15 mL
3 tbsp.	water	50 mL
1 cup	sliced OR slivered almonds	250 mL
6 oz.	chocolate chips almonds for sprinkling	170 g

ALMOND BUTTER CRUNCH

Melts in your mouth — the best candy ever!

Boil to hard-crack stage, 310°F (152°C), the sugar, butter, syrup and water. (Please use a candy thermometer.) • Remove from heat, add almonds, stir and pour onto cookie sheet. Work quickly. • Melt chocolate chips and spread over candy. • Sprinkle with extra almonds. • Refrigerate until very cold. • Break into pieces.

1 cup	white sugar	250 mL
½ cup	white Karo syrup	125 mL
1½ cups	peanuts	375 mL
2 tbsp.	butter	30 mL
½ tsp.	vanilla	2 mL
1 tsp.	baking soda	5 mL

MICROWAVE PEANUT BRITTLE

Grease a cookie sheet and cover with foil. • Use a wooden spoon to mix the ingredients together. • Mix the sugar, syrup and peanuts in a microwave-safe bowl; cook 3 minutes, with spoon in bowl. • Remove and stir, place back in microwave oven another 3 minutes and again leave spoon in bowl. • Remove, stir in butter and cook another 3 minutes. • Working very quickly, stir in vanilla and baking soda. • Spread on cookie sheet and cool • Break into pieces and it is ready to serve.

10 oz.	can Eagle Brand sweetened condensed milk, (do not substitute)	300 mL

CARAMEL SAUCE

Place 1, or more, unopened cans of milk in a large kettle of boiling water. • Keep at boiling point for 3 hours, being careful to keep can well covered with boiling water at all times. • Remove from water and cool. • When cool, remove both ends of the can and push out contents. • Beat until liquid and smooth. • Serve over ice cream. • Unopened, it will keep in the refrigerator for months. • Opened, it will keep for several weeks.

To prevent the bottom crust on pies becoming soggy, grease pie pans with butter. The crust will be soft and flaky.

GRAND MARNIER SAUCE

2	egg yolks	2
¼ cup	brown sugar	50 mL
¼ cup	Grand Marnier	50 mL
1 cup	whipping cream	250 mL
1-2 tsp.	corn syrup	5-10 mL

Beat egg yolks until light, gradually adding brown sugar, then liqueur. • Whip cream and corn syrup until stiff and fold egg mixture into cream. • Chill at least an hour. • Spoon onto servings of fresh fruit compote.

WHIPPED CREAM SAUCE

1	egg, separated	1
½ cup	icing sugar	125 mL
1 tsp.	vanilla	5 mL
dash	salt	dash
¾ cup	heavy cream	175 mL
1-2 tbsp.	rum (optional)	15-30 mL

Beat egg white until stiff and add sugar gradually while beating. • Beat egg yolk until thick and lemon colored. • Fold egg white mixture and egg yolk mixture together and add flavoring and salt. • Whip cream until stiff and fold into the egg mixture. • Add rum if desired. • You can prepare the sauce ahead up to whipping the cream. Just before serving, whip the cream and add the rum. • This has long been our family favorite on carrot or plum pudding.

RUM SAUCE

¼ cup	butter	50 mL
½ cup	brown sugar	125 mL
1 cup	boiling water	250 mL
2 tbsp.	cornstarch, softened in ¼ cup (75 mL) cold water	30 mL
2 tbsp.	lemon juice	30 mL
¼ cup	amber OR white rum	50 mL

Melt butter in a small saucepan and add brown sugar. • Add boiling water and cornstarch mixture. • Stir over medium heat. • Add lemon juice and stir until thickened. • Add rum to suit taste! • This is nice spooned over traditional Christmas pudding or baked apples, but especially good with hot apple pie.

When measuring molasses, dip the measuring cup into flour, first, then every bit of molasses will run out, so the correct measurement will be obtained.

Meringue will always stand up high and perfect if a generous pinch of baking soda is added to beaten egg whites.

202

Special Offerings

MARGUERITA

6½ oz.	can frozen limeade	188 mL
6½ oz.	can water	188 mL
6½ oz.	can tequila	188 mL
3¼ oz.	Triple Sec (½ can)	94 mL
	ice, to fill blender	

Pour above ingredients into blender and blend until frothy. • Makes 6 drinks.

MAI TAI

½ oz.	lemon & lime sweet sour mix	15 mL
1 oz	orange juice	30 mL
1 oz.	pineapple juice	30 mL
1 oz.	passion fruit juice	30 mL
½ oz	grenadine	15 mL
½ oz.	orange Curaço	15 mL
¾ oz.	brandy	20 mL
1½ oz.	white rum	40 mL
1½ oz.	gold rum	40 mL
	fruit garnish	
½ oz.	151 proof rum	15 mL

Add all ingredients except garnish and 151 proof rum to a 15 oz. (425 mL) glass, half filled with ice cubes. • Now stir until well mixed. Garnish with fresh pineapple spear, or slice of orange and cherry. Leave room on top to float 151 proof rum. Do not stir after adding float. • Add straw, sip slowly, relax and let the rest of the world go by. • See photograph page 16A.

ORANGE JULEP

6¼ oz.	can frozen orange juice	178 mL
1 cup	cold water	250 mL
10-12	ice cubes, broken	10-12
1 cup	milk	250 mL
¼ cup	sugar	75 mL

Blend together for 1 minute and serve. • Great on a hot day!

10 lbs.	tomatoes	5 kg
10	drops Tabasco OR chili sauce	10
10	drops fresh lemon juice	10
½ cup	sugar	125 mL
1 tsp.	salt	5 mL

HOMEMADE TOMATO JUICE

Wash the tomatoes, remove core and blossom ends. • Cut into small pieces and cook slowly until soft. • Press through food mill to remove seed and skin. • Reheat juice to boiling point. • Add rest of the ingredients. • Fill hot sterile jars to within ½" (1.3 cm) of the top, partially seal and process in canner for 10 minutes; seal tightly. • Store in cool dark place. • Should keep for several months. • **Note:** You may vary additives to suit personal taste.

½ cup	roka dressing	125 mL
6 oz.	Cheez Whiz	170 g
8 oz.	cream cheese with pimiento	250 g
8 oz.	cream cheese	250 g
½ cup	green sweet relish seasoned salt	125 mL

QUICK GOURMET CHEESE DIP

Mix ingredients together and serve hot or cold, as you wish. • Serve with vegetables, crackers, taco chips, or French bread.

	salmon	
1 tsp.	salt	5 mL
	onion, thickly sliced	
2 cups	white vinegar	500 mL
2 cups	water	500 mL
1½ tbsp.	pickling spices	22 mL
¼ cup	olive oil	50 mL
1 tsp.	salt	5 mL

PICKLED SALMON

Fillet the salmon and remove skin. Cut into serving pieces, lay in pan and sprinkle on 1 tsp. (5 mL) salt. Let sit for 30 minutes. Rinse in warm water and pat dry. • Combine brine ingredients. Bring to a boil and simmer for 30 minutes. • Layer salmon, a thick slice of onion, salmon and so on to fill a 1-quart (1 L) jar. Then pour hot brine over salmon and seal jars. • Refrigerate for 24 hours before serving. • This appetizer is delicious with crackers, toasts or breads. • It will keep for months.

Adding cold milk to cooked potatoes while mashing will cause them to go soggy; add hot milk instead.

CHICKEN WINGS AND OYSTER SAUCE

3 lbs.	chicken wings	1.5 kg
	salt	
1 tbsp.	light soy sauce	15 mL
1 tsp.	dark soy sauce	5 mL
2 tsp.	white wine	10 mL
3 tbsp.	flour	45 mL
	oil for deep frying	

SAUCE

½ cup	oyster sauce	125 mL
½ cup	chicken stock OR water	125 mL
2 tsp.	light soy sauce	10 mL
2 tsp.	sugar	10 mL
½ tsp.	M.S.G. (optional)	2 mL

GARNISH

	green onions, finely cut or cut flat

Wash and cut wings in 3 pieces. Place in big bowl and sprinkle with salt, soy sauces, and wine. Mix, then add flour. • Heat oil to 350°F (180°C) and fry wings, a few at a time, until brown. • Combine the sauce ingredients in a large saucepan and stir well. Add chicken wings and cook slowly covered with a heavy lid, or in oven in a flat pan at 325°F (160°C). • Garnish and serve on bed of rice or Chinese noodles. • Serves 4..

LOU'S HORS D'OEUVRES

1	pkg. chicken livers	1
1 lb.	bacon	500 g
2 x 5 oz.	cans whole water chestnuts	2 x 150 g
2 cups	soy sauce	500 mL

The day before, if you are thinking cooking, start marinating the whole chestnuts by first draining them, then covering them in soy sauce. The longer they marinate, the better they'll taste. • If you weren't fortunate enough to find fresh chicken livers, don't forget to thaw them out. • Cut the bacon strips in half. (So they are shorter, not narrower!) Now, place a chicken liver beside 1 of the chestnuts, and wrap in bacon. If you are a persistent type, you will probably discover a way to stretch the bacon so it will go around the whole assembly. If you are not persistent, don't panic, you're having fun, right? • Now, how's your motor control? Holding this assembly in 1 hand, grab for a toothpick with the other, and pierce this potential as if it were a club house sandwich you didn't want to fall over. Except in this case, it's an hors d'oeuvre you don't want to have fall apart. (You end up with too many hors d'oeuvres if they fall apart . . . but more variety!) Place the result of your efforts on a greased baking pan, or cookie sheet, or something you can stick in a 400°F (200°C) oven. Now do just that — stick it in a 400°F (200°C) oven, for about 20 minutes. (But end this step if it looks like they are starting to dry out. Then stroke out 20, and write in 15.) Then turn on the broiler, and zap them for another 5 minutes. • Now feed your face, and if you approve, those of your guests. • ENJOY! • See photograph page 48A.

6 cups	water	1.5 L
2	small ribs celery with leaves, cut in half	2
1½ tsp.	salt	7 mL
4	whole peppercorns	4
1 lb.	chicken livers, trimmed	500 g
1 cup	unsalted butter, in 1" (2.5 cm) pieces	250 mL
¼ cup	Calvados (apple brandy) OR Applejack	50 mL
¼ cup	coarsely chopped onion	50 mL
2 tsp.	dry mustard	10 mL
1	small clove garlic	1
½ tsp.	freshly grated nutmeg	2 mL
⅛ tsp.	ground cloves	0.5 mL
pinch	ground red (cayenne) pepper	pinch
½ cup	dried currants	125 mL

DEEGAN'S PÂTÉ MAISON

Heat water, celery, ½ tsp. (2 mL) salt and the peppercorns in medium saucepan over high heat to boiling. Add livers; return to boil; lower heat to medium-low. Cook 10 minutes. Drain livers; discard celery and peppercorns. • Combine livers, butter, Calvados, onion, mustard, remaining 1 tsp. (5 mL) salt, garlic, nutmeg, cloves and red pepper in medium bowl. • Process in batches in food processor until smooth. Stir in currants. Pour into 3-cup (750 mL) crock. Cover surface of pâte with plastic wrap. • Refrigerate until firm, 4-6 hours. • Let stand at room temperature for 1 hour before serving. Serve with crisp crackers and cornichons. • Makes about 2½ cups (625 mL).

1	chicken	1
2 tbsp.	butter, melted	30 mL
5	small onions	5
2 tbsp.	curry powder	30 mL
6 cups	stock	1.5 L
½ tsp.	salt	2 mL
3 oz.	almonds, crushed	85 g
1	lemon, juice of	1

MULLIGA-TAWNY SOUP

Cut chicken in small pieces and fry in melted butter. • Fry onions in same butter. • Mix curry and stock and let simmer for 2 hours. • Add fried chicken and onions to stock and, just before serving, add salt, almonds and lemon juice.

Always soak raisins before adding them to your fruit breads so they will not absorb moisture from the bread, making it dry.

EGG ROLLS

2	pkgs. frozen egg roll wrappers	2
1 lb.	ground pork	500 g
	garlic powder, to taste	
2 tbsp.	cornstarch	30 mL
2 tbsp.	soy sauce	30 mL
1-1½ lbs.	fresh bean sprouts	500-750 g
6.5 oz.	can broken shrimp	184 g
10 oz.	can mushroom stems and pieces	284 mL
	corn oil for deep frying	
4	green onions, minced	4
	salt, to taste	
1 tbsp.	sugar	15 mL
1 cup	chopped celery (optional)	250 mL
	egg white	

Defrost egg roll wrappers. • Sprinkle ground pork with garlic, cornstarch and soy sauce. Mix well. Set aside. • Rinse and drain bean sprouts, shrimp, and mushrooms. • Heat wok, add 3 tbsp. (45 mL) oil. Add pork mixture, stir-fry at high heat until meat is no longer pink. Add balance of the ingredients and stir-fry. • Place a spoonful of mixture on wrapper. Seal with egg white. • Deep fry until golden brown. • Freezes well. • Warm in oven and serve with plum sauce and hot mustard. • Makes about 50.

MEAL-IN-A-BOWL SOUP

1 lb.	ground beef	500 g
½ cup	chopped onion	125 mL
4 cups	beef broth	1 L
1¼ cups	water	325 mL
10 oz.	pkg frozen peas	283 g
2	large potatoes, peeled and cubed	2
1 cup	sliced fresh mushrooms	250 mL
1	large carrot, chopped	1
1	small zucchini, sliced	1
1½ tsp.	crushed dried basil	7 mL
¾ tsp.	ground sage	3 mL
½ tsp.	salt	2 mL
⅛ tsp.	pepper	0.5 mL

Cook ground beef and onion until meat is browned and onion is tender. Drain off fat. • Stir in beef broth, water, peas, potatoes, mushrooms, carrot, zucchini, basil, sage, salt and pepper. Bring to a boil, lower heat, cover and simmer about 15 minutes, stirring occasionally. • NOTE: You can substitute 5¼ cups (1.3 L) of water and 3 tbsp. (45 mL) instant beef bouillon granules for the beef broth and 1¼ cups (325 mL) water. • Serves 6.

4	strips bacon, chopped	4
1	small onion, chopped	1
2	stalks celery, chopped	2
½	green pepper, chopped	½
1	garlic clove, minced	1
¼	bay leaf	¼
2 x 10 oz.	tins whole baby clams, undrained	2 x 284 mL
½ cup	water	125 mL
2 cups	diced raw potatoes	500 mL
1 tsp.	H. P. Sauce	5 mL
½ tsp.	salt	2 mL
⅛ tsp.	pepper	0.5 mL
¼ cup	salad oil	50 mL
¼ cup	flour	50 mL
½ cup	18% cream	125 mL
2 cups	milk	500 mL

CLAM CHOWDER

To a large pot, add the bacon, onion, celery, green pepper and garlic; sauté gently for 5 minutes, stirring often. ● Add the bay leaf, the liquid from the clams, the water, diced potatoes, H.P. Sauce, salt and pepper and simmer until the potatoes are barely tender. ● Combine oil and flour and stir into the chowder mixture to thicken. ● Add the clams, cream and milk and bring to a boil! ● Remove the bay leaf. ● Serves approximately 6. ● See photograph page 64A.

1	small OR medium onion	1
4-6	pork chops	4-6
4	potatoes, cut up	4
10 oz.	can cream of mushroom soup	284 mL
¼ tsp.	rosemary	1 mL
¼ tsp.	marjoram	1 mL
¼ cup	wine (optional)	50 mL
½ cup	chopped celery (optional)	125 mL
	garlic, to taste (optional)	
1 tsp.	horseradish (optional)	5 mL

CHOPPED SOUP

An easy casserole dish that is just as good when it is reheated.

Cut up onion and add to pork chops in heavy saucepan. Brown quickly, but do not burn or overcook. ● Add potatoes, soup and seasonings to pan. Let simmer for 45 minutes. ● This is a very forgiving dish! You can add the following if you like, wine (I prefer white but red is OK too), celery, garlic, horseradish, or try your own favorites.

Before serving cream soups, beat with your egg beater for a few seconds and a wonderful smooth soup will result.

ROCKY MOUNTAIN BOUILLABAISSE

This Bouillabaisse is not authentic. Especially so far away from an ocean. However, since there arguably is no such thing as "the real thing", and fresh seafood is available, I have no qualms about suggesting this recipe as a real winner. The hallmark of a good Bouillabaisse is how you cook it and how it tastes, rather than the strictness of the formula or the pedigree of the ingredients. (Even in Marseilles debates rage over which fish to use or whether it's proper to use shellfish.) So I have developed a Western-Canadian version which has satisfied many, and disappointed few.

3-4 lbs.	fresh white solid-type fish fillets (cod, turbot OR red snapper) cut in ¾" (2 cm) squares	1.5-2 kg
1½ lbs.	large fresh prawns, cleaned and shelled (approx. 5-6 per person)	750 g
1½ lbs.	mussels in the shell, washed	750 g
1½ lbs.	clams in the shell, washed	750 g
1½ lbs.	crab OR 1 large meaty crab leg per person	750 g
¼ cup	olive oil (do not substitute)	50 mL
1	large onion, (not Spanish) chopped	1
1-2	garlic cloves, crushed, OR to taste	1-2
19 oz.	can peeled whole tomatoes OR equivalent in fresh (6-8)	540 mL
2	celery stalks, chopped	2
2	carrots, chopped	2
2	bay leaves, broken up	2
½ tsp.	freshly ground fennel	2 mL
¼ tsp.	freshly ground anise	1 mL
½-¾ tsp.	ground saffron	2-3 mL
	freshly ground black pepper, to taste	
1 tsp.	parsley	5 mL
¾ oz.	orange brandy OR Grand Marnier	22 mL
4 oz.	white Dubonnet	113 mL

To peel tomatoes for any use, place in boiling water 15 seconds. Then in cold water, and the skin slips off easily.

ROCKY MOUNTAIN BOUILLABAISSE
(continued)

Well ahead of time prepare the fish and seafood. Start cooking approximately 1 hour before serving. • Prepare the stock by heating the olive oil in a large saucepan (this pot can be used to prepare the whole dish). Add the onions and the garlic. Simmer for 3-4 minutes, add the tomatoes, celery, carrots and bay leaves. After 5 minutes on medium heat, add half of the fresh fish cubes with 6 cups (1.5 L) of cold water. Simmer for 30 minutes, adding the fennel, anise, saffron, pepper and parsley. • Approximately 20 minutes before serving, add the orange brandy and Dubonnet. Stir in the remaining fish cubes. Add remaining spices to taste. Add and gently stir in the mussels, clams and crab legs. Three minutes before serving, drop in the prawns, cover with lid, turn off the heat and it's ready to serve. • Don't be afraid to add extra water to make the stock go further, but not after you have added the shellfish. • Serve with a zesty Caesar Salad, fresh French bread and your favorite white wine, followed with a filling dessert of your choice. • It's an easy dish to prepare and serve with the company "in-the-kitchen" if you have prepared the ingredients ahead. Great summer or winter! • Serves 6-8. • See photograph on back cover.

19 oz.	can diced beets	540 mL	**COLD BEET SOUP**
2 cups	buttermilk	500 mL	
2 cups	cold chicken stock OR 2 bouillon cubes OR Chicken-In-A-Mug in water	500 mL	
2-3	hard-boiled eggs, chopped	2-3	
1	medium cucumber, peeled, sliced, slices quartered	1	
3-4	green onions OR chives, chopped	3-4	
2 tbsp.	chopped dill salt and pepper lemon juice	25 mL	

Combine all ingredients in a bowl. • Place in refrigerator and enjoy when chilled!

2 tbsp. (30 mL) lemon juice or vinegar added to 1 cup (250 mL) of milk will sour it immediately. Always put the lemon juice in the measuring cup first.

LENTIL SOUP

A most hearty meal, recorded in the bible 3,500 years ago. These notes follow, as closely as possible, the ancient recipe.

1 lb.	lentils (about 2 cups [500 mL])	500 g
2	slices bacon, diced	2
1	large onion, sliced	1
½	green pepper, diced	½
2	garlic cloves, crushed	2
1	carrot, sliced	1
2 qts.	beef stock OR 2 beef cubes plus water	2 L
¼ tsp.	thyme	1 mL
1	bay leaf	1
2	potatoes, in ½" (1.3 cm) cubes	2
1	stalk celery, sliced	1
2 tsp.	apple cider vinegar	10 mL
	salt and pepper	
	frankfurters, knackwurst OR garlic ring	

Wash the lentils in cold water, drain and set aside. • In a pot large enough for the soup and the sausages, fry together, for about 4 minutes, the bacon, onions, green pepper, garlic and carrot. • Add the beef stock or water and bouillon cubes, the lentils, thyme and the bay leaf. Simmer for 1 hour. • Add the diced potatoes and the celery., Simmer for another hour. • During the last 20 minutes, add the vinegar and salt and pepper to taste. Drop the sausages into the pot for heating. With the soup, our family eats slices of dark rye bread or crusty rolls. And of course a bottle of dry red wine is a must! — No wonder Essau sold his birthright to his brother Jacob for a meal of lentil soup: "Then Jacob gave Essau bread and pottage of lentils; and he did eat and drink, and rose up and went his way: thus Essau despised his birthright" Genesis XXV:34. • Serves 6.

IMPOSSIBLE PIE

2 cups	chopped zucchini	500 mL
½ cup	chopped onion	125 mL
1 cup	chopped tomato	250 mL
¼ cup	grated Parmesan cheese	75 mL
1½ cups	milk	375 mL
¾ cup	biscuit mix	175 mL
3	eggs	3
½ tsp.	salt	2 mL
¼ tsp.	pepper	1 mL

Preheat oven to 400°F (200°C). • Grease a 10" (25 cm) quiche pan, or a 10½" (1 L) pie plate. • Sprinkle zucchini, onion, tomato and cheese in pan. • Beat remaining ingredients until smooth on high speed for 1 minute. • Pour into pan. • Bake for approximately 35 minutes, or until knife inserted in center comes out clean. • Cool for 5 minutes.

1	medium onion, sliced	1
1	green pepper, in ½" (1.3 cm) squares	1
¼ cup	sweet pickle relish	75 mL
¼ cup	vinegar	50 mL
½ cup	barbecue sauce (hickory best)	125 mL
2 cups	brown sugar	500 mL
2 tsp.	dry mustard	10 mL
¼ tsp.	Tabasco Sauce	1 mL
½ tsp.	instant coffee	2 mL
2 x 28 oz.	cans baked beans	2 x 796 mL
6	slices bacon, diced	6

BAPTISTE BARBECUE BEANS

Combine all ingredients in a saucepan and simmer 10 minutes. • This recipe is better if left to sit overnight and then reheated and served. • Serves 6-8.

1 lb.	bacon, in ½" (1.3 cm) dice	500 g
6	large potatoes, peeled	6
1	small head of lettuce	1
1	large onion, finely chopped	1
1 cup	mayonnaise salt, to taste	250 mL

SLIP 'N' GO DOWN

Fry bacon pieces while you boil potatoes until tender. • Chop lettuce into thick slices. • Drain potatoes and mash. • Add remaining ingredients and mix gently. • Serve immediately. • Goes well with poultry, ham or roast pork. Also excellent for a barbecue buffet as bacon and potatoes can be done ahead of time and reheated in the microwave and then remaining ingredients added.

1 cup	uncooked long-grain rice	250 mL
12 oz.	kernel corn	341 mL
2 x 7½ oz.	cans tomato sauce	2 x 213 mL
¾	can water	¾
½ cup	chopped onion	125 mL
¾ lbs.	lean ground beef salt and pepper, to taste	365 g
4	bacon strips, cut in half	4

LAYERED CASSEROLE

Place in layers: rice, corn, 1 can tomato sauce and ½ can of water, onions, uncooked beef, second can tomato sauce and ¼ can of water. Season to taste. Cover with bacon. • Cover, bake at 350°F (180°C) for 1 hour. Then bake uncovered for ½ hour more. • Serves 4-6.

SWISS CHEESE FONDUE

Good dish for wintertime

7 oz.	Emmenthaler cheese (Swiss)	200 g
10½ oz.	Gruyére Cheese (Swiss)	300 g
4 tbsp.	kirsch brandy	60 mL
1 tbsp.	cornstarch	15 mL
1	loaf white Italian bread	1
1	garlic clove	1
2 cups	dry white wine (Swiss Fendant)	500 mL
	nutmeg and pepper	

Have all ingredients ready ahead of time. Grate the cheeses, which must be natural, not pasteurized. • Mix the kirsch brandy and the cornstarch. Slice the Italian bread into ¾" (2 cm) cubes. Each cube should have a crust on 1 side. • Rub a ceramic pot with a clove of garlic. • Fill with 2 cups (500 mL) of dry white wine (Fendant type), put on stove at medium heat until wine is simmering (do not boil). • Then add, slowly, the grated cheese, constantly stirring with a wooden spoon. • Keep the heat high, but do not boil! • When the shredded cheese has dissolved in the wine, add the mixture of kirsch and cornstarch, stirring constantly. • Add nutmeg and pepper to taste. • Place the ceramic pot over medium fondue heat. • Each guest dips his cube of bread into the cheese fondue with a fork. Use a second fork to eat fondue. Serve tea or white wine. • It is important to use a ceramic pot, not metal!! • Serves 4.

EVERYMAN'S THERMIDOR AU GRATIN

½ cup	butter	125 mL
½ cup	flour	125 mL
1 tsp.	salt	5 mL
pinch	cayenne	pinch
¼ tsp.	dry mustard	1 mL
2½ cups	milk	625 mL
¼ cup	butter	50 mL
½ lb.	fresh mushrooms, sliced	250 g
1 tbsp.	minced onion	15 mL
3 cups	poached cod OR haddock chunks	750 mL
2 tbsp.	sherry	30 mL
¼ cup	Parmesan and/OR Romano cheese	75 mL
½ cup	bread crumbs	125 mL

Melt butter over low heat. • Add flour, salt, cayenne and mustard. Stir until smooth. • Add milk slowly. Stir and cook until thickened and smooth. Remove from heat. • Melt ¼ cup (50 mL) butter, sauté mushrooms and onion. • Add mushrooms, onion, fish and sherry to sauce. • Mix gently, then pour into a buttered casserole. • Sprinkle with cheese and bread crumbs. • Bake in a 350°F (180°C) oven for 15 minutes until bubbly hot. • Serves 6.

SMOKED FISH

	trout OR salmon fillets (skin left on 1 side)	
8 cups	water	2 L
1 cup	coarse OR pickling salt	250 mL
½ cup	brown sugar	125 mL
1½ oz.	lemon juice	30 mL
1 tsp.	garlic salt	5 mL
3-4	slices of onion	3-4

Both trout and salmon work very well for this recipe. Depending upon the size of your smoker use 6 fillets or more. Cut fillets in serving-sized pieces leaving the skin on. • Combine remaining ingredients and stir until salt is dissolved. Soak fillets in the marinade (brine) for approximately 1 hour and 15 minutes. • Place fish on the racks of your smoker, skin side down, with the thicker pieces on the bottom rack. • Smoke fish for 4-6 hours. • This recipe is for small home electric smokers using hickory-flavored wood chips.

CURRIED SHRIMP

¼ cup	chopped onion	50 mL
3 tbsp.	butter	45 mL
4 tbsp.	flour	60 mL
¾ tsp.	sugar	3 mL
1 tsp.	curry powder	5 mL
⅛ tsp.	ginger	0.5 mL
½ cup	chicken broth	125 mL
2 cups	milk	500 mL
2 cups	shrimp	500 mL
4-5 cups	cooked rice	1-1.25 L
½ cup	chopped celery OR water chestnuts (optional)	125 mL
¼ cup	chopped pimiento (optional)	50 mL
	extra ginger (optional)	

Sauté the onion in the butter. • Add the flour, sugar, curry and ginger to make a roux. • Slowly add the chicken broth and the milk. • Stir until smooth and thick. • Lastly, add the shrimp and serve on a bed of rice. (I cook the rice in the microwave and add the chopped celery, or water chestnuts, the chopped pimiento and increase the ginger to ½ tsp.[2mL].)

Try serving leftover vegetables by sprinkling them with grated cheese and browning the resulting casserole in the oven.

Add a few drops of vinegar to the water when you boil rice, and it won't stick to the pan.

BARBECUE SHRIMP

Without the barbecue.

1½ lbs.	medium shrimp, shelled, deveined	750 g
¾ cup	butter OR margarine	175 mL
2 tbsp.	Dijon mustard	30 mL
1½ tsp.	chili powder	7 mL
¼ tsp.	basil	1 mL
¼ tsp.	thyme	1 mL
2 tsp.	black pepper	10 mL
½ tsp.	oregano	2 mL
2-3	garlic cloves, chopped	2-3
2 tbsp.	chopped onion	30 mL
1 tbsp.	seafood seasoning OR equivalent	15 mL
½ tsp.	Tabasco	2 mL

Prepare shrimp. Use a wok or pot that can be put in the oven. On surface heat, medium to high, add all the ingredients, except the shrimp, and mix well. ● When the margarine has melted, add the shrimp and coat well. ● Place in preheated 370°F (190°C) oven for 20 minutes. ● Serve hot. ● NOTE: Should you choose to do so, the shells can be left on the shrimp, allow your guests to shell them.

LINGUINI WITH CLAM SAUCE

1	garlic clove, crushed	1
1	onion, finely chopped	1
2 tsp.	olive oil	10 mL
½ cup	dry white wine	125 mL
2 cups	chicken broth	500 mL
2 x 5 oz.	cans baby clams	2 x 142 g
4 oz.	can shrimp (optional)	113 g
6.5 oz.	crab meat (optional)	184 g
dash	ground pepper	dash
3	dashes Tabasco sauce	3
1 tsp.	oregano	5 mL
6 oz.	cream cheese, cubed	170 g
1 lb.	linguini noodles	500 g
	grated Parmesan	
	chopped parsley	

In a 4-quart (4 L) saucepan, sauté the garlic and onion in oil until the onion is soft and transparent (do not brown). ● Add wine and chicken broth, then clams with liquid; add seafood, if desired. ● Add the pepper, Tabasco and oregano. ● Simmer (do not boil) for a full 30 minutes. ● Add cream cheese and stir into sauce mixture until well-blended. ● Cook the linguini in boiling salted water — linguini noodles should never be cooked longer than 10 minutes. Drain well and rinse in cold water to remove starch and then warm under hot water. ● Add to sauce and let pasta sit in sauce for 3-4 minutes to absorb flavor. ● Serve on a large platter. ● Sprinkle with Parmesan cheese and parsley. ● Serve immediately. ● Serves 6-8.

3 tbsp.	paprika	45 mL
2½ tbsp.	salt	30 mL
1 tbsp.	onion powder	15 mL
1 tbsp.	garlic powder	15 mL
1 tbsp.	cayenne pepper	15 mL
2 tsp.	white pepper	10 mL
2 tsp.	black pepper	10 mL
1½ tsp.	dried thyme leaves	7 mL
1½ tsp.	dried oregano leaves	7 mL

BLACKENED FISH (OR STEAKS)

The seasoning mix for this dish can be premixed in large quantities and stored in a 6-8 oz. (170-250 g) spice tin.

For good results, to blacken steak or fish, a very hot skillet is required and, therefore, very high heat is needed. 30,000 plus B.T.U. gas grill (a charcoal fire will not do) will work out of doors. If you are going to cook this indoors, then insure that your hood vent fan is on; any other fan in the house is on; open all the windows and quite possibly you may have to resort to opening the doors. Don't forget to turn your smoke alarm off. • This method of cooking does produce smoke, however, the end result does justify this slight inconvenience. • NOTE: Altering the cayenne pepper will determine the hotness of the fish or steak.

8-10 oz.	per person either: red fish, pompano, tyle fish, red snapper or Salmon steaks, ½"-¾" (1.3-2 cm) thick unsalted butter	250-285 g

BLACKENED FISH

Heat a cast iron skillet over very high heat until it is extremely hot (a minimum of 10 minutes). • When the skillet is hot, prepare the fillets by liberally coating both sides of fish with melted unsalted butter then sprinkling seasoning mix generously and evenly on 1 side, patting it in by hand. • Place the fillets, seasoned side down, in the hot skillet and pour 1 tsp. (5 mL) melted butter on top of each fillet. BUTTER MAY FLARE, SO BE CAREFUL. • Cook uncovered over high heat until the underside is charred (approximately 2 minutes). • Before turning, sprinkle the fillet with seasoning mix, generously and evenly, and after turning the fish over, again pour 1 tsp. (5 mL) butter on top. • Cook until fish is ready (approximately 2 minutes more). • Serve fillets quickly on warm plates.

---

steaks, not more than ¾" (2 cm) thick

STEAKS

Using the same seasoning mix, brush the steak with unsalted butter and then sprinkle the seasoning mix generously and evenly on both sides of the steak, pressing it in. • Into the cast iron skillet, heated over high heat (at least 10 minutes), place 1 steak at a time and cook over the very high heat until the underside starts to develop a heavy black crust (2-3 minutes). Turn the steak over and cook for another 2-3 minutes. The steak should not be more than ¾" (2 cm) thick.

PEPPER STEAK

A recipe which will please the most discriminating taste!

1	large steak, cubes OR strips	1
½ cup	soy sauce	125 mL
1 tsp.	ground ginger	5 mL
1 tsp.	sugar (optional)	5 mL
4-6	drops hickory liquid smoke, (optional)	4-6
1 tsp.	Worcestershire sauce (optional)	5 mL
2 cups	finely chopped onions	500 mL
1 tbsp.	vegetable oil	15 mL
	Hy's Seasoning Salt, to taste	
¼ tsp.	garlic powder OR 2 garlic cloves, finely crushed (optional)	1 mL
1 cup	chopped fresh mushrooms OR 2 cups (250 mL) frozen mushrooms, precooked	250 mL
¼ cup	cubed green pepper	50 mL
2 cups	nearly boiling water	500 mL
	cornstarch	
	cold water	
	Tabasco (optional)	
	chopped celery	

Choose your own cut of steak, however, round steak is very suitable. HINT: Slightly frozen steak is most easily cut. Place cut steak in a deep mixing bowl (not metal). • Combine soy sauce, water, ginger, sugar and stir to dissolve. If additional flavor is desired, add hickory liquid smoke and/or Worcestershire sauce to the marinade. Pour marinade over steak and marinate, at room temperature, for 2-4 hours, stirring occasionally. Onions may be marinated with the meat, or cooked separately. • Heat oil in wok or frying pan, add meat; use Hy's Seasoning Salt to taste. Brown only. Garlic fans may add additional garlic. Add onions, if not in the marinade. Continue cooking until onions are soft. Add mushrooms and green peppers, stir-fry with meat for 5 minutes. Add marinade and hot water, bring to boil, stirring constantly; reduce heat, simmer for 30 minutes. Thicken with cornstarch in cold water to obtain desired consistency, simmer for 5-10 mintues. Tabasco sauce may be added to meet your desired taste. Sautéed chopped celery may be added for additional flavor. • Serve with warm brown or whole wheat-rolls, or on rice which has been cooked in Clamato juice with ½ tsp. (2 mL) of sugar. Quick-cooking rice is most effective. This dish may be prepared in advance or frozen for future use. Advance preparation often produces a deeper flavor. HINT: Taste continuously while cooking to savor the full effect of your spices. Italian Seasoning added to simmering mixture is excellent.

4½ lbs.	lean ground beef	2 kg
1 cup	water	250 mL
2 tbsp.	liquid smoke	30 mL
¼ cup	quick-cure salt	50 mL
½ tsp.	pepper	2 mL
1 tsp.	garlic salt	5 mL
1 tsp.	M.S.G.	5 mL

SALAMI SAUSAGE

Combine all ingredients and put in covered bowl in refrigerator for 24 hours. ● Roll into 3 or 4 rolls. ● Place on wire rack on cookie sheet. Bake at 225°F (110°C) for 5 hours. ● Freezes well.

2 lbs.	hamburger	1 kg
1½ tsp.	salt	7 mL
1 tsp.	poultry seasoning	5 mL
10 oz.	tomato juice	284 mL
1	chopped onion	1
1¾ cups	sifted flour	425 mL
1 tsp.	baking powder	5 mL
½ tsp.	salt	2 mL
4	eggs	4
2 cups	milk	500 mL

YORKSHIRE STEAK

Heat oven to 450°F (230°C). ● Mix first 5 ingredients and spread in a greased pan. Bake 10 minutes. Skim off fat. Break up meat with fork. ● Sift dry ingredients together. ● Beat eggs well. Beat in milk and flour alternately. Pour over meat and bake for 30 minutes. ● Serve with tomato sauce or gravy.

1 lb.	brown and serve sausage, OR bulk sausage meat	500 g
½ cup	butter OR margarine	125 mL
½ cup	orange marmalade	125 mL
1	pkg. Bran Muffin mix, OR favorite Bran Muffin recipe	1

WELSH SAUSAGE BAKE

Brown sausage and drain. ● Melt butter in a 10″ x 12″ (3-4 L) baking dish. ● Stir in marmalade. ● Arrange sausages on top of butter-marmalade mixture. ● Prepare muffin mix and spoon on top of sausage. ● Bake at 350°F (180°C) for 30-35 minutes. ● Cut into squares. ● Immediately invert onto large serving platter.

If you boil sausage for about 5 minutes before frying, or coat it with flour, it won't shrink.

BARBECUED SPARERIBS

Use side ribs as they are less expensive than back ribs and contain more meat, however, the following steps of preparation are necessary. • Cut and discard the tail at the last good rib as this piece is tough. Remove the membrane, which will be found on the inside of the ribs. Scrape away excess fat. • Barbecue these ribs without a barbecue, on the oven rack, in the Chinese fashion. Place a single oven rack in the uppermost position in the oven and to the underside attach the spareribs by utilizing coat hangers which have been cut and formed into small meat hooks, so that the ribs are hanging vertically. By proper positioning several racks of spareribs can be cooked at one time. Place under the ribs a large pan of water to catch fat drippings. • To cook the ribs, coat each rack of ribs with the Barbecue Sauce, below, and place in 375°F (190°C) oven. Do not open the door; cook for 45 minutes. Raising the heat to 450°F (230°C), roast for another 15 minutes. During the whole hour of cooking, the oven door should not be opened. Remove ribs from oven, cut each rack of ribs into single ribs and place into a pot containing sufficient warm (not boiling) Barbecue Sauce so that all ribs will be covered. Simmer for 1 hour prior to serving. • It is not recommended that the Barbecue Sauce be utilized a second time.

BARBECUE SAUCE

36 oz.	tomato ketchup	1.125 L
24 oz.	red wine vinegar	750 mL
8 oz.	vegetable oil	250 mL
6	onions, chopped	6
3 cups	water	750 mL
¾ cup	Worcestershire sauce	175 mL
4 tbsp.	dry mustard	60 mL
2 tbsp.	salt	30 mL
2 tbsp.	paprika	30 mL
½ tsp.	Tabasco sauce	2 mL
1 tbsp.	garlic powder	15 mL
2	lemons, juice and pulp added to sauce, skins to be removed and discarded after simmering	2
12 oz.	honey	375 mL

This produces a succulent barbecue rib due to the simmering of the rib in the barbecue sauce prior to serving. • The quantity of sauce is, therefore, greater and any sauce not utilized to cover the ribs in the simmering stage may be saved for a period of time, if refrigerated. • Combine ingredients except honey in a heavy non-reactive saucepan and mix well. Bring to a boil and reduce the heat and simmer until the sauce begins to thicken, approximately 30 minutes. • After sauce thickens add honey, stirring to blend. • This will make approximately 18 cups (4.5 L) of sauce.

1 tbsp.	salt	15 mL	
1 tsp.	onion powder	5 mL	
¾ tsp.	garlic powder	3 mL	
½ tsp.	white pepper	2 mL	
½ tsp.	dry mustard	2 mL	
½ tsp.	rubbed sage	2 mL	
½ tsp.	ground cumin	2 mL	
½ tsp.	dried thyme leaves	2 mL	
12	pork chops, ½" (1.25 cm) thick	12	
	vegetable oil, for frying		
1¼ cups	all-purpose flour	300 mL	

CAJUN PORK CHOPS

Combine first 8 ingredients in a small bowl to make seasoning mix. • Sprinkle pork chops with 2 tbsp. (30 mL) seasoning mix, patting it in with your hands. Set aside. • In a large skillet, over medium-high heat, heat ¼" (0.6 cm) oil until hot, about 2 minutes. • Just before frying, dredge each chop in the seasoned flour mixture, shaking off excess. • Fry in hot oil until golden brown, about 4-5 minutes per side. • Change oil if sediment starts to burn. • Drain chops on a paper towel. • Serve with Garlic Butter, below.

¾ cup	butter	175 mL	
2 tsp.	minced garlic	10 mL	
4 tsp.	minced fresh parsley	20 mL	
1 tbsp.	Tabasco sauce	15 mL	

GARLIC BUTTER

Melt butter in small saucepan, over high heat, until half melted, shaking pan almost constantly. • Add garlic and cook until butter is melted and foam on the surface is barely browned, about 2-3 minutes, shaking pan occasionally. • Stir in parsley and Tabasco Sauce; cook until sauce is lightly browned and very foamy, about 1-2 minutes. • Remove from heat and immediately drizzle over Cajun Pork Chops, above. • Yields ⅔ cup (150 mL) sauce.

4-6	center-cut pork chops	4-6	
	salt and pepper, to taste		
12 oz.	beer	341 mL	
3 tbsp.	brown sugar	50 mL	
¾ cup	ketchup	175 mL	

WESTERN PORK CHOPS

Brown the pork chops, season with salt and pepper and place in a baking dish. • Mix the remaining ingredients and pour over the chops. • Bake for 1 ½ hours, covered, in a 375°F (190°C) oven. • Remove cover for last 15 minutes. • Serve with rice and a salad. • Sauce can be poured over rice and leftover sauce can be used for Sloppy Joes. • Serves 4-6.

PORK CHOPS AND BROWNED RICE

6-8	medium pork chops	6-8
1 cup	raw rice	250 mL
1	onion, chopped	1
19 oz.	can tomatoes	540 mL
½ cup	chopped green pepper (optional)	125 mL
	salt and pepper	

Brown chops in frying pan. Remove, leaving 2 tbsp. (30 mL) fat. • Brown rice and onion. • Add tomatoes and green pepper to rice and onion mixture. • Pour tomato mixture into greased casserole, add salt and pepper to taste. • Place chops on top of mixture in casserole; cover. • Cook at 350°F (180°C) for at least 1 hour. • NOTE: You may need to add a little water during cooking. • "Fred's Favorite" from university days. • Serves 6-8.

BAKED DEVILLED PORK CHOPS

8	pork chops, trimmed of excess fat	8
	garlic salt, to taste	
1	large onion, finely chopped	1
4 tbsp.	lemon juice	60 mL
1 cup	ketchup	250 mL
1 tsp.	dry mustard	5 mL
2 tbsp.	brown sugar	30 mL
2 tsp.	Worcestershire sauce	10 mL

Sprinkle chops with garlic salt and brown in a skillet. Transfer them to a large baking dish. • Combine the onion, lemon juice, ketchup, mustard, brown sugar and Worcestershire sauce. • Spoon this mixture over the pork chops. • Cover with foil, or lid, and bake in a 325°F (160°C) oven for 1 hour. • Serves 8.

COUNTRY CHICKEN

1 cup	white sugar	250 mL
1 tsp.	dry mustard	5 mL
1 tsp.	paprika	5 mL
1 tsp.	salt (optional)	5 mL
⅛ tsp.	pepper	0.5 mL
1 cup	cider vinegar	250 mL
½ tsp.	garlic powder	2 mL
¾ cup	ketchup	175 mL
1 tbsp.	Worcestershire sauce	15 mL
1-2 tsp.	curry powder	5-10 mL
1	frying chicken, cut-up OR chicken parts	1

Mix all of the ingredients, except the chicken, in a saucepan and simmer for 5 minutes. • Place cut-up chicken in a single layer in baking dish, pour hot sauce over and bake at 350°F (180°C) for 1½ hours. • Baste chicken with sauce about every 20 minutes. • Unused sauce may be frozen. • Serves 4.

½ cup	finely chopped onions	125 mL
½ cup	butter OR margarine	125 mL
1 tsp.	turmeric powder	5 mL
½ tsp.	cinnamon powder	2 mL
½ tsp.	ginger powder	2 mL
½ tsp.	chili powder, OR to taste	2 mL
3 lbs.	whole chicken, cut into 2"-3" (5-7.5 cm) pieces OR chicken breasts	1.5 kg
1 cup	potato cubes, 1-2" (2.5-5 cm)	250 mL
	hot water	
6-8	whole cloves	6-8
2-4	2" (5 cm) cinnamon sticks	2-4
8-10	cardamom pods OR powder	8-10
6-8	bay leaves	6-8
2	medium tomatoes, chopped	2

CHICKEN CURRY

In a 6-quart (6 L) metallic pan, fry the chopped onions in butter at medium heat to a light golden-brown. • Add the first 4 spices at 1 minute intervals, stirring all the time. • After 5 minutes of cooking the spices, increase the heat to high and add the chicken pieces. Stirring well, cook for 10 more minutes, then decrease the heat to low-medium; cook at this heat for the next 45 minutes, stirring often to make certain the contents are not sticking to the bottom of the pan. • Now add the potatoes and hot water to the desired consistency, bring to a boil and cook again at low-medium heat for another 30 minutes. • Add the next 5 ingredients, at 1 minute intervals, and cook for another 10 minutes or so. • Check with a fork to see if the potatoes are cooked. • Serves 6-8.

1	chicken thigh OR boneless breast, per person	1
2-4 oz.	white wine	60-120 mL
8 oz.	whipping cream	250 mL
2-3 tbsp.	Dijon mustard	30-45 mL

CHICKEN DIJON

Fry chicken in open pan, approximately 20 minutes, until cooked to your satisfaction. • Place chicken in casserole dish — retain juices and add the white wine. Pour over chicken. • Beat the whipping cream. Cover chicken with the cream. • Place Dijon mustard on top of the whipped cream. • Place in oven and bake at 350°F (180°C) for 30 minutes, until browned.

If you see someone without a smile give him one of yours.

CHICKEN WITH ALMONDS

3	whole chicken breasts, boned	3
	salt and pepper, to taste	
½ cup	butter OR margarine, divided	125 mL
1 tbsp.	minced onion	15 mL
¼ cup	slivered almonds	75 mL
1 tsp.	tomato paste	5 mL
1 tbsp.	flour	15 mL
1¼ cups	chicken bouillon	300 mL
pinch	tarragon	pinch

Cut chicken breasts in half and remove skin. Sprinkle with salt and pepper. ● Melt 6 tbsp. (90 mL) of the butter in a skillet. ● Add chicken and brown slowly, turning occasionally for about 25 minutes. ● Remove chicken. ● Add remaining 2 tbsp. (30 mL) of butter. ● Add onions and almonds. Cook over low heat until almonds are browned. ● Blend in tomato paste and flour. ● Gradually add chicken bouillon and cook, stirring constantly, until mixture thickens and comes to a boil. ● Add browned chicken to mixture in skillet. ● Sprinkle with a pinch of tarragon. Lower heat and simmer 20 minutes. ● Serves 6.

DANISH ROAST DUCK

1	large duck	1
1 tbsp.	salt	15 mL
	pepper, to taste	
1 lb.	apples	500 g
½ lb.	prunes, pitted	250 g
1	onion, chopped (optional)	1
2 cups	water	500 mL
	cream and flour, for gravy (optional)	
	red currant jelly	

Clean duck, rinse well in cold water and dry. Rub well with salt and pepper on the inside. Peel and quarter apples. Mix with prunes and stuff duck with this fruit along with chopped onion, if desired. Roast in medium hot oven, 350°F (180°C) for 1¼ to 1½ hours. Add water and baste duck regularly. ● When duck is almost done, pour off the gravy and finish roasting at about 475°F (240°C) for 10-15 minutes until skin becomes brown and crisp. (If there is a ventilator in oven, it should be open.) ● Skim fat off gravy. Add cream and thicken with a little flour, previously dissolved in cold water. Add a few teaspoons (10 mL) of red currant jelly and salt and pepper to taste. ● Serve with red cabbage and boiled or caramel potatoes — and red currant jelly. ● VARIATION: Dressing may be used in chicken or turkey.

An old chicken can be made tender by rubbing with vinegar a few hours before cooking.

1	whole chicken, cut-up and skinned	1
1½ oz.	pkg. dried onion soup mix	40 g
½ cup	Russian salad dressing	125 mL
½ cup	apricot jam	125 mL

RUSSIAN CHICKEN

Mix soup, dressing and jam together in a bowl. • Place chicken in baking dish or small roasting pan. • Pour ingredients over chicken. Cover. • Place in oven and bake at 325°F (160°C) for 75-90 minutes. • Popular pot-luck dish. Goes well with steamed rice topped with sauce from the chicken.

---

12 oz.	can tomato paste	375 mL
½ cup	Ener-G Vinegar, made according to directions on jar	125 mL
½ cup	water	125 mL
½ tsp.	salt (optional)	2 mL
1 tsp.	ground oregano	5 mL
⅛ tsp.	ground cumin	0.5 mL
⅛ tsp.	ground nutmeg	0.5 mL
⅛ tsp.	ground black pepper	0.5 mL
½ tsp.	mild mustard powder	2 mL
¼ tsp.	ground garlic	1 mL

KETCHUP

Yeast-free, gluten-free.

Mix the above together. • Makes 2 cups (500 mL).

½ cup	dry mustard	125 mL
½ cup	hot water	125 mL
6 tbsp.	Ener-G Vinegar	90 mL
⅛ tsp.	dried tarragon	0.5 mL
¼ tsp.	garlic powder	1 mL
½ tsp.	molasses	2 mL

MUSTARD

Yeast-free.

Stir mustard, water and 2 tbsp. (30 mL) of Ener-G Vinegar together. Let sit for at least 2 hours. • Mix the remaining vinegar, tarragon and garlic together and let sit for 30 minutes. • Strain tarragon from the second mixture and add liquid to the mustard mixture. Mix in molasses. • Pour mustard into pan and set pan over simmering water. Cook until thick, about 20 minutes. The mustard will become even thicker when cool. • Let cool and put into glass jar. Store refrigerated. • Yields approximately 1 cup (250 mL).

To remove the cornsilk from corn on the cob easily, brush towards stalk end with a damp toothbrush, every strand of cornsilk will come off.

FRENCH DRESSING

½ cup	Ener-G Vinegar	125 mL
1½ cups	salad oil	375 mL
½ tsp.	freshly ground pepper	2 mL
½ tsp.	dry mustard	2 mL

Yeast-free.

Shake all ingredients together well in a screw-top jar. • For variety, add ½ cup (125 mL) sour cream, or garlic to taste. • Yields 2 cups (500 mL).

BARBECUE SAUCE

Yeast-free, gluten-free.

1 tsp.	salt	5 mL
¼ tsp.	pepper (mild OR hot, to taste)	1 mL
1 tsp.	paprika	5 mL
1 tsp.	powdered garlic	5 mL
½	onion, chopped	½
½ cup	water	125 mL
1 cup	ketchup, page 225	250 mL
¼ cup	Ener-G Yeast-Free Vinegar	50 mL

Mix all ingredients together. Simmer for 20 minutes. • Let cool before using.

TACO SAUCE

For chips, as a condiment, or as a seasoned tomato sauce for cooking.

8	large tomatoes, peeled	8
2	medium onions	2
2-3	jalapeño peppers (use green chilies for a mild sauce)	2-3
1 tsp.	black pepper	5 mL
1 tsp.	salt	5 mL
1 tsp.	garlic powder	5 mL
¼-½ tsp.	oregano	1-2 mL
½ tsp.	celery seed OR 1 tsp. (5 mL) celery salt	2 mL
½ tsp.	red pepper (cayenne)	2 mL
½ tsp.	Worcestershire sauce	2 mL
½ cup	vinegar	125 mL
1 tsp.	Mrs. Dash Seasoning (optional)	5 mL

Finely chop the tomatoes, onion and peppers. • Place all ingredients in saucepan and bring to a boil. Reduce heat and simmer until thickened, approximately 30 minutes. • Seal in 1 or 2 cup (250 or 500 mL) containers. Process in hot water bath for 25 minutes. • Serve chilled for chips or taco salad, as a sauce for meatloaf or as a portion of the tomato sauce in chili or spaghetti sauce. • Makes 6-8 cups (1.5-2 L) of sauce.

4	egg yolks	4
½ tsp.	H.P. OR	2 mL
	Worcestershire sauce	
	OR 2 tbsp. (30 mL)	
	lemon juice	
1 cup	butter	250 mL
	paprika OR cayenne	

NO-FUSS HOLLANDAISE SAUCE

Beat eggs until foamy and stir in sauce or lemon juice. • Melt butter. • Put beaten egg mixture into saucepan and partially cook over low heat, stirring continuously. • Slowly drizzle melted butter into egg mixture while still stirring and cook until thickened. • Serve at once. • A sprinkle of paprika, or cayenne, may be added when served. • NOTE: Sauce may separate if cooked too long, let stand too long, or is cooked over too hot a heat. To smooth, beat in 1 tbsp. (15 mL) of cold water or an ice cube. • Different herbs may be added for flavor, depending on with what you serve it. Enjoy!

1 cup	flour	250 mL
sprinkle	salt	sprinkle
1 tsp.	baking powder	5 mL
sprinkle	poultry seasoning OR	sprinkle
	sage	
½ cup	milk	125 mL
4 tbsp.	lard OR salad oil	60 mL

DUMPLINGS FOR STEW

Mix all ingredients well (must be stiff). • Drop, 1 spoonful at a time, in a well-cooked, juicy stew. • Cover with lid. DO NOT LIFT LID FOR 15 MINUTES. • Keep stew simmering while dumplings cook.

FESTIVE RUM CAKE

Before you start, measure out the necessary rum and sample for quality. Good, isn't it?

Select a large mixing bowl, measuring cup, spatula and all that stuff. Check the rum again. You want to be sure, eh? Now, with an electric beater, beat 1 cup (250 mL) butter, in a large fluffy bowl. Add 1 tsp. (5 mL) shugar and beat again. Add 2 large eggsh and 2 cups (500 mL) of fried druit. Beat until very high. Shample the rum again.

Now shift in 3 cups of paking powder, a punch of rum, 1 tsp. (5 mL) of toda, 1 cup (250 mL) of pepper — ugh, maybe that should be shalt. Check the rum while you deshidect aext, shift in half-pint (250 mL) of lemon juice and fold in the chopped buttermilk. Shtrain the nuts and add. Make shure they're right shide up.

Sample rum.

Now add 1 babbleshpoon srawn bugar and mish well. Greash and set cake pan at 350°F (180°C).

On thecond shot forget the whole thing, shample the rest of the rum bo to ged!

85% WHOLE-MEAL BREAD

This recipe was donated by a former London policeman, who worked next to a marvellous bakery. Before he came to Canada, the baker taught him to make this bread which has been entered in many contests — always winning first prize.

6 cups	whole-meal flour (whole-wheat)	1.5 L
1 cup	regular white flour	250 mL
1 tbsp.	salt	15 mL
1 tbsp.	fast-rising dried yeast	15 mL
1 tsp.	brown sugar	5 mL
2½ cups	warm water ,110-115°F (43-46°C)	625 mL
2	metal bread pans, 9" X 5" X 3" (2 L)	2

Measure flours into mixer bowl and add salt. Run mixer at medium speed to disperse salt. ● Place yeast and sugar in a warm measuring jug and add ½ cup (125 mL) warm water, stirring briskly until dissolved. Add warm water to yeast mix to make up to 2½ cups (625 mL). ● With mixer running at medium speed, add about half of the yeast mixture to the "well" in the middle of the flour and allow it to form a lumpy dough. Add the remaining liquid a little at a time so that all the dry flour is picked up. Add a little more water, if required to produce a "springy" dough. ● Make 2 or 3 batches in this manner according to the number of loaves required, remembering that you will need 2 pans per batch. ● Turn all the dough into a lightly flour-dusted mixing bowl, cover with 2 or 3 dry tea towels and set to rise in a warm place, 75-80°F (24-27°C) for about 1 hour, or until doubled in bulk. ● Turn the dough out onto a lightly floured counter and cut into 2 equal pieces per batch. One by one, fashion into a round shape about ¾" (2 cm) thick using the knuckles of both hands in a rocking motion. This is the only kneading required! Grasp the sides, pull out to twice the width, fold sides to middle and repeat the flattening process. Now make a VERY tight roll, and with a chopping action, seal both ends. ● Place in tins and press well down. Return them to the warm area, and again cover with tea towels. ● After 20 minutes, turn oven on and allow to come up to 425°F (220°C) having set a shelf at mid-oven height. Place all tins on the same shelf, bake for 20 minutes. Lower heat to 375°F (190°C) and continue to bake for another 20 minutes. Turn out onto a wire rack to cool. ● As there are no special preservatives added, it is advisable to freeze the loaves that you will not consume within 2 days. However, loaves should not be bagged and frozen for at least 12 hours after they come out of the oven. ● If you prefer to do the whole thing by hand, just double or triple the quantities listed and mix in a large bowl. See photograph page 64A.

To moisten brown sugar which has hardened, place a couple of apples in the container, and cover tightly.

GOOD'N EASY PASTRY MIX RECIPES

Good 'n Easy Pastry Mix is a commercially available product which is wheat-free, gluten-free and corn-free, with no preservatives.

IMPORTANT BAKING HINTS

Water — Because nongluten flours retain water differently than gluten flours, liquid measurements are approximate. When adding liquids, do so gradually until the consistency is similar to an equivalent wheat-based batter. • When rolling out cookies, or pie crust, use any allowable flour, i.e. tapioca, rice, potato starch. Be certain that all pans and utensils (sifter) are free from gluten flours. • If using foil-covered cookie sheets for cookies, grease the foil. • Sifting — because nongluten flours tend to cake and lump during storage, sift mixes before using. • Read recipe completely and carefully before you begin.

1	pouch Good'n Easy Pastry Mix	1	
½ cup	sugar	125 mL	
¼ cup	shortening	50 mL	
2-3 tbsp.	cold water	30-45 mL	
½ tsp.	flavoring	2 mL	

BASIC COOKIES
gluten-free

See Baking Hints, above, before baking. • Place oven rack in center of oven. Preheat oven to 375°F (190°C). • Sift Good'n Easy Pastry Mix with sugar. Cut in shortening. Make well in dry ingredients and pour in water and flavoring. Mix well. • Roll into ¾" (2 cm) balls, place 2" (5 cm) apart and flatten with fork. (These spread a bit.) Bake 7-10 minutes on ungreased cookie sheet. Remove with spatula to rack while still hot. • Yield 2½-3 dozen.

COOKIE VARIATIONS

For **rolled cookies** roll ⅛" (0.3 cm) thick using non-gluten flour to dust rolling surface. Cut in shapes and follow Basic Cookie baking instructions, above.

For **drop cookies** use 4-5 tbsp. (60-75 mL) cold water and drop on ungreased cookie sheet. Add ½ cup (125 mL) nuts, raisins, baking chips, dried fruit, etc. after the water and flavoring are added. Use either white or brown sugar.

4 tsp.	lemon juice	20 mL
2-3 tbsp.	cold water	30-45 mL
2 tsp.	lemon rind	10 mL

LEMON DROPS
gluten-free

Replace water and flavoring in Basic Cookies, above, with above ingredients. • Drop onto ungreased cookie sheet. • Follow Basic Cookie baking instructions.

CHIFFON CAKE

gluten-free

4	large eggs, separated	4
3 tbsp.	cold water	45 mL
1 cup	white sugar	250 mL
1 tsp.	vanilla OR other flavouring	5 mL
1	pouch Good'n Easy Pastry Mix, sifted	

Move oven rack to lowest position. Preheat oven to 375°F (190°C). • Be sure bowl, pan and all utensils are free from grease. Do not use plastic bowl. • Beat egg whites until stiff peaks form; set aside. • In a separate bowl, beat together egg yolks and water until fluffy. Gradually add sugar and beat well. Beat in flavoring. Gradually blend in pastry mix. Do not over-mix. Gently fold beaten egg whites into egg yolk mixture. • Pour into ungreased 10" x 4" (3 L) tube pan. Gently cut through batter to remove air bubles. • Bake 40-45 minutes. Test with skewer or toothpick. • Hang inverted to cool. • Remove from pan when cool. • Cut with a serrated knife.

PIE PASTRY

gluten-free

1	pouch Good'n Easy Pastry Mix, sifted	1
6 tbsp.	hard shortening	90 mL
2-4 tbsp.	cold water	30-60 mL

Place oven rack in lowest position. Preheat oven to 425°F (220°C). • Cut shortening into Good'n Easy Pastry Mix. Add only enough water to barely moisten. Mix until flour is dampened. • Form into ball. Cut in half. • Roll each half separately between 2 sheets of waxed paper lightly dusted with tapioca starch, potato starch, or fine rice flour. • Line 8" (20 cm) or 9" (22 cm) pie plate with 1 rolled half of the pastry. • For double crust pie, fill shell and cover with other half of rolled pastry. Crimp edges. Bake according to filling directions. • For single crust pie, prick bottom before baking. Bake at 425°F (220°C) for 7-10 minutes. Cool and fill. • Baked or unbaked shells may be frozen for future use.

EASY BANANA BREAD

gluten-free

½ cup	mashed ripe banana	125 mL
½ cup	white sugar	125 mL
3-4 tbsp.	milk OR water	45-60 mL
2	large eggs	2
1	pouch Good'n Easy Quick Bread Mix, sifted	1
2 tbsp.	melted shortening	30 mL

Place rack in center of oven. Preheat oven to 350°F (180°C). • Grease a 9" x 3" (2 L) loaf pan. • Beat together banana, sugar, milk or water and eggs. Mix in Good'n Easy Quick Bread Mix and melted shortening. Blend well. Spoon into pan. • Bake for 40-50 minutes. Test with skewer. • Remove from pan while warm. • Cool on rack.

3	large eggs	3
9 tbsp.	milk OR 6 tbsp. (90 mL) cold water	135 mL
3 tbsp.	liquid shortening	45 mL
½ tsp.	sugar (optional)	2 mL
1	pouch Good'n Easy Quick Bread Mix, sifted	1

GOOD'N EASY QUICK BREAD

gluten-free

See Baking Hints, page 229, before baking. • Place oven rack in center of oven. Preheat oven to 375°F (190°C). • Grease a 9" x 3" (2 L) loaf pan. • Lightly beat eggs in a bowl. Beat in milk, or water, oil and sugar. Add Good'n Easy Quick Bread Mix. Mix until well blended. Spoon into loaf pan. • Bake for 30 minutes. Test with a skewer or toothpick inserted in center. • Remove from pan and cool on a rack. • To cut the soy flavor, add 1 tsp. (5 mL) lemon juice to the liquids.

VARIATION:

Hamburger Buns: Bake at 350°F (180°C) in 6 well-greased custard baking dishes, 10 or 12 oz. (300 or 341 mL) size, for 25 minutes. • Muffins: Bake at 375°F (190°C) in greased muffin tins for 12-15 minutes. • Remove buns or muffins from baking dish or tin while hot. Cool on rack. • Yields 1 dozen.

½ cup	canned pumpkin	125 mL
½ cup	sugar	125 mL
2	eggs	2
2 tbsp.	milk OR water	30 mL
2 tbsp.	vegetable oil	30 mL
1 tsp.	cinnamon	5 mL
½ tsp.	cloves	2 mL
¼ tsp.	nutmeg	1 mL
1	pouch Good'n Easy Quick Bread Mix, sifted	1

PUMPKIN BREAD

gluten-free

Place oven rack in center of oven. Preheat oven to 350°F (180°C). • Grease loaf pan. • Beat together pumpkin, sugar, eggs, milk or water, oil and spices. Add Good'n Easy Quick Bread Mix and blend well. Pour into pan. • Bake 40-50 minutes. • Remove from pan while warm. Cool on rack.

VARIATIONS FOR EASY BANANA, PUMPKIN AND BASIC BREAD

Add ½ cup (125 mL) raisins, currants, chopped dates or chopped nuts to the dry Good'n Easy Quick Bread Mix before adding it to the liquid ingredients.

A dash of salt in cream or eggs makes them whip faster. It really works.

DELUXE BANANA BREAD

gluten-free

3	large eggs, separated	3
1½ cup	mashed ripe banana	375 mL
¾ cup	brown sugar	175 mL
2 tbsp.	melted shortening	30 mL
1	pouch Good'n Easy Quick Bread Mix, sifted	1

Place oven rack in center of oven. Preheat oven to 350°F (180°C). • Grease a 9" x 3" (2 L) loaf pan. • Beat egg whites until stiff. Set aside. • In another bowl, lightly beat egg yolks. Beat in bananas, then sugar, then shortening. Mix in Good'n Easy Quick Bread Mix until smooth. Fold in stiffly beaten egg whites. • Pour into pan and bake for 1 hour, or until done. Test with a skewer. • Remove from pan. Cool on rack.

CRÊPES

gluten-free

1	pouch Good'n Easy Quick Bread Mix, sifted	1
1½ cups	water	375 mL
2	eggs	2
½ tsp.	sugar (optional)	2 mL

Blend together and let stand 5 minutes. • Pour onto medium-hot greased 6" (15 cm) pan, tilting pan to spread batter. • Cook until lightly browned. Turn once to brown other side. • Makes 12-16 crêpes.

OLD-TIME GINGERSNAPS

¼ cup	butter	50 mL
2 cups	granulated sugar	500 mL
2	eggs, well-beaten	2
½ cup	molasses	125 mL
2 tsp.	white vinegar	10 mL
3¾ cups	all-purpose flour	925 mL
1½ tsp.	baking soda	7 mL
2-3 tsp.	ground ginger	10-15 mL
½ tsp.	ground cloves	2 mL
½ tsp.	cinnamon	2 mL

Preheat oven to 325°F (160°C) and grease cookie sheets. • Thoroughly mix ingredients in order given and form into small balls. Place on greased cookie sheets. • Bake 12 minutes. • Store in tin box to retain chewy consistency. • Makes 10 dozen cookies.

In making rolled cookies chill cookie dough for about ½ hour. The dough will be easier to handle and will require much less flour, therefore will make a tender cookie.

2½ cups	flour	625 mL
1 tsp.	cardamom	5 mL
1 tsp.	cinnamon	5 mL
¼ tsp.	white pepper	1 mL
1 cup	sugar	250 mL
1 cup	butter	250 mL
2	eggs	2
2 tsp.	grated lemon rind	10 mL

PEBBER-NODDER

Peppernuts, a Christmas specialty!

Sift dry ingredients into a large mixing bowl. Add butter, eggs and grated lemon rind. Mix well. • Mix with hands until dough is smooth. • Let stand about 1 hour, or longer, in refrigerator. • Roll into long "worms" as thick as your little finger and cut pieces from the "worms" no longer than your fingernail (man's).
• Bake on greased cookie sheet in oven at 325°F (160°C) until golden brown.
• Store in jar with tight-fitting lid in cool place.

½ cup	butter OR margarine	125 mL
½ cup	shortening	125 mL
1 cup	white sugar	250 mL
1 cup	brown sugar	250 mL
2 cups	rolled oats	500 mL
¾ cup	coconut	175 mL
2	eggs	2
1 tsp.	baking powder	5 mL
½ tsp.	baking soda	2 mL
½ tsp.	salt	2 mL
1 tsp.	vanilla	5 mL
½-1 cup	mixed peel, raisins OR nuts	125-250 mL
½ cup	wheat germ	125 mL
1½ cups	flour	375 mL

DAD'S MUNCHERS

Beat with electric mixer in order given. Drop by spoonfuls on greased cookie sheets. • Bake at 350°F (180°C) for 10 minutes. • Makes about 3 dozen.

½ cup	butter	125 mL
1 tsp.	cream	5 mL
1 tsp.	almond extract	5 mL
1½ cups	icing sugar	375 mL
1½ cups	fine coconut	375 mL
7-8	halved red and green maraschino cherries	7-8
7-8	graham wafers, finely rolled	7-8

CAPE BRETON SURPRISE BALLS

Unbaked!

Cream butter and cream. • Add almond extract, icing sugar and fine coconut; mix well. • Take small piece of dough and pat flat in the hand. • Place half cherry in center and roll into a ball, then in wafer crumbs. • Chill overnight.
• Makes about 30 balls.

233

PUFF BALL DOUGHNUTS

3	eggs	3
1 cup	sugar	250 mL
2 cups	milk	500 mL
2 tsp.	lemon extract OR 1 tsp. (5 mL) vanilla OR 1 tsp. (5 mL) nutmeg	10 mL
3½ cups	unsifted all-purpose flour	875 mL
1 tbsp.	baking powder	15 mL
½ tsp.	salt	2 mL

Beat eggs, add sugar and beat well; add milk and flavoring of your choice. • Mix flour, baking powder and salt together and add to egg and sugar mixture. • Drop by teaspoon (5 mL) into deep fat at 370°F (190°C). • Doughnuts will turn over by themselves. If not, turn with fork, BUT DO NOT PIERCE. Drain on paper towel. Roll in sugar, if desired. • Makes 20-30, depending on how much batter on spoon.

MICROWAVE APPLE CRISP

6 cups	sliced apples	1.5 L
2 tbsp.	melted butter	30 mL
¼ cup	brown sugar	50 mL
2 tsp.	cinnamon	10 mL
2 tsp.	lemon juice	10 mL
1 cup	graham wafer crumbs	250 mL

Add apples slices to melted butter, cook in microwave 3 minutes. • Stir in brown sugar, cinnamon and lemon juice, and cook in microwave 4 minutes; stir. • Sprinkle graham cracker crumbs over the top. Cook 2 minutes. • Serve warm with ice cream or whipped cream. • Serves 4.

LEMON POPPY SEED CAKE

19 oz.	Lemon Supreme Cake Mix	520 g
3 oz.	pkg, lemon instant pudding	85 g
½ cup	poppy seeds	125 mL
½ cup	vegetable oil	125 mL
1 cup	lukewarm water	250 mL
4	eggs, beaten	4
2 tsp.	rum OR brandy flavoring	10 mL

Mix all of the above ingredients, spoon into 2 greased loaf pans or layer cake pans and bake at 350°F (180°C) oven for 45-50 minutes. • Makes 2 loaves or a double layer cake.

A few whole cloves in the kettle of frying fat will give the doughnuts a better flavor.

1 cup	glazed cherries	250 mL
1 cup	chopped moist figs	250 mL
1 cup	chopped pitted dates	250 mL
½ cup	chopped citron peel	125 mL
½ cup	blanched almonds	125 mL
2	medium carrots, grated	2
1½ cups	loosely packed, chopped fresh suet	375 mL
2½ cups	sifted all-purpose flour	625 mL
1 tsp.	baking soda	5 mL
1 tsp.	baking powder	5 mL
1 tsp.	salt	5 mL
1 tsp.	cinnamon	5 mL
¼ tsp.	ginger	1 mL
¼ tsp.	allspice	1 mL
¼ tsp.	nutmeg	1 mL
½ cup	white sugar	125 mL
2	eggs, beaten	2
½ cup	honey	125 mL
1 cup	buttermilk	250 mL
1 tsp.	vanilla	5 mL

STEAMED FRUIT PUDDING (CHRISTMAS)

Measure fruit and nuts, grated carrots and suet into large mixing bowl. ● Measure sifted flour, add baking soda, baking powder, salt and spices and add to the fruit mixture; blend thoroughly. ● In a separate bowl, mix sugar, eggs, honey, buttermilk and vanilla. Beat well. Add to flour mixture and mix well. ● Put in sterilized 1-quart (1 L) jars to ⅔ full and seal with tight covers. Place jars in boiling water in a canner. Cook for 3 hours. ● Makes 3 quarts (3 L).

6	oranges	6
2 cups	sugar	500 mL
2 cups	water	500 mL
2 tsp.	lemon juice	10 mL
½ cup	orange liqueur (Cointreau or Grand Marnier)	125 mL

FLOATING ORANGE SLICES

Zest the oranges. Simmer zest for 10 minutes; drain. ● Add to zest, the sugar, water and lemon juice. Simmer, uncovered, for 15 minutes. ● Peel the oranges, slice thinly. Marinate with the orange liqueur for 1 hour. ● Pour hot syrup over oranges. ● Cool and serve.

WINDOW CLEANER

1 tbsp.	cornstarch	15 mL
1 tbsp.	Fleecy	15 mL
1 quart	warm water	1 L

235

FRENCH BANANA ECLAIR

Party-sized!

½ cup	water	125 mL
¼ cup	butter	50 mL
¼ tsp.	salt	1 mL
½ cup	flour	125 mL
2	eggs	2
2 cups	whipping cream	500 mL
2 tbsp.	sugar	30 mL
2	large ripe bananas	2
2 tbsp.	Kahlúa	30 mL
1 cup	icing sugar	250 mL
¼ cup	cocoa	75 mL
1 tbsp.	melted butter	15 mL
1 tsp.	vanilla	5 mL
3-4 tbsp.	boiling water	45-60 mL

Bring water, butter and salt to boil in saucepan over medium heat. Add flour all at once, stirring vigorously with spoon until dough forms a ball and leaves sides of pan. Remove from heat; beat in eggs, 1 at a time, until dough is stiff and glossy. Set aside about half of dough. • On a greased baking sheet, form remaining dough into 1 long oblong, about 2" (5 cm) wide. Spoon reserved dough in mounds along top of oblong. • Bake in hot oven, 400°F (200°C) for 40 minutes. With a sharp knife, make slits along sides of eclair 2" (5 cm) apart, to let steam escape. Return to oven and continue baking 10 mintues longer. Remove to rack. Slice off top. Remove any soft dough inside. Cool completely. • Whip cream until soft peaks form. Gradually add sugar, whipping until stiff. Mash bananas to make 1 cup (250 mL) and fold into whipped cream along with Kahlúa. Fill eclair, replace top. • Combine icing sugar with cocoa, melted butter and vanilla. Stir in enough boiling water to make thin glaze. Drizzle over eclair. • Chill at least 1 hour. • Slice crosswise. • Makes 8-10 servings.

CARAMEL CORN

2 cups	light brown sugar	500 mL
½ cup	light corn syrup	125 mL
½ lb.	butter	250 g
½ tsp.	baking soda	2 mL
pinch	cream of tartar	pinch
dash	salt	dash
8 quarts	dry popped corn	8 L

Mix sugar, syrup and butter in heavy saucepan; bring to a boil and cook for 5 minutes. • Remove from heat; add baking soda, cream of tartar and salt. • Immediately pour over popped corn. Mix lightly, but thoroughly. • Place in a large roaster; bake at 200°F (100°C) for 1 hour. • Pour on waxed paper and cool.

Popcorn will pop better if slightly moistened with water just before placing in popper.

CHILDREN

1 cup	unpopped popcorn	250 mL
1 cup	butter	250 mL
2 cups	packed brown sugar	500 mL
½ cup	corn syrup	125 mL
¼ tsp.	salt	1 mL
½ tsp.	baking soda	2 mL
1 tsp.	vanilla	5 mL

CARAMEL CORN

Pop the corn; set aside. ● Boil butter, sugar, syrup, and salt together for 5 minutes without stirring. Remove from heat. Add baking soda and vanilla. ● Pour over popped corn; stir to coat evenly.

1 cup	raw wheat germ	250 mL
4-5 cups	rolled oats	1-1.25 L
¾ cup	chopped pecans	175 mL
½ cup	sesame seeds	125 mL
½ cup	shelled sunflower seeds	125 mL
½ cup	unsweetened coconut	125 mL
¼ cup	sugar	50 mL
½ tsp.	salt	2 mL
¾ cup	vegetable oil	175 mL
½ cup	water	125 mL
½ cup	honey	125 mL
2 tsp.	vanilla	10 mL
½ cup	raisins	125 mL
½ cup	chopped dried fruit	125 mL

SUPER GRANOLA

Combine dry ingredients, except fruits, in a large bowl. Combine vegetable oil, water, honey and vanilla in blender. Pour over dry ingredients and mix well.
● Place granola on 2, 10″ x 15″ (25 cm x 35 cm) baking sheets. Bake for about 20-25 minutes at 300°F (150°C). Stir the granola approximately every 5 minutes. Granola is done when it is golden brown. Cool and add raisins and dried fruit.
● Store in airtight containers in a cool dry place. ● Serve as a cereal with milk, as a dry snack, or sprinkle on yogurt or ice cream. ● Makes approximately 10 cups (2.5 L).

SESAME BARS

4 cups	rolled oats	1 L
1 cup	melted margarine	250 mL
1 cup	brown sugar	250 mL
½ cup	sesame seeds	125 mL

Mix all ingredients. • Press HARD into a cookie sheet, 18″ x 12″ (45 cm x 30 cm). • Bake at 350°F (180°C) for 2 minutes, or more, until light brown. • Mark in squares while warm. • Cut when cool. • NOTE: If you like nutty chewy things, this is delicious! Make sure it is pressed well in pan, or it will crumble.

CANDY CAKE SQUARES

1 cup	butter OR margarine	250 mL
2 cups	brown sugar	500 mL
4 cups	rolled oats	1 L
½ tsp.	baking soda	2 mL
1 tsp.	vanilla	5 mL

Bring butter and sugar to boil on stove and add rolled oats, baking soda and vanilla. • Mix well and pat into a 7″ x 10″ (17.5 cm x 25 cm) pan. • Bake in 375°F (190°C) oven until golden brown, about 20 minutes. • Let cool before cutting.

COCOA KRISPIE CAKE

Gluten-free.

¾ cup	corn syrup	175 mL
¾ cup	sugar	175 mL
¾ cup	peanut butter	175 mL
2 tbsp.	butter	30 mL
4½ cups	rice krispies	1.125 L
¼ cup	butter	75 mL
2 tbsp.	milk	30 mL
1½ cups	icing sugar	375 mL
⅔ cup	cocoa	150 mL

Cook corn syrup and sugar over medium heat until sugar dissolves and mixture bubbles. Remove from heat and blend in peanut butter and 2 tbsp. (30 mL) of butter. Combine with rice krispies and stir until well-coated. Press ⅔ of mixture into a 9″ x 13″ (22 cm x33 cm) pan or a 9″ (1 L) pie plate. • Prepare Chocolate Filling by melting butter with milk over low heat. Remove from heat; sift in icing sugar and cocoa. Blend thoroughly. • Spread filling over krispie base. Sprinkle balance of krispie mix over chocolate filling. • Refrigerate a few hours, or overnight.

Juices from pies which have run over and onto the bottom of the oven can be prevented from filling the oven with smoke and a burnt odor, by sprinkling the juice at once with salt.

238

1	egg	1
½ cup	cocoa	125 mL
½ cup	butter OR margarine	125 mL
1½ cups	flour	375 mL
½ cup	sour milk	125 mL
1 tsp.	baking soda	5 mL
1 cup	sugar	250 mL
½ cup	hot water	125 mL
1 tsp.	vanilla	5 mL

CHOCOLATE CUPCAKES

An easy recipe for children.

Don't stir until all ingredients are put into mixing bowl. • Mix well and bake in greased and floured muffin tins, or lined with paper cupcake cups, at 350°F (180°C) for 25 minutes.

---

3 lb.	pkg. chocolate pudding and pie filling using:	1.5 kg
7½ qts.	milk	7.5 L
5-7 cups	ground chocolate cookie wafers (prefer Oreos)	1.25-1.75 L
2 cups	whipping cream, whipped OR 4 pkgs. Dream Whip	500 mL
10-20	bananas	10-20
	chocolate cookies for garnish	

BLACK MAGIC

This is the favorite dessert at the Youth Emergency Shelter. It was invented by our cook, Helena Smith, and feeds 50 teenagers!

Cook the chocolate pudding and refrigerate several hours before assembling. • Crush the cookies (the blender works well). • Whip the cream. • In a very large bowl, put a layer of cookie crumbs, about 2 cups (500 mL). Spoon a thick layer of cooled pudding on top of cookies. Slice a layer of bananas on top of that. Repeat crumbs, pudding and bananas (be generous). Cover last layer of bananas with pudding. Spread the whipped cream on top and decorate with whole cookies. • NOTE: This is not a diet item! • Serves 50.

---

28 oz.	can peach halves	796 mL
½ cup	light brown sugar, firmly packed	125 mL
⅛ tsp.	cinnamon	0.5 mL
6 tbsp.	cornflakes	90 mL
1 tbsp.	butter	15 mL
2 cups	vanilla ice cream	500 mL

PEACHES AND CREAM

Gluten-free.

Preheat oven to 375°F (190°C). • Drain peaches, reserving ½ cup (125 mL) liquid. Arrange, cut side up in an 8″ x 8″ x 2″ (20 x 20 x 5 cm) baking dish. Add reserved liquid. • Combine sugar and cinnamon. Sprinkle evenly over peaches. • Top each peach half with 1 tbsp. (15 mL) cornflakes and a dot of butter. • Bake 15 minutes. • Serve warm with ice cream.

NAN'S BAKED LEMON PUDDING

1 tbsp.	butter	15 mL
⅔ cup	sugar	150 mL
3 tbsp.	flour	45 mL
1	lemon, juice of	1
2	eggs, separated	2
1 cup	milk	250 mL

Mix together the butter, sugar and flour. Add the lemon juice, egg yolks and milk. • Stiffly beat the egg whites and fold into first mixtures. • Pour into an 8" x 8" (20 cm x 20 cm) cake tin, or casserole dish. Place dish in pan of hot water and put in a 350°F (180°C) oven for 30 minutes. • Dad's and kids love it!!! • Serves 4-6.

CARAMEL BALLS

4	bars MacIntosh Toffee OR 1 jar butterscotch topping	4
¼ cup	butter	50 mL
⅔ cup	can condensed milk	150 mL
1	bag marshmallows cereal: corn flakes OR Special K, crushed	1

Combine and melt toffee, or topping, butter and milk. • Dip marshmallows into mixture and then into crushed cereal.

MONSTER COOKIES

14	eggs	14
3 cups	brown sugar	750 mL
1 tbsp.	vanilla	15 mL
8 tsp.	baking soda	40 mL
3 cups	margarine	750 mL
4 cups	peanut butter, (3 lbs. [1.5 kg])	1 L
18 cups	oatmeal	4.5 L
2½ cups	chocolate chips, (1 lb. [500 g])	625 mL
2½ cups	Smarties, (1 lb. [500 g])	625 mL

Mix ingredients. • Drop by spoonfuls onto cookie sheet. • Bake 10-12 minutes at 375°F (190°C).

When making cookies add 1 tsp. (5 mL) jam or jelly. The cookies will have a little better flavor and stay moist longer.

13 oz.	tin evaporated milk	369 mL
8 oz.	pkg. mini marshmallows	250 g
16 oz.	pkg. chocolate chips	500 g
1 cup	chopped walnuts	250 mL
½ cup	margarine	125 mL
7 oz.	pkg. coconut	200 g
2 cups	graham wafer crumbs	500 mL
2 qts.	vanilla ice cream	2 L

ICE CREAM CHOCOLATE DELIGHT

Combine first 4 ingredients in a double boiler. Heat and stir until all is melted. Remove from heat and cool. ● In a saucepan, over medium heat, add margarine and coconut. Cook until coconut is slightly brown, then add graham crumbs. Press ¾ of the coconut mixture into a 9″ x 13″ (22 cm x 33 cm) pan. Then add a layer ½″ (1.3 cm) thick of vanilla ice cream. Pour half of the marshmallow mixture over ice cream. Then repeat layers, ending with crumbs on top. ● Freeze. ● Slice and serve when ready.

2 cups	vanilla ice cream	500 mL
16 oz.	can frozen orange juice	500 mL
1	egg	1
1½ cups	milk	375 mL

EGGNOG POPS

Mix first 3 ingredients together. ● Gradually beat in the milk and pour into popsicle molds. ● Freeze.

3 oz.	pkg. chocolate pudding (not instant)	85 g
3½ cups	milk	875 mL
1 cup	sugar, or less	250 mL

FUDGSICLES

Prepare pudding according to directions, but substitute 3½ cups (875 mL) milk. ● Blend until smooth. ● Pour into popsicle molds and freeze.

½ cup	butter OR margarine	125 mL
1 cup	peanut butter	250 mL
2 x 6 oz.	pkgs. butterscotch chips	2 x 170 g
½ x 8 oz.	pkg. miniature marshmallows	½ x 250 g

BUTTER-SCOTCH SQUARES

Melt first 3 ingredients in saucepan, over low heat. Remove from heat and let cool. ● Add the miniature marshmallows and pat into an 8″ x 8″ (2 L) greased pan. ● Let set 2 hours. ● Cut in small squares.

PRETZEL BREAD

My children make these for Easter morning!

1	yeast cake, dissolved in 1 cup (375 mL) warm water	1
1 tsp.	salt	5 mL
1 tbsp.	sugar	15 mL
4 cups	flour	1 L
1	egg, beaten	1
	coarse salt	

Dissolve the yeast cake in the warm water; add the salt and sugar. • Blend in the flour. • Knead dough until smooth. • Cut into small pieces. Roll into ropes and twist into pretzel shape. • Place on lightly greased cookie sheet. • Brush with beaten egg. • Sprinkle with coarse salt. • Bake immediately at 425°F (220°C) for 12-15 minutes. • VARIATION: For hard pretzels, use only 1¼ cups (300 mL) flour and add ¼ cup (50 mL) melted butter. Shape smaller and bake until brown.

CORN DOGS

1	egg	1
1 cup	milk	250 mL
½ cup	cornmeal	125 mL
1 cup	all-purpose flour	250 mL
½ tsp.	salt	2 mL
1 tsp.	baking powder	5 mL
12	wieners	12
2	slices Cheddar cheese (12 strips)	2
	vegetable oil	

Mix first 6 ingredients in shallow bowl to make batter. • Split wieners and insert a strip of cheese. • Dip wiener into cornmeal batter and drop into hot oil, 375°F (190°C). • Cook until golden brown. • Drain on paper towels. • Insert skewer in corn dog and serve with mustard and ketchup. • Kids love them — no buns to fall apart! • Makes 12.

PLAY DOUGH RECIPE

1 cup	flour	250 mL
½ cup	salt	125 mL
1 cup	water	250 mL
1 tbsp.	vegetable oil	15 mL
2 tsp.	cream of tartar	10 mL
	food coloring	

Mix and heat over low. heat. • Stir a few minutes until thick and rubbery. • Remove from heat, cool and knead until pliable. • Store in a covered container.

Do you know how strawberries got their name? In the 15th century, they were brought to market and strung on straws . . . so, naturally they were called strawberries.

INDEX

WIVES OF ROTARIANS

248

ROTARIANS

Share AMONG FRIENDS with a friend

Please send _____ copies of AMONG FRIENDS, at $15.95 per book, plus $1.50 (total order) for postage and handling:

    Number of books _____ x 15.95 $ _____
    Handling Charge _____ $ 1.50
    Total enclosed _____ $ _____
    Visa # _____ Expiry Date _____

U.S. or International orders payable in U.S. funds.

NAME: _____

STREET: _____

CITY: _____ PROV./STATE: _____

COUNTRY: _____ POSTAL CODE/ZIP: _____

A Great Gift Idea

Please make check, visa or money order payable to: **AMONG FRIENDS**
                                   P.O. Box 6127, Station "A"
                                   Calgary, Alberta, Canada T2P 1X5

For volume orders please call:
V. & D. Martin — (403) 243-3693
Gerry Watkins C.A. — (403) 244-4562
Lucille Steinhauer — (403) 236-4488

Price subject to change

Share AMONG FRIENDS with a friend

Please send _____ copies of AMONG FRIENDS, at $15.95 per book, plus $1.50 (total order) for postage and handling:

    Number of books _____ x 15.95 $ _____
    Handling Charge _____ $ 1.50
    Total enclosed _____ $ _____
    Visa # _____ Expiry Date _____

U.S. or International orders payable in U.S. funds.

NAME: _____

STREET: _____

CITY: _____ PROV./STATE: _____

COUNTRY: _____ POSTAL CODE/ZIP: _____

A Great Gift Idea

Please make check, visa or money order payable to: **AMONG FRIENDS**
                                   P.O. Box 6127, Station "A"
                                   Calgary, Alberta, Canada T2P 1X5

For volume orders please call:
V. & D. Martin — (403) 243-3693
Gerry Watkins C.A. — (403) 244-4562
Lucille Steinhauer — (403) 236-4488

Price subject to change

Share AMONG FRIENDS with a friend

Please send _____ copies of AMONG FRIENDS, at $15.95 per book, plus $1.50 (total order) for postage and handling:

Number of books _____ x 15.95	$ _____	
Handling Charge _____	$ 1.50	
Total enclosed _____	$ _____	
Visa # _____ Expiry Date _____		

U.S. or International orders payable in U.S. funds.

NAME: _____

STREET: _____

CITY: _____ PROV./STATE: _____

COUNTRY: _____ POSTAL CODE/ZIP: _____

A Great Gift Idea

Please make check, visa or money order payable to: **AMONG FRIENDS**
P.O. Box 6127, Station "A"
Calgary, Alberta, Canada T2P 1X5

For volume orders please call:
V. & D. Martin — (403) 243-3693
Gerry Watkins C.A. — (403) 244-4562
Lucille Steinhauer — (403) 236-4488

Price subject to change

===

Share AMONG FRIENDS with a friend

Please send _____ copies of AMONG FRIENDS, at $15.95 per book, plus $1.50 (total order) for postage and handling:

Number of books _____ x 15.95	$ _____	
Handling Charge _____	$ 1.50	
Total enclosed _____	$ _____	
Visa # _____ Expiry Date _____		

U.S. or International orders payable in U.S. funds.

NAME: _____

STREET: _____

CITY: _____ PROV./STATE: _____

COUNTRY: _____ POSTAL CODE/ZIP: _____

A Great Gift Idea

Please make check, visa or money order payable to: **AMONG FRIENDS**
P.O. Box 6127, Station "A"
Calgary, Alberta, Canada T2P 1X5

For volume orders please call:
V. & D. Martin — (403) 243-3693
Gerry Watkins C.A. — (403) 244-4562
Lucille Steinhauer — (403) 236-4488

Price subject to change